HOLLYWOOD MOVIE SONGS

Collectible Sheet Music

Marion Short

Photography by Roy Short

Schiffer Publishing Ltd

4880 Lower Valley Road, Atglen, PA

Designed by "Sue"
Photo layout by Randy Hensley
Type set in Bernhard Mod BT/Times New Roman

ISBN: 0-7643-0698-7
Printed in China
1 2 3 4

Published by Schiffer Publishing Ltd.
4880 Lower Valley Road
Atglen, PA 19310
Phone: (610) 593-1777; Fax: (610) 593-2002
E-mail: Schifferbk@aol.com
Please visit our web site catalog at
www.schifferbooks.com
or write for a free catalog

This book may be purchased from the publisher.
Please include $3.95 for shipping.

In Europe, Schiffer books are distributed by
Bushwood Books
6 Marksbury Rd.
Kew Gardens
Surrey TW9 4JF England
Phone: 44 (0)181 392-8585; Fax: 44 (0)181 392-9876
E-mail: Bushwd@aol.com

Please try your bookstore first.

We are interested in hearing from authors
with book ideas on related subjects.

Even in its day sheet music was acquired and cherished not only for performance but also for a vague but real "cultural delight." It is easy to disparage a preoccupation with personal property, but it is important, too, to understand that the possession of items of beauty should be seen as serving to elevate the owner, the listener, or the beholder. Historical collections reflect and foster owners who are thereby the more humane, more filled with delight, good taste, and understanding of human history, and thus more responsive to one's fellow citizenry and the democratic society that was part of the collective national vision.

D. W. Krummel
Bibliographical Handbook of American Music
University of Illinois Press, 1988

Acknowledgments

 I am very grateful to my sheet music friends and associates who added to the beauty and completeness of this book. Roy Bishop, James Nelson Brown, and Harold Jacobs provided rare sheet music from three of the best collections on the West Coast to fill in the gaps, and also offered insight into the pricing dilemma. My thanks to all for their pricing advice.

The prices used in the value guide have been carefully researched and reflect buying trips across the country as well as dealer prices. Criticism received from most dealers with whom I have been in contact regard the prices as on the low side. On the other hand, most buyers find them to be realistic and fair. An acceptable price seems to depend on whether one is buying or selling. So I continue to founder in the treacherous shoals.

The book would not have been possible without the extraordinary photography of Roy Short, and my deepest thanks to him for his patience and hard work.

Both the author and publisher wish to thank all owners of copyright who, in the interest of historical reference, have graciously allowed the use of their music covers to enhance the book and to aid cinema scholars in the pursuit of knowledge.

Special thanks to the able staff at Schiffer Publishing for helping to make the book readable as well as beautiful, and to publisher Peter Schiffer for his kind words of encouragement and for the jar of special honey from his farm, "undiddled with by humans."

Contents

INTRODUCTION

Hollywood. The name means different things to different people. To some it is merely a place northwest of Los Angeles in California, the center of the American motion picture industry. For me it is magic, glamour, escapism, fantasy, and absorbing drama. Playing the music from old movies evokes the mood and experience of seeing the movie anew. Pictorial covers of the stars add to the mystique.

Movie sheet music covers are most appealing as collectibles. I grew up with movies in the 1930s and 1940s during the period now referred to as Hollywood's Golden Age. Collecting and preserving the sheet music is an extension of my love affair with Hollywood. I see in sheet music the best of both worlds, the world of music and the world of motion pictures. The movie is commemorated, as are the stars and the songs. In possessing the music, I own a little bit of Hollywood past.

The old Grand theater in Rochester, New York, was the scene of my early exposure to the world of the cinema. As a child growing up during the Depression years I was taken to the movies on Tuesday and Thursday nights when a free dish was given with the purchase of tickets. Mother was intent on having a whole set, so if our schoolwork was done, we children were included in the trek to the theater on Dish Nights with our parents, and again on Saturday for the children's matinee.

The matinee took up most of the day, as it included cartoons, previews of coming attractions, the Movietone newsreel, "cliff-hanger" serial installments, and the main course—at least two full-length movies. And if that wasn't enough we could hang around for a second showing.

Our first stop on Saturday mornings before the matinee was the small neighborhood store near the theater that sold penny candy. And I don't mean a penny a piece! In those halcyon days, glass cases full of "ten for a penny" candies beckoned to us, and we could buy a small assorted bagful for one penny. The proprietor would wait patiently as we carefully studied all the varieties and slowly selected "two of those, three of this, one of that, two more of that" until our little bag was full.

Saturday at the Movies
Ecstatic children pose in front of the Metro theater, displaying the free door prizes they received at a Saturday matinee of double features during the Depression. Note the convenient candy store next door.

Dish Night!
The 1930s were lean years for Hollywood, and theater marquees across the country beckoned to the public with inducements of free dishes and multiple features.

The warm, savory smell of fresh popcorn wafted tantalizingly through the lobby as we entered the theater. Lavishly illustrated posters and lobby cards of coming attractions were displayed as we followed a uniformed usher to our seats. Though slightly shabby and down-at-the-heels from heavy use, the Grand theater had all the accoutrements of a grand opera house in the European tradition—crystal chandeliers, heavy velvet draperies, plush seats and carpeting, loge seating for the more affluent, and a pervasive aura of expectancy (see right). One could overlook that the chandeliers had missing prisms and were heavily coated with dust, the draperies had lost their nap, and the plush seats and carpeting were worn and threadbare. The magic was still there.

Once we were seated inside the theater, if the projectionist was late in starting, some in the audience would start clapping in unison to get his attention. Heaven help the poor man if the celluloid failed or if he forgot to change reels, for a cacophony of foot stomping, boos, and whistles would erupt until he got things fixed. We sat in rapt attention through most of the movies, but sometimes during the mushy scenes we squirmed, giggled, and talked in whispers until the action resumed. We would enthusiastically hoot and hiss the villain and cheer the good guys. Communication was never a problem in those days—very simple and direct.

On Sunday the program changed again with two first class or "A" movies, or at the very least, an "A" movie and a less stellar "B" movie. We were indiscriminate in our enthusiasm, enchanted with anything forthcoming on the silver screen. We assiduously followed the screen stars' lives in movie magazines, and learned the names of the most minor film players from the screen credits of the many movies we saw.

Temptation
The mere mention of the magical place known as Hollywood in a movie title was enough to attract large audiences. Popular **Bing Crosby** played a crooner in *Going Hollywood*, with **Marion Davies** as his adoring fan. This was the best of the Arthur Freed/Nacio Herb Brown songs in the film. (1933) $5.

Hooray for Hollywood
Dick Powell's dulcet singing tones were heard in *Hollywood Hotel*, in which he wins a talent contest and goes to Hollywood in search of stardom. The movie was filmed at the venerable old Hollywood Hotel at the corner of Hollywood and Highland, one time gathering place for movie people. Song was written by Johnny Mercer (W) and Richard Whiting (M). (1937) $50 *($120)*

Loew's Paradise Movie Theater
The Grand Theater in Rochester, New York, was in no way as grand as Loew's Paradise in the Bronx, but had its day of splendor, albeit on a much smaller scale. *Photo by Henry Groskinsky.*

The theater courted our business with Bingo games and talent shows and raffles and promotions, as well as the Dish Nights and Saturday matinees. Bank Night was popular in the middle to late 1930s, and money was given to holders of lucky tickets. We and the rest of the world were willing victims, and succumbed to the charms of the cinema, singing along with great gusto with the bouncing ball during the musical interludes.

In the darkened theater as the drapes slowly opened, the big screen with its lights and shadows would come alive and transport us for a few hours from the mediocre ordinariness of a Depression childhood to a storybook world of escapism. Little did we know that this period in cinema history was to be of such short duration. We were blissfully unaware that Jeanette MacDonald and Nelson Eddy would not live forever, and that Shirley Temple would grow up. Those were indeed the "good old days." And the magic of Hollywood and the movies lingers on for me in my collection of old sheet music.

But Definitely
Shirley Temple played a rich child who gets lost and ends up in the care of a vaudeville couple played by **Alice Faye** and **Jack Haley** in *Poor Little Rich Girl*. Naturally, Shirley joins the act, and ends up on the radio where her overjoyed father discovers her. Mack Gordon and Harry Revel wrote the songs. (1936) $12.

Ah! Sweet Mystery of Life
In their first movie together, *Naughty Marietta*, **Jeanette MacDonald** and **Nelson Eddy** created a sensation and established themselves as Hollywood's leading singing duo, warbling the wonderful music of Victor Herbert. British printing. (1935) $5.

Sheet music was published for a surprising number of movies—from the theme songs of the earliest silents to the later sound movies. Pictures of the stars and scenes from the movie adorned the covers in clever attractive graphic presentations similar to the lobby cards and posters that promoted the movie in the theater. The golden years of Hollywood from the debut of the talkies are well-represented, creating a historical record of movies, stars, and studios, that is invaluable for researchers or hobbyists. Though those wonderful years in early Hollywood are past, and many of our favorite stars are gone, they will live forever, frozen in time on the covers of this fine old music.

Collecting movie music can be done from many approaches. Most commonly, one collects covers of one's favorite movie star. Some people collect songs from silent movies with cover pictures of early film stars and movies, or concentrate on accumulating songs from movies of the 1930s or the 1940s. Others collect studios such as Warner Brothers or First National, or music imprinted with the early Vitaphone sound trademark. A favorite composer and/or lyricist of movie songs is sometimes the starting point. Theme collecting in such special categories as *film noir*, war movies, comedies, Academy Award songs, or musicals are other ways. Where several songs from a movie were printed with the same cover, some zealous collectors try to get the complete set.

Sittin' on a Backyard Fence
Each of the songs in *Footlight Parade* has a different background photo and color, not a usual occurence in movie music sets. Most have the same cover design, merely changing the title. In this imaginative production number, Busby Berkeley used a troupe of long-legged chorines dressed in cat costumes. (1933) $5.

Ah, the Moon Is Here
Footlight Parade was a backstage musical with emphasis on the problems of producing a show in the 1930s. Such a story line created many opportunities for a song, and **Dick Powell,** Frank McHugh, and the girls rose to the occasion to sing this one by Irving Kahal (W) and Sammy Fain (M). This is the hardest song to find in the set.*Collection of Harold Jacobs.*$35

Shanghai Lil
Ruby Keeler and **James Cagney** did some fancy tap-dancing in *Footlight Parade.* The production number included an exotic opium den with garishly painted prostitutes, a brawl in a Chinese bar, and a patriotic finale, complete with marching sailors and an oversized portrait of President Roosevelt. $6.

Honeymoon Hotel
Dick Powell and **Ruby Keeler** play young newlyweds who head for the Honeymoon Hotel in Busby Berkeley's production number for *Footlight Parade.* Words by Al Dubin and music by Harry Warren. $5

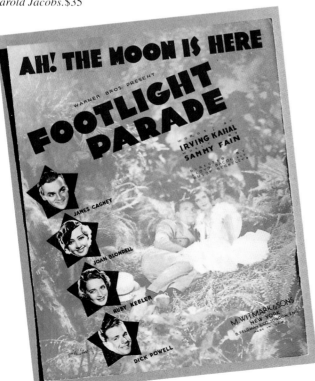

By a Waterfall
Busby Berkeley went all out in this brilliant kaleidoscopic water fantasy in *Footlight Parade*. He used a five-tier water tower from which his bathing beauties dived into a huge well-lit pool. The production number lasted for almost 15 minutes of dazzling special effects. Kahal and Fain wrote this song. $4

Movie sheet music is attracting more collectors every day, but prices are still relatively reasonable, and a fine collection of the more commonly found pieces can be acquired without heavy expenditures. No matter what is collected, it will undoubtedly be a good investment, as well as a cherished memento from the past.

The book is arranged in two parts. The first section starts in the late 1920s when talking pictures took over, with a little background on the transition from silent movies to sound. This is followed by an overview of Hollywood movie songs through the Depression years and World War II. The 1950s and beyond are also touched upon, as certain stars, movies, and songs were too important to omit. Concentration here is mainly on the 1930s and 1940s, the decades of the greatest output of film music. Significant trends are followed for each decade, and pertinent sheet music is used to illustrate these developments. Also included are illustrations of the Academy Award winning songs for the first thirty years since their inception.

The second section is an alphabetical album of famous film stars with thumbnail biographical sketches of each, a listing of their movies that yielded sheet music, and photos of each star on selected song sheet covers. We have tried to use representative songs; if a star was honored with an Oscar, that movie cover is used if possible. Some less notable movie songs are included when interesting graphics warrant their use. Some quite common pieces are also included to sate the beginning collector, and some very rare pieces are shown to whet the appetite of the more advanced collector. Certain conventions observed in the book, perhaps, need an explanation. It should be noted that (W) and (M), when encountered, mean respectively "Words by" and "Music by." When two prices are given in the captions under the photos and in the Song Index at the end of the book, the first price is the usual price paid, and the second price in parentheses and *italics* is a documented price known to have been paid at a dealer's auction. Dates given with film titles are generally the years of first release in the United States, or as close as can be ascertained, given the frequent discrepancies that crop up in movie research materials.

Most of the stars in the profiles were chosen as the most collectible in the movie sheet music marketplace. The vastness of the available material prevented inclusion of everyone's favorite star or movie, and despite attempts at objectivity, personal preferences have undoubtedly crept in. We can only hope that there is something to please and satisfy all our readers.

—Marion Short

CHAPTER 1: TRANSITION TO SOUND

Music as an adjunct to motion pictures was used from the earliest days of the silents. It was frequently played on movie sets by company musicians during filming to cover up stage noise, to create atmosphere, and to get the actors in the right mood for their scenes.

Music was also used by exhibitors in theaters to drown out projector noise and to enhance the drama. Accompanists ranged from earnest musicians playing lachrymose music like "Hearts and Flowers" on battered upright pianos in small theaters to professional symphony orchestras playing specially composed scores in grand motion-picture palaces. Both popular and classical music sources were raided for interpretive themes, and special music with the photos of stars on the cover was often composed and published to promote a particular movie.

When sound movies exploded into popularity in 1929, movie-related sheet music was published in great quantities. The fertile field of early musical revue type movies like *The Broadway Melody*, *Hollywood Revue of 1929*, and *Gold Diggers of Broadway* yielded many different songs from the same movie with the same cover, and practically every important movie released thereafter had its accompanying promotional sheet music.

Don Juan
John Barrymore co-starred with **Mary Astor** in the historic sound movie *Don Juan*, an early experiment by Warner Brothers using a synchronized musical score. This complimentary copy shows the couple in a passionate embrace that wasn't entirely feigned. They were rumored to be romantically involved at the time. Photo on left is opera singer Anna Case who introduced the theme song. $20

Vitaphone Song Excerpts
This advertisement on the back cover of a song sheet teases with one-liner tunes from Warner Brothers and First National movie musicals using the Vitaphone sound system. Samples like these encouraged sheet music sales.

Fox Movietone Follies Excerpts
Excerpts from four of the songs from *Fox Movietone Follies of 1929* are shown on back cover of sheet music. Tin Pan Alley composer Con Conrad was lured to California, where he collaborated with Sidney Mitchell and Archie Gottler on the movie songs.

Pilly Pom Pom Plee
Striking graphics and leggy chorines on a bold yellow background highlight the cover of the First National Vitaphone talkie *Footlights and Fools*. It was an effective vehicle for vivacious cover star **Colleen Moore**. She played a dual part—a fiery musical comedy star and a quiet "plain Jane" type—showing the wide range of her acting skill. (1929) $10

The death knell for independent Tin Pan Alley publishers was sounded when Warner Brothers, in their insatiable quest for music, bought up three major music houses in 1928—Harms, Remick, and Witmark—providing them with a huge reservoir of songs to use in their films. They also contracted with the American Society of Composers, Authors & Publishers (ASCAP) to use works by members of the society, another vast backlog of songs. Metro-Goldwyn-Mayer followed suit by acquiring Leo Feist and Robbins music companies, and Fox Pictures bought up the music firm of DeSylva, Brown and Henderson.

The changing times are reflected on the sheet music covers. No longer did music publishers control the output and promotion of popular music. Hollywood was the new lord, and now decreed that published music would promote feature films. Artwork changed from the cartoon-like flappers, Art Deco, and ethereal Manning covers of the 1920s to covers featuring photos of popular stars from the latest movies. The era of the illustrator was approaching an end, giving way to Hollywood photographic art.

Lamentations are not in order for the loss of illustrated covers because collecting songs from Hollywood movies is also an interesting and stimulating challenge. It could prove to be a valuable investment as well. Hollywood memorabilia is becoming much sought after by collectors, and prices are escalating.

Early Experiments

Interest in adding sound to motion pictures started as early as 1889 in the United States at a Thomas Edison lab with W. K. L. Dickson's invention of the Kinetophone that synchronized phonograph records with action on the screen. By 1912 Edison had produced several one reel talking pictures using this synchronization technique, but a 1914 fire in the Edison labs forestalled additional progress.

Other experiments using the phonograph in synchronization with movies were also conducted in Europe with successful demonstrations at the Paris Exposition of 1900. Further European experiments on a different tack produced a more stable method of matching sound to film—the Tri-Ergon Process that recorded the sound track directly on the film next to the picture.

In America the wiring pioneer Dr. Lee De Forest, who was skeptical of Edison's sound-on-disk technique with its propensity for breakdown, was working on the sound-on-film process. In 1923 he exhibited his Phonofilm system in selected theaters showing movie shorts of speeches and monologues by such luminaries as President Coolidge and Eddie Cantor, and the following year went a step further by producing a two-reel talkie with Una Merkel, *Love's Old Sweet Song*. But De Forest's endeavors failed to stimulate interest in the movie world. The De Forest system, integrated with the European Tri-Ergon Process, was eventually used by Fox studios in their Movietone sound system. By the mid-1920s both approaches to adding sound to movies were becoming viable—the Vitaphone sound-on-disk system of Warner Brothers, and the Movietone sound-on-film system of Fox studios.

Warner Brothers, a relatively small studio in the throes of financial doldrums, gambled that sound movies were the wave of the future and took the leap, waging a publicity campaign promoting Vitaphone, and forging ahead with their first feature-length sound production. They heralded the coming of the sound era on August 6, 1926, with a lavish premiere at their New York theater introducing the John Barrymore swashbuckler *Don Juan*, in which a musical score on large wax disks accompanied the film in synchronization. The first half of the program featured musical shorts of renowned opera stars and performances by the New York Philharmonic Orchestra filmed at the old Manhattan Opera House in New York. At the colorful opening, ticket-takers dressed in 15th century *Don Juan* period costumes handed out complimentary souvenir copies of the movie's theme song.

Opening Night in New York
After the glamorous premiere of *Don Juan*, curious New York audiences braved the heat and humidity of an August summer to view the new Vitaphone sound phenomenon in a Warner's refrigerated theater.

Opening Night in Los Angeles
Headlines in the trade paper *Variety* were enthusiastic over Warner Brothers' Vitaphone sound system after the sellout Los Angeles opening of *Don Juan* at Grauman's Egyptian Theater in October of 1926. "Remarkable first night crowd acclaims Vitaphone.... Perfect synchronization of sound and motion causes spectators to gasp."

The success of the *Don Juan* venture prompted Warners to make other sound movies in the same vein—with synchronized music and sound effects, but still no dialogue. *The Better 'Ole* (1926) was a slapstick comedy film starring Syd Chaplin, talented brother of Charlie Chaplin, who played a cockney soldier during World War I. Its opening presentation also included Vitaphone shorts featuring Al Jolson and George Jessel. Another Vitaphone sound flick, *When a Man Loves* (1927), co-starred John Barrymore and Dolores Costello in a costume drama with able support from Eugenie Besserer, Warner Oland, and Myrna Loy.

The Jazz Singer

Though Vitaphone's system of matching sound recording on disk with a film projector was handicapped by frequent interruptions in synchronization, it still led the field in sound pictures. On October 6, 1927, with much fanfare, Warner Brothers made cinema history by releasing its first talking motion picture *The Jazz Singer* at Warner's Theater in New York. The use of synchronized dialogue and sound to advance the telling of the story was the magic touch. The movie was a sensation, and the public wanted more sound pictures.

The Jazz Singer was basically a silent movie with the old subtitles on the screen. It also had a synchronized orchestral score based on excerpts from the works of classical composers and exquisite Hebraic cantorial music sung by Cantor Joseph Rosenblatt. Warner Oland played Jolson's father, and Eugenie Besserer, his sympathetic mother. As the sentimental subtitles tell us, "God made her a woman and love made her a mother." Lovely little May McAvoy played the actress who helped the jazz singer break into the theater. When she first heard him perform she gazed soulfully into his eyes commenting through subtitle, "There are lots of jazz singers, but you have a tear in your voice."

For movie audiences the main attraction of *The Jazz Singer* was popular star Al Jolson talking and singing on the screen. Two sequences of synchronized speech and several popular songs from his Broadway shows performed in Jolson's inimitable, enthusiastic style dazzled audiences, and drew crowds of people to theaters across the country. Songs by Jolson in *The Jazz Singer* were already top sheet music sellers—"Dirty Hands, Dirty Face," "Toot, Toot, Tootsie," "Blue Skies," "Mother of Mine," and "My Mammy." In addition Jolson performed a touching rendition of "Kol Nidre" in the synagogue scene at the end of the movie.

Mother of Mine, I Still Have You
Al Jolson's famous line on the vaudeville stage was "You ain't heard nothing yet!" and he proved it in *The Jazz Singer*, the first feature length movie using the Vitaphone sound system that used spoken dialogue and songs. George Jessel was originally slated for the role, but Warner Brothers refused to meet his price, and the dynamic performer Jolson was selected. He sang his best known stage songs and improvised snappy dialogue that delighted audiences. (1927) *Collection of Harold Jacobs.* $6

My Mammy
Songs sung by **Al Jolson** in *The Jazz Singer* sold piles of sheet music including this famous hit originally in the stage show *Sinbad*. He performed it in blackface in the theater scene at the end of the movie. (1921) $5

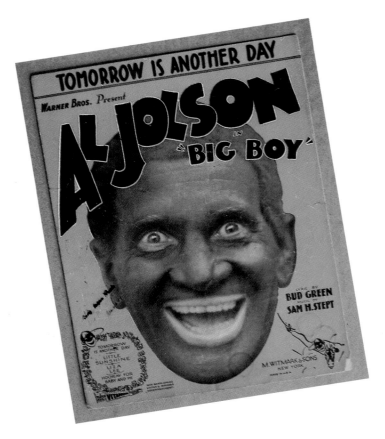

Tomorrow Is Another Day
Al Jolson's vivacity comes across on this sheet music cover from the Warner Brothers movie *Big Boy*, a racing picture in which he portrayed a Negro jockey (in blackface) who wins the Kentucky Derby, a role he reprised from his 1925 stage show. (1930) $15

Al Jolson (1886-1950) was an established vaudeville star long before he entered the movies. He was born Ase Yoelson in Russia, and arrived in this country as a boy. Like the fictional father in the *Jazz Singer* scenario, Jolson's real-life father wanted him to become a cantor, but Al resisted and joined a circus as a ballyhoo man. He later became a cafe entertainer and toured in vaudeville as a blackface comedian and "mammy" singer. From that time on he rapidly became the reigning king of musical shows in New York, starring in nine Broadway hits between 1911 and 1925. His name became a household word through widespread sales of his phonograph records, and his face appeared on countless sheet music covers from as early as 1912. With *The Jazz Singer* his fame became worldwide, and his place in cinema history was firmly established as star of the first talking picture.

Swanee
Jolson songs are popular with collectors. A whole new generation came to know him and his unique style through the Columbia movie *The Jolson Story*. **Larry Parks** portrayed Jolson, but it was the real Al Jolson who sang the songs off-screen causing a surge in sales of records of the sound track. The hit movie won Academy Awards for best scoring of a musical and best sound recording. (1946) $3

15

The Vitaphone System

In the late summer of 1928, Warner Brothers absorbed First National studios, and sheet music with the familiar Vitaphone banner began to appear. All the feature films made at Warner Brothers and First National in 1928-1929 (some 67 of them) used the Vitaphone sound system, and sheet music from these movies have the Vitaphone logo. Vitaphone was represented on sheet music from 1928 to 1934, but with its frustrating synchronization imperfections, it was eventually phased out in favor of the more reliable sound-on-film system.

The first all-talking feature film made by Warner Brothers was *The Lights of New York* in 1928, followed by *The Singing Fool*, again starring Al Jolson. The public was clamoring for more of Jolson, and sheet music and record sales soared as songs from *The Singing Fool* became popular across the country.

Glad Rag Doll
The early Vitaphone sound movie *Glad Rag Doll* had a lot of kinks in it, and reportedly had little else going for it except the exquisite beauty of **Dolores Costello**, who played a show girl pursued by a rich man. Music for this theme song was composed by Dan Dougherty and Milton Ager with lyrics by Jack Yellen, who also wrote a special recitation for the song. (1929) $5

Sonny Boy
Other songs from *The Singing Fool*, Vitaphone's part-talkie movie, included "It All Depends on You," "I'm Sittin' on Top of the World," "Keep Smiling at Trouble," "Golden Gate," "There's a Rainbow 'Round My Shoulder," and "The Spaniard Who Blighted My Life." The biggest seller by far was "Sonny Boy," shown here with **Al Jolson** and little **Davey Lee** on the cover. Jolson reputedly made a fortune from royalties on this song alone. (1928) $4

Under a Texas Moon
Michael Curtiz directed the romantic adventure *Under a Texas Moon*, one of his earlier efforts for Warner Brothers. It starred **Frank Fay** as a Mexican desperado and **Raquel Torres** as his love interest, and had the added bonus of Vitaphone sound and Technicolor. (1930) $5

The Movietone System

Movietone was Vitaphone's competitor in the development of a sound system for movies. Developed by the William Fox film company, it recorded sound directly on film, much as it is done today. It was a big improvement over Vitaphone's sound-on-disk technique. At first the Fox company concentrated on Movietone newsreels, and audiences were thrilled to view screenings of such exciting events as the departure of Charles Lindbergh and his welcome back in Washington. Simultaneously Fox was also making part-talkie feature length movies with Movietone sound, and by 1929 Fox Film Corporation had produced 47 Movietone sound pictures.

A Night of Happiness
Cover star **Lois Moran** made the transition from silents to talkies co-starring with singer/pianist **Joseph Wagstaff** in the exciting movie musical *A Song of Kentucky*, another sound vehicle using the Movietone sound system. (1929) $5

Right:

Movietone Promotional Ad
In its early sound days, Fox Movietone concentrated on presenting famous contemporary personalities in short sound features. Clockwise from bottom right: **Chic Sale, Robert Benchley, Benito Mussolini, George Bernard Shaw, Charles Lindbergh, Joe Cook, Bobby Clark** and **Paul McCullough**, with **King Alfonso XII** of Spain in center.

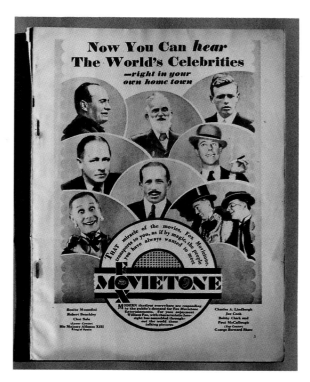

Left:

Flower of Delight
John Ford directed *The Black Watch*, his first all-sound film using the Fox Movietone sound system. The setting was in India, and **Myrna Loy** played an exotic Indian princess to **Victor McLaglen**'s British officer. (1929) $15

Ride on Vaquero
Warner Baxter and **Mary Duncan** appear on cover in a scene from the Fox Movietone production of *Romance of the Rio Grande*. Baxter had played leads in silent movies but met with more success with his first sound movie *In Old Arizona* playing the bandit, the Cisco Kid, for which he won an Academy Award. (1929) $6

17

Other Sound Systems

To keep up with the demand, other studios scrambled to add sound to their pictures. Paramount Famous Players-Lasky made 49 Movietone movies, and Universal, M-G-M, United Artists, and Columbia also jumped on the Movietone bandwagon. RKO Pathé Exchange and Tiffany-Stahl Productions used Photophone, a system almost identical to Movietone. Tiffany-Stahl named its sound system "Tiffany T-o-n-e." At the same time, theater distributors around the world were frantically converting to sound equipment to handle the new phenomenon, preferably Movietone or one of the other sound-on-film systems that had fewer problems.

To You
The Tiffany-Stahl all-talking production of *Woman to Woman* co-starred **Betty Compson**, a major silent film star, with **George Barraud.** The movie included three songs, and sound was provided by the Tiffany-Tone system. (1929) $7

A Kiss to Remember
Tiffany-Stahl Studios made some noteworthy silent movies and several talkies of the "soap opera" variety, before drifting into the B-western genre in the 1930s. *My Lady's Past* was an early sound offering that used the Tiffany-Tone sound system, an offshoot of the Photophone sound-on-film system. The film featured cover stars **Joe E. Brown** and **Belle Bennett.** (1928) $18

True Blue Lou
Paramount Studios opted for the Movietone system in their all talking, singing, dancing production *The Dance of Life*, a classy movie with good songs, a good plot, and the talents of Broadway stars **Hal Skelly** and winsome **Nancy Carroll.** (1929) $5

Casualties of the Talkies

The transition period to sound only lasted a couple of years, but was fraught with confusion and sometimes panic. Stars whose voices were unsuitable were replaced, and the Broadway stage was raided for talent. Directors had to rethink their technique, always keeping in mind the importance of the proximity of the actors to microphones, which, in the early days before the microphone boom, were stationary radio mikes spotted around the set, hidden in props, or suspended by ropes.

In the rush to adapt to sound there was often some overlapping of silents and "talkies." Silent movies in production frequently added hodgepodge sound effects, musical scores, and sporadic dialogue in combination with subtitles to please the horde of sound-hungry movie viewers. In the years 1928-1929 a great proliferation of silent movies, sound movies, part-talkies, and all-talkies flooded the screen. But by 1930 the silent era was virtually at an end, and talking pictures took over. Silent stars with stage experience generally moved smoothly into sound movies, leaving behind many famous and gifted movie stars of the silents who failed to make the transition.

When My Dream of Love Comes True
Beautiful **Corinne Griffith** starred in *Prisoners*, a Vitaphone sound picture. She was a popular star of the silents with a long list of successful movies when she tackled the sound problem. She was criticized for talking through her nose. After her few talkies bombed, she faced the bitter reality that she should retire gracefully from the screen to pursue a writing career. (1929) $5

Paradise
Exotic **Pola Negri**, a reigning star of Hollywood silents, attempted to cross the sound barrier in RKO's *A Woman Commands*. She sang this lovely Nacio Herb Brown song in the movie, but her deep voice and thick foreign accent impeded her presentation. The film flopped, and she returned to Europe to try to revive her slumping career. (1932) $3

Left:

Love's First Kiss
During the silent era **John Gilbert** was the highest paid movie star in the country, a handsome, dashing, and charismatic leading man. His career was ruined when surprised audiences found that his voice failed to match his commanding screen presence, and his love scenes drew snickers. As his career slid downhill, he turned to alcohol and died a broken man at age 41. He is seen here with **Garbo** in *A Woman of Affairs*. (1929) $20

A Year from Today
Norma Talmadge, star of *New York Nights*, was the queen of silent melodramas in the 1920s, popular with audiences as a tearful heroine. She tried valiantly to adapt to the demands of sound by taking elocution lessons, but her rather nasal Brooklyn accent doomed all hopes and she retired from the screen after two sound movies. (1929) $6

Broadway's Influence

By the end of 1929 many Tin Pan Alley composers were lured to Hollywood, attracted by generous contracts and the promise of greater fame even than their Broadway successes had brought them. Nacio Herb Brown and the team of DeSylva, Brown, and Henderson were soon joined by Irving Berlin, the Gershwin brothers, Cole Porter, Jerome Kern, Vincent Youmans, and Richard Rodgers. Movie versions of Broadway musicals were popular fare for audiences, and Broadway tunesmiths were happy to cooperate on the productions.

Keepin' Myself for You
Broadway composer Vincent Youmans brought his stage musical *Hit the Deck* to the Hollywood screen with **Jack Oakie** playing the sailor Bilge Smith and **Polly Walker** as Looloo, the owner of a seaside hash house, whose sudden wealth changes her life. (1929) $4

Turn on the Heat
The Broadway team of DeSylva, Brown, and Henderson wrote the original film score for *Sunny Side Up*, a hit Hollywood musical featuring the popular romantic couple **Janet Gaynor** and Charles Farrell. Other songs include "If I Had a Talking Picture of You" and "I'm a Dreamer, Aren't We All?" (1929) $4

Opposite page:

Singin' in the Rain
The spectacular M-G-M movie *Hollywood Revue of 1929* featured this Arthur Freed and Nacio Herb Brown song. The all-star lineup included **Marie Dressler, Marion Davies, Joan Crawford, John Gilbert, Norma Shearer, Buster Keaton,** and **Jack Benny.** (1929) $5

Were You Just Pretending
No, No, Nanette transferred successfully from the Broadway theater to the motion picture screen. An amusing plot, great songs, a talented cast, and some dazzling Technicolor sequences guaranteed a solid hit. (1930) $8

Love Sings a Song in My Heart
Laura La Plante played Magnolia in Universal's *Show Boat*, seen here on an alternate cover for the movie. Critics found the movie to be an uninspired production, citing over-emoting by the actors, clumsy direction, and a lack of continuity partly because it was filmed as a silent movie with songs and dialogue added later. (1929) $5

Ol' Man River
Joseph Schildkraut as Gaylord Ravenal and **Alma Rubens** as Julie co-starred in the first movie version of *Show Boat*. Schildkraut began as a matinee idol on the stage, moving into character roles in later movies culminating in an Oscar for Best Supporting Actor in *The Life of Emile Zola* in 1937. Poor little Alma Rubens was addicted to heroine and died in 1931. (1929) $4

As established stars in Hollywood fell by the wayside when their voices failed to meet the demands of sound, stage stars and musical comedy stars joined the influx of talent to replace them. Sophie Tucker starred in *Honky Tonk*, and Rudy Vallee in *The Vagabond Lover*—both with lots of good songs. Ziegfeld stars Fanny Brice, Marilyn Miller, Helen Morgan, and Eddie Cantor also headed west to make early sound movies. Broadway chorus girls looking for stardom, like Ruby Keeler and Barbara Stanwyck, came to Hollywood around this time to start their movie careers.

I'm the Last of the Red Hot Mammas
Famous vaudevillian **Sophie Tucker** dominated the screen in *Honky Tonk* in a strong portrayal of a mother who is determined to give her daughter a better life than she had. She was cast as a nightclub entertainer, and the plot gave her ample opportunity to belt out some great interpretations. (1929) $7

If You Want the Rainbow
Fannie Brice crossed over from the stage to star in the part-talkie movie *My Man* in which she played a struggling performer who hits the big time as a Broadway star. Her vibrant personality and sure way with a song captivated audiences. Other songs from her repertoire that she sang in the movie were "I'd Rather Be Blue" and "Second Hand Rose." (1928) $4

A Little Kiss Each Morning
Rudy Vallee with his Connecticut Yankees band was one of the top performers on record and radio in the country when he starred in the Radio Picture *The Vagabond Lover*. Despite his wooden acting technique, the movie was a solid hit as audiences flocked to see their idol. (1929) $5

What Wouldn't I Do for That Man
Helen Morgan performed this song in both movies, *Applause* and *Glorifying the American Girl*. She was particularly praised for her portrayal of a down-at-the-heels aging burlesque star who shields her daughter from her squalid life style and ends up a suicide. Director Rouben Mamoulian is now recognized for his innovative camera work and sound track manipulation, which opened new doors in movie-making technique. (1929) $6

If I'm Dreaming
Jerome Kern's 1920 successful hit show *Sally* was tapped in Hollywood's search for new material, with **Marilyn Miller** creating her original Broadway stage role. She is seen toe dancing on this song cover from the movie version with the Alberta Rasch dancers in the background. (1930) $5

The White Dove
Lionel Barrymore directed the Technicolor all-talking picture *The Rogue Song* co-starring Metropolitan Opera baritone **Laurence Tibbett** with **Catherine Dale Owen**. The script was based on Franz Lehar's operetta *Gypsy Love*, with this Lehar song written especially for the movie. Interestingly, the music sheets outlasted the movie, as no known prints are extant today. (1930) $4

Star-Studded Musical Revues

The procession of star-studded musicals in 1929 included two outstanding movie hits, *The Broadway Melody* from M-G-M and *The Gold Diggers of Broadway* from Warner Brothers. The success of these all-singing, all-talking movies created a surge of competing movie musicals, many of which were presented in the revue format using talented headliners in featured acts with little or no plot line.

M-G-M made *Hollywood Revue of 1929*, and Fox released *Fox Movietone Follies* that same year. Warner Brothers followed suit with its all-star extravaganza *The Show of Shows*. Universal presented *The King of Jazz* in 1930 with Paul Whiteman's orchestra showcasing young Bing Crosby and the Rhythm Boys, and Paramount joined the club with *Paramount on Parade*. Songs from these movies became instantly popular and were snapped up by the public.

Walking with Susie
Former silent star, pert **Sue Carol** (top) is one of the beauties on this song cover from the William Fox production of *Fox Movietone Follies*, which used the same sound-on-film system that the studio used in its Movietone Newsreels. (1929) $5

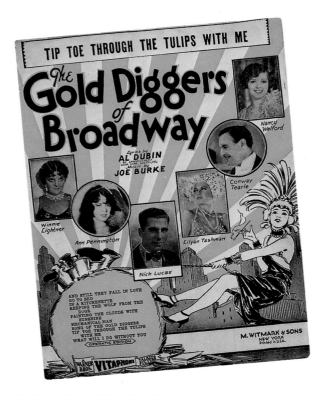

Tip Toe Through the Tulips With Me
Nick Lucas sang this in *The Gold Diggers of Broadway*, a Warner Brothers early Vitaphone sound offering that was notable for its use of two-color Technicolor as well as memorable songs by Al Dubin and Joe Burke. (1929) $4

Singin' in the Bathtub
Warner Brothers' *The Show of Shows* was an all-star extravaganza that included such luminaries as John Barrymore reciting a Shakespearean soliloquy, Ted Lewis's orchestra, Myrna Loy as an Oriental princess, and appearances by Richard Barthelmess, Loretta Young, Ann Sothern, and Alice White, among others. Winnie Lightner performed this song in the movie. (1929) $4

Song of the Dawn
King of Jazz, Universal Studio's offering to the lineup of super-musicals, featured the music of **Paul Whiteman** and his band. This classic musical revue was directed by Broadway's John Murray Anderson, and was praised as "nothing short of superlative." John Boles with 500 cowboys sang this song by Jack Yellen (W) and Milton Ager (M) in the movie. (1930) $4

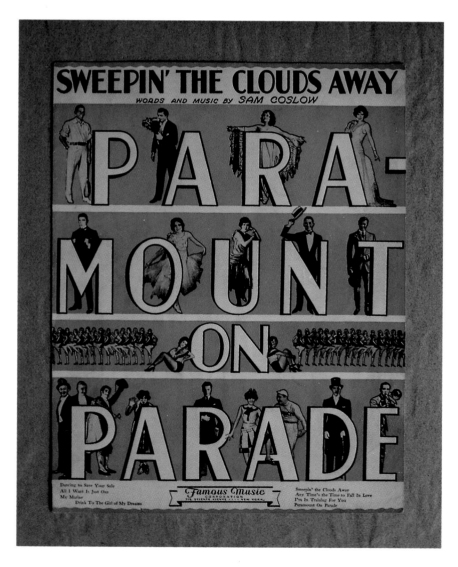

Sweepin' the Clouds Away
Paramount Studios, not to be outdone, mounted *Paramount on Parade*, a sparkling plotless revue using practically every star and would-be star on the lot. Some stars identified on cover are **Nancy Carroll** (2nd line "O") with **Margaret Lindsay, Maurice Chevalier,** and **Gary Cooper** to her left. A dignified, dapper **William Powell** stands behind the "D," with **Jack Oakie** on his right, and **Buddy Rogers** on his left. (1930) $5

Deanna Durbin

Norma Shearer

The 1930s
★ ★ ★ ★ ★

Shirley Temple

Alice Faye

Fred Astaire & Ginger Rogers

Bing Crosby & Joan Bennett

Joan Crawford & Clark Gable

Judy Garland

Loretta Young & Charles Boyer

Jeanette MacDonald & Nelson Eddy

Jean Harlow & Allan Jones

CHAPTER 3: 1930s PHENOMENA

The country was in the throes of the Depression in the early 1930s, and theater attendance plummeted. Many moviegoers preferred to stay home and listen to the radio rather than go out to the show. To stimulate faltering attendance, ticket prices were lowered and double features were offered, often with cartoons, newsreels, trailers, and short subjects. Some theaters had Dish Nights and free dishes were given out with a ticket, inducing customers to return until they had the whole set. Screeno, Bingo, and Banko games were played between features, and prizes were raffled off to holders of winning tickets.

The public was drawn to a wide variety of films including horror movies, gangster movies, and a plethora of charming musicals. Movies offered inexpensive escapism from grim reality, and became immensely popular. Weekly attendance at picture shows increased from 50 million in 1932 to 85 million in 1936.

The chief movie studios at the start of the 1930s were Columbia, Goldwyn Studios, Paramount, Metro-Goldwyn-Mayer, Warner Brothers, Pathé, RKO Radio, Universal, United Artists, Fox, Hal Roach, Tiffany-Stahl, and Walt Disney. At the close of the decade the so-called "Big Five" movie studios had emerged—Warner Brothers, M-G-M, Paramount, RKO, and Twentieth Century-Fox. They owned their own theater chains and had complete artistic control over their product and its release. The lesser studios at this time were Universal, Columbia, and United Artists. Republic and Monogram were two so-called "Poverty Row" studios that made mainly Westerns and B-movies respectively.

Along with the vast music library it acquired from Tin Pan Alley, Warner Brothers studio also had the enormously talented choreographer Busby Berkeley, who astounded audiences with his special effects in movies like *42nd Street* and the *Gold Diggers* series. M-G-M produced sparkling musicals featuring the talented twosomes Mickey Rooney and Judy Garland, and Nelson Eddy and Jeanette MacDonald. RKO launched the dazzling dance team of Fred Astaire and Ginger Rogers, Twentieth Century-Fox had the winsome moppet Shirley Temple, and Universal was in the running with soprano Deanna Durbin. The star system moved into high gear, and unknown starlets who could sing and dance were catapulted to stardom at the whim of a studio head.

Busby Berkeley

The legendary choreographer Busby Berkeley was recruited from the Broadway stage in the 1930s, bringing his innovative concepts with him. He took the basically immobile camera and "gave it legs." Instead of having performers parade their acts in front of a static camera, he choreographed the camera to move with the activity, sometimes featuring closeups of dancers' legs or their smiling faces, or creating brilliant kaleidoscopic effects by shooting from top, bottom, or side angles, and introducing techniques in photography that revolutionized the industry.

Berkeley's first film, *Whoopee*, produced by Samuel Goldwyn and Florenz Ziegfeld, starred Eddie Cantor, and featured some great songs by Gus Kahn and Walter Donaldson including "Makin' Whoopee" and "My Baby Just Cares For Me." His stunning choreography and grand scale photography foreshadowed the brilliance that became associated with Berkeley in later films.

Berkeley's musical settings in 1930s movies captured the genius of his great talent. His most prolific year was 1933 with fabulous production numbers in four successful movies—*42nd Street*, *Gold Diggers of 1933*, *Footlight Parade*, and *Roman Scandals*. His exciting dance ensembles were dramatically enhanced by his clever and daring use of inventive camera angles and creative lighting.

Gold Diggers of 1933 featured Depression songs with a theme of optimism. Who can forget bright and brassy young Ginger Rogers in a gown of gold coins belting out "We're In the Money" with a special chorus in "pig Latin," and the snappy dance routines of charming hoofer Ruby Keeler as the understudy who made good when she replaced the star? "Pettin' In the Park" with Dick Powell and Ruby Keeler was a lavish Berkeley production number that used lots of pretty blondes and a midget who leaps from a baby buggy to leer lasciviously at the petting couples. Joan Blondell sang "Remember My Forgotten Man," a mournful Harry Warren tune that was a tribute to the Depression army of out-of-work homeless war veterans standing in food lines for handouts, and begging for dimes on rainy street corners. The dramatic march in the lengthy finale was an inspired bit of drama in an unforgettable scene. Stars like Dick Powell, Ruby Keeler, Ginger Rogers, and Joan Blondell remain eternally fresh, young, and appealing in this delightful movie.

In *Gold Diggers of 1935* the imaginative Berkeley dazzled audiences with the spectacle of 65 girls dressed in white playing 65 white baby grand pianos in "The Words Are In My Heart" number. Songs from Berkeley 1930s musicals were big sheet music sellers, getting a tremendous boost by being featured in these popular movies. He continued his inventiveness in the 1940s with *Strike Up the Band*, *Ziegfeld Girl*, *Lady Be Good*, *For Me and My Gal*, *Girl Crazy*, and *The Gang's All Here*. He also created a spectacular water ballet for the Esther Williams movie *Million Dollar Mermaid* in 1951.

Busby Berkeley Musicals

My Baby Just Cares for Me
Eddie Cantor reprised his original Broadway role in this movie version of *Whoopee*. Busby Berkeley's creativity set a new standard of excellence for musical production numbers. (1929) $4

Shadow Waltz
Fresh-as-a-daisy **Ruby Keeler**, framed in the window, was entranced with **Dick Powell**'s singing in the next apartment. As a budding songwriter, he saved the day by backing the show and writing the song for this glamorous production number created in Busby Berkeley's lavish style for *Gold Diggers of 1933*. $4

You're Getting to Be a Habit with Me
Forty Second Street sparkled with inspired Busby Berkeley production numbers and songs by Al Dubin and Harry Warren. The story line ran that the leading lady in a musical show (**Bebe Daniels**) broke a leg, giving a struggling chorine (**Ruby Keeler**) her big chance on stage. **Dick Powell** played the virile tenor love interest. (1933) $4

The Girl at the Ironing Board
Dames was memorable for Busby Berkeley's creative production numbers and good songs by Al Dubin and Harry Warren including "I Only Have Eyes for You," "Try to See It My Way," and "Dames." **Joan Blondell** smiles prettily as she labors at the ironing board on this song cover (the most valuable in the set). (1934) $50

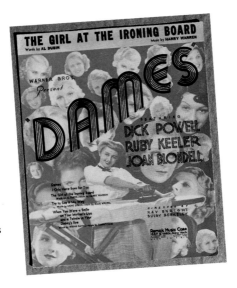

Build a Little Home
Roman Scandals, set in Caesar's Rome, gave Busby Berkeley a fertile field on which to stage his dances and production numbers. **Eddie Cantor** starred, and also notable was Ruth Etting, who sang the torch song "No More Love," while a slave market of blonde "nude" women in chains writhed on a revolving set. (1933) $6

With Plenty of Money and You
Joan Blondell, one-time wife of Dick Powell, is the lovely statuesque blonde posing on the cover of a popular song by Al Dubin and Harry Warren from *Gold Diggers of 1937*. (1937) $6

Child Stars

Bright and wholesome child stars charmed and delighted audiences in the 1930s—talented singers and superlative actors who could bring tears to the eyes and a lump to the throat of the most sophisticated movie viewer. Topping the list of juvenile superstars of the 1930s were Shirley Temple, Judy Garland, and Deanna Durbin. Mickey Rooney, Jackie Cooper, Freddie Bartholomew, and the Our Gang Kids were other favorites. Less renowned but very popular in their heyday were Jane Withers, Bobby Breen, Gloria Jean, and the Dionne quintuplets. Animated cartoons, always popular with both young and old, were topped by Walt Disney's monumental feature-length production of *Snow White and the Seven Dwarfs*, released at Christmas time in 1937.

On Account-a I Love You
The country had already fallen in love with beguiling little four-year-old **Shirley Temple** when she made *Baby Take a Bow,* seen with cover stars **James Dunn** and **Claire Trevor.** Her singing, dancing, and acting were so astounding that it even was rumored that she was a midget. Fortunately she continued growing and dispelled the rumors. (1934) $30

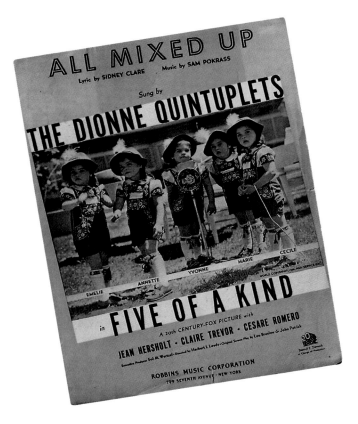

All Mixed Up
The darling **Dionne Quintuplets** were world famous and the public devoured news items about them. They charmed audiences in the movie *Five of a Kind* when they were only four years old. The popular youngsters appear on the cover of this song by Sidney Clare and Sam Pokrass. (1938) *Collection of James Nelson Brown.* $15

Meet the Beat of My Heart
The Hardy family series was top box-office owing to the charm and talent of **Mickey Rooney** as the sincere callow youth, Andy Hardy. *Love Finds Andy Hardy* was the fourth in this popular series, and it introduced **Judy Garland** into the cast, and also a cute ingenue called Lana Turner. (1938) $20

If I Had My Way
Petite **Gloria Jean** was fourteen when she co-starred with **Bing Crosby** in *If I Had My Way*. Universal Studio was grooming her to replace Deanna Durbin who was moving into more adult roles, but despite her sweet good looks and a voice like an angel, she failed to hit the big time as she matured, and is best remembered as a charming adolescent. (1940) $7

Someone to Care for Me
Deanna Durbin made her feature debut in *Three Smart Girls*, a sentimental story about three sisters who try to bring their parents together. With her clear light coloratura singing and youthful prettiness and enthusiasm, she delighted movie audiences and became one of Universal Studio's major stars. (1936) $10

Keep That Twinkle in Your Eye
Jane Withers was sometimes cast as the bratty nemesis of little Shirley Temple, but in *Paddy O'Day* she proved her worth as an independent star. As an immigrant who arrives at Ellis Island to find that her mother has died, she gives a moving performance as a plucky kid moving into the world of entertainment. (1935) *Collection of Harold Jacobs.* $25

Down Where the Trade Winds Blow
Bobby Breen (born 1927), a great little singer from Canada, became a national celebrity when he sang on Eddie Cantor's radio show in 1936. He was a popular child star at RKO until his voice began to change. He was ten years old when he starred in *Hawaii Calls*, playing a stowaway on a ship going to Hawaii. (1937) $15

Right:
Ten Pins in the Sky
Freddie Bartholomew was London-born and acted on the English stage and screen before coming to Hollywood. He was a gifted child actor in a string of fine performances, notably in *David Copperfield*, *Little Lord Fauntleroy*, and *Captains Courageous*. He co-starred with exuberant **Judy Garland** in *Listen Darling*, the two of them playing teenage matchmakers. (1938) $40

Skippy
Jackie Cooper played in several "Our Gang" comedies before becoming one of Hollywood's most popular juvenile actors. He was nominated for the Best Actor Academy Award for his role in *Skippy*. Other successful 1930s films where he effectively stirred the emotions were with colorful Wallace Beery in *The Champ*, *The Bowery*, and *Treasure Island*. Cooper made a smooth transition to television as an actor, director, and producer. In private life he has distinguished himself as a high-ranking officer in the U. S. Naval Reserve. (1930) $15 *($40)*

Talented Twosomes

Jeanette MacDonald and Nelson Eddy

Talented twosomes were popular in the 1930s. Jeanette MacDonald and Nelson Eddy starred in eight screen operettas together—*Naughty Marietta*, *Rose Marie*, *Maytime*, *The Girl of the Golden West*, *Sweethearts*, *New Moon*, *Bitter Sweet*, and *I Married an Angel*. She was young and beautiful, and he was stalwart and handsome, and they sang to each other at incredible volumes while entwined in each other's arms. They were beloved as "America's Singing Sweethearts" for the purity and beauty of their movie personae, and faithful fans still pack revival theaters to enjoy the golden-voiced couple.

I'm Falling in Love with Someone
The operetta *Naughty Marietta* was transferred beautifully to the screen with **Jeanette MacDonald** portraying a French princess who runs off to America and meets and falls in love with handsome Indian scout **Nelson Eddy.** Douglas Shearer won an Oscar for his outstanding sound recording of the music. (1935) $5

Snow White and the Seven Dwarfs Song Folio
Walt Disney's first feature length animated cartoon earned a Special Oscar, custom designed with Snow White representing Oscar flanked by seven little dwarf Oscars descending in a row. Hollywood's top child star, diminutive Shirley Temple, made the presentation to Walt Disney beaming enthusiastically, "Isn't it beautiful and shiny, Mr. Disney?" (1938) $35

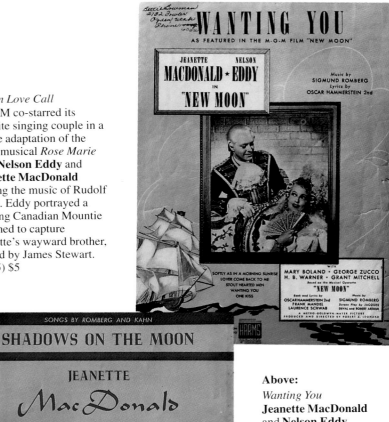

Left:

Indian Love Call
M-G-M co-starred its favorite singing couple in a movie adaptation of the stage musical *Rose Marie* with **Nelson Eddy** and **Jeanette MacDonald** singing the music of Rudolf Friml. Eddy portrayed a dashing Canadian Mountie assigned to capture Jeanette's wayward brother, played by James Stewart. (1935) $5

Shadows on the Moon
Jeanette MacDonald was a saloon keeper, and **Nelson Eddy** was a dashing bandit in the musical melodrama *The Girl of the Golden West*. It was a beautifully scenic movie with songs by Sigmund Romberg (M) and Gus Kahn (W). (1938) $6

Summer Serenade—Badinage
Jeanette MacDonald and **Nelson Eddy** broke away from period costumes in *Sweethearts*, a musical comedy about a married stage couple who want to leave Broadway for Hollywood. Victor Herbert again provided the music with lyrics by Bob Wright and Chet Forrest. (1938) $5

Above:

Wanting You
Jeanette MacDonald and **Nelson Eddy** were paired for a sixth time in *New Moon*, a romantic adventure based on the successful operetta. The wonderful Hammerstein/Romberg score also included "Softly As in a Morning Sunrise," "Lover Come Back to Me," and "Stout Hearted Men." (1940) $8 *($20)*

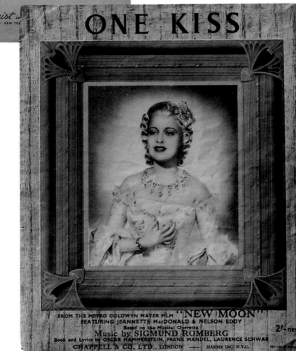

Right:

One Kiss
Jeanette MacDonald was at her loveliest in *New Moon* singing this Sigmund Romberg song with lyrics by Oscar Hammerstein II. The setting was 1700s New Orleans, and her romantic partner was again Nelson Eddy. This is a British printing. (1940) $6

Ziguener
Noel Coward's original British stage musical *Bitter Sweet* was a perfect vehicle for **Jeanette MacDonald** and **Nelson Eddy** when brought to the screen by M-G-M. The combination of Coward's wonderful music, brilliant Technicolor, and the popular couple made a pleasing package. (1940) $5

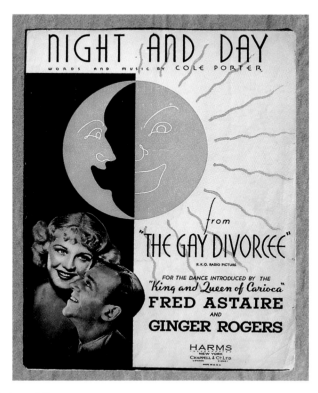

Night and Day
Ginger Rogers with **Fred Astaire**, at their sparkling best, were a winning combination in *The Gay Divorcee*. This great popular classic was written by Cole Porter. (1934) $7

Ginger Rogers and Fred Astaire

The great dancing partners Ginger Rogers and Fred Astaire danced their way through a series of fine movie musicals, and are found on sheet music covers of songs by Broadway's top composers. Cole Porter music was featured in *The Gay Divorcée* in 1934; George Gershwin wrote songs for *Shall We Dance* in 1937; Irving Berlin scored the songs for *Top Hat* (1935), *Follow the Fleet* (1936), and *Carefree* (1938); and Jerome Kern wrote the songs for *Swingtime* in 1936. (Some of these song covers were Academy Award winners and can be viewed in Chapter 6.)

The Piccolino
Irving Berlin's original film score for the RKO Radio movie *Top Hat* was written expressly for the talents of **Ginger Rogers** and **Fred Astaire**, and included other worthy songs, "Top Hat, White Tie, and Tails," "Isn't This a Lovely Day," "No Strings," and "Cheek to Cheek." (1935) $10

Let's Face the Music and Dance
The entertaining musical *Follow the Fleet* co-starred **Fred Astaire** as a sailor and **Ginger Rogers** as a dance hall girl who once again create their dancing magic on the screen. Fred introduced this fine Irving Berlin song in the film that has since become an enduring standard. (1936) $5

Let's Call the Whole Thing Off
An original score with hit songs by George and Ira Gershwin was one of the highlights of *Shall We Dance*. The talented team of **Astaire** and **Rogers** delighted audiences with their dancing, capped off with a clever roller skating sequence. (1937) $5

They Can't Take That Away from Me
The magic was still there. In their last picture together, *The Barkleys of Broadway*, **Fred Astaire** and **Ginger Rogers** continued to entertain audiences with their great dancing and perfect chemistry. This song was written by the great Gershwin brothers, George and Ira. (1949) $5

Other Twosomes

William Powell and Myrna Loy were another charismatic screen couple introduced in 1930s movies. They made the first of their sophisticated mystery comedies in 1934, *The Thin Man*, based on author Dashiell Hammett's characters. The charming sleuths with their wry humor and beguiling pet dog, Asta, were so popular that they subsequently made five more *Thin Man* movies, and also co-starred in several non-*Thin Man* vehicles.

Dick Powell and Ruby Keeler, Janet Gaynor and Charles Farrell, Mickey Rooney and Judy Garland, and Joan Crawford and Clark Gable were other couples frequently paired in the 1930s with many sheet music covers promoting their movies.

Smoke Dreams
William Powell and **Myrna Loy** followed their successful movie *The Thin Man* with this equally popular sequel, *After the Thin Man*, seen on cover with their faithful dog Asta. The great supporting cast included young James Stewart as the murderer. (1936) $15

Flirtation Walk
The charming couple **Dick Powell** and **Ruby Keeler** co-starred in the military musical *Flirtation Walk*, a patriotic film dedicated to West Point Academy. The score was by Mort Dixon and Allie Wrubel. (1934) $8

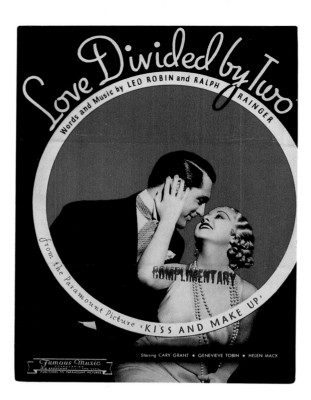

Love Divided by Two
Cary Grant cut a handsome swath in *Kiss and Make Up* as a society beautician in Paris. Co-star **Genevieve Tobin** played his shallow wife in the movie whom he dumps for his secretary. (1934) $6

Thanks a Million
In *Thanks a Million*, popular leading man **Dick Powell** played a young singer with persuasive powers who wins office as governor. Also in the cast were (top to bottom) **Fred Allen, Paul Whiteman, Ann Dvorak, Rubinoff,** and **Patsy Kelly.** (1935) $4

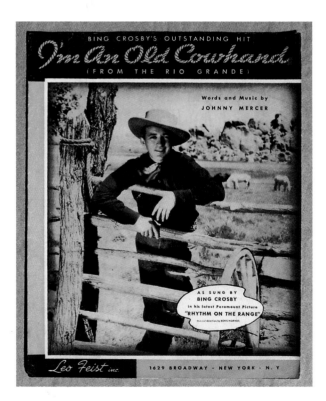

I'm an Old Cowhand
Bing Crosby was a superstar in the 1930s, good-looking, and with an easy manner and special way with a song that made him popular with both men and women. He starred in the lighthearted Western musical *Rhythm on the Range* crooning this Johnny Mercer song to the top of the heap. (1936) $5

Mimi
The inimitable **Maurice Chevalier** charmed movie audiences with his portrayal of a Parisian tailor in *Love Me Tonight*, a highly praised musical with songs by Lorenz Hart and Richard Rodgers. (1932) $5

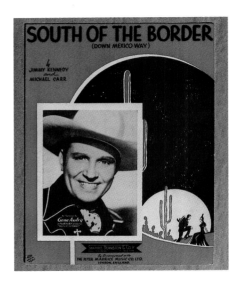

South of the Border
Gene Autry was popular with both men and women. He had a winning way with a song, and sang this favorite ballad in the Republic movie *South of the Border*. (1939) $6

Gangster Movies

Gangsters and gun molls, boys who go bad, and shady lawyers were often the themes of movies in the 1930s, and many movies were made that showed the stark realism of life behind bars. Warner Brothers led the pack with gangster movies starring its crop of "bad men"—Edward G. Robinson, James Cagney, Humphrey Bogart, Paul Muni, John Garfield, and the Dead End Kids on the wrong side of the law. Despite attempts at censorship, these movies continued to be good box office attractions during the Depression, popular with the public. There's not a lot of sheet music for gangster movies as the seriousness of the subject was not conducive to musical production.

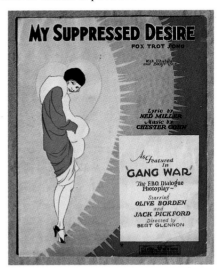

My Suppressed Desire
F.B.O. Studio, one of Joseph Kennedy's business ventures, produced *Gang War*, a lurid depiction of underworld corruption. It was an early sound movie that presaged the popularity of gangster movies in the 1930s. It starred Olive Borden, a former Sennett Bathing Beauty, and Jack Pickford in his last picture. (1928) $5

How Could You?
San Quentin was a typical 1930s prison film that used the talents of cover stars **Pat O'Brien** as a prison yard captain and **Ann Sheridan,** his girlfriend who is also **Humphrey Bogart**'s sister in the movie. Bogart, the imprisoned felon, peers from behind prison bars in the background. (1937) $5

It Had to Be You
In the gangster film *The Roaring Twenties*, **James Cagney** at his cocky best opts for a life of crime as a big-time bootlegger after World War I army service. Also co-starred were **Humphrey Bogart** and **Priscilla Lane**. (1939) $45

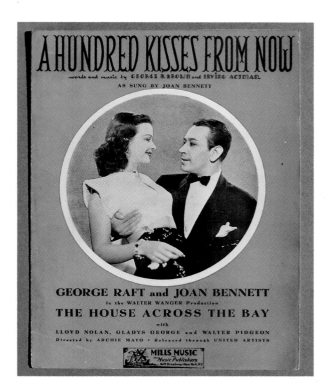

Angels with Dirty Faces
The classic gangster movie *Angels with Dirty Faces* tells of two boys who grew up together in Hell's Kitchen—one becoming a priest, and the other a killer. The movie starred **James Cagney, Pat O'Brien,** and the **Dead End Kids,** with Humphrey Bogart playing a hardened criminal. (1938) *Collection of James Nelson Brown.* $25 ($36)

A Hundred Kisses from Now
The House Across the Bay was the infamous prison on the island of Alcatraz. **George Raft** played an escaped prisoner with a vendetta to get his unfaithful wife, **Joan Bennett,** who was responsible for his imprisonment. Miss Bennett sang this song by Al Siegel in the film. (1940) *Collection of Harold Jacobs.* $75

A Love Song of Long Ago
They Gave Him a Gun co-starred **Spencer Tracy, Gladys George,** and **Franchot Tone** in a story of a war-hardened veteran who became a gangster after the war. Tone was the bad guy, Tracy was the good guy, and Gladys George was the love interest. (1937) *Collection of James Nelson Brown.* $30

Nearer and Dearer
Ladies were not immune to imprisonment, and *Ladies of the Big House* showed what life behind bars meant to the female sex. **Sylvia Sidney** was effective as an embittered lady inmate who was framed for murder, with co-star **Gene Raymond** as her love interest. Haven Gillespie (W) and Egbert Van Alstyne (M) wrote the song. (1931) *Collection of Harold Jacobs.* $100

Danny Kaye

The 1940s
★ ★ ★ ★ ★

John Wayne & Martha Scott

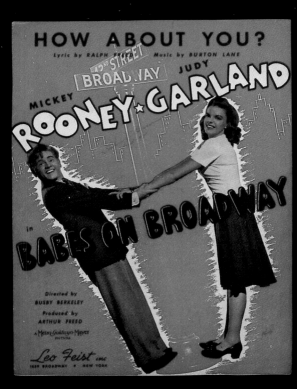

Mickey Rooney & Judy Garland

Betty Grable & Victor Mature

Eleanor Parker & Dennis Morgan

Barbara Stanwyck

Sonja Henie

Rita Hayworth

Alice Faye & John Payne

Deanna Durbin

Susan Hayward & Dana Andrews

CHAPTER 4: THE FABULOUS FORTIES

In 1939, *Gone With the Wind* was released to great critical acclaim. The stunning production ushered in the decade of the fabulous forties, an era of outstanding productivity in Hollywood movies. A star-studded premiere in Atlanta, Georgia, introduced the monumental movie, and audiences that clamored to see this highly publicized venture came away awed by the epic proportions of the lavish production. Margaret Mitchell, author of the best-selling book upon which the movie was based, was well pleased with the result. The movie won top accolades at the Academy Awards presentations—ten Oscars in all.

Gone With the Wind has been reshown again and again through the years, and is now available on videocassette for home viewing. Its freshness, charm, and historical accuracy continue to dazzle audiences of a new generation.

World War II at the Movies

In 1941 the United States entered the war, which instead of diminishing theater attendance, increased it. Long lines waiting for admission to movie theaters were a common sight. The public's appetite for entertainment was insatiable, and movies were better than ever.

Serious wartime dramas as well as escapist musicals were the fare. The survival of a courageous English family during the Blitz was told in *Mrs. Miniver*, and daily life at the American homefront was depicted in such films as *Since You Went Away*. Audiences viewed stories about our gallant fighting forces emphasizing the danger and heroism on the battlefield, and the painful separation from home and family. The grimness of life in Nazi Germany was depicted in such films as *Mortal Storm* and *Hitler's Children*.

My Own True Love
The theme song from the Max Steiner score for *Gone With the Wind* was originally published in 1939 with an innocuous cover drawing of a tree. Lyrics by Mack David were later added to the Tara theme, and the song was re-released with this attractive cover of **Vivien Leigh** and **Clark Gable.** (1954) $4

Wartime Dramas

Midsummer's Day
Mrs. Miniver co-starred **Greer Garson** and **Walter Pidgeon** as a gallant English couple who survive the onslaughts of World War II in England. The widely acclaimed movie captured seven Oscars at the awards ceremony. Gene Lockhart, veteran screen actor, wrote the song. (1942) *Collection of Harold Jacobs.* $25

Since You Went Away
One of Holly-wood's best wartime movies was *Since You Went Away*, a tribute to American families who carried on at the homefront during the tribulations of separation and loss. The all-star cast included from top—**Claudette Colbert, Jennifer Jones, Joseph Cotten, Shirley Temple, Monty Woolley, Lionel Barrymore,** and **Robert Walker Sr.** (1944) $4

I'll See You in My Dreams
Three trainees for the U.S. Women's Army Corps were thrown together in World War II in *Keep Your Powder Dry*. Clockwise from bottom are **Lana Turner, Laraine Day,** and **Susan Peters.** Shortly after making the movie Miss Peters was crippled in a tragic boating accident and never walked again. This classic 1924 song was written by Gus Kahn (W) and Isham Jones (M). (1944) $8

I'll Get By
In *A Guy Named Joe*, **Spencer Tracy** played a fighter pilot who came back from the dead to guide fledgling pilot Van Johnson. Halfway through the filming Van Johnson was seriously injured in a car wreck, but the studio decided he was so good that they would wait for his recovery to complete the picture. **Irene Dunne** was Tracy's co-star. This song is an enduring standard written in 1928 by Roy Turk (W) and Fred Ahlert (M). (1943) $4

The Song of the Seabees
Dennis O'Keefe, Susan Hayward, and **John Wayne** co-starred in *The Fighting Seabees*, with the men fighting the Japanese in the South Pacific, and fighting each other for the attentions of Miss Hayward. The movie stimulated patriotism in its glorification of the fighting Construction Battalion. (1944) *Collection of Harold Jacobs.* $30

Gung Ho!
The U.S. Marines were the focus of this dramatic true life story of the raid on the Japanese-held Makin Island in the South Pacific during World War II. **Randolph Scott** (center cover) was the leader of the "gung ho" squadron in the movie. The dramatic song cover shows the battle-ready marines in action. (1943) *Collection of Roy Bishop.* $50

Someday, I'll Meet You Again
Humphrey Bogart effectively portrayed an escaped convict from Devil's Island who helped the free French fight the Germans in *Passage to Marseille*. **Michele Morgan** was the female lead. Romantic ballad was by Ned Washington (W) and Max Steiner (M). (1944) $7

To the End of the End of the World
Rated as one of the finest movies to come out of World War II, *They Were Expendable* benefited from the direction of John Ford, and the sage advice of veteran Naval officer **Robert Montgomery** (r) who played the lead. **John Wayne** was equally convincing as one of the PT boat's heroic crew, and **Donna Reed** threw in a bit of romance. (1945) *Collection of Harold Jacobs.* $40

No Surrender!
Hangmen Also Die was an impressive anti-German movie directed by Fritz Lang about a doctor on the run who had assassinated a top-ranking Gestapo leader. Co-stars **Brian Donlevy** and **Anna Lee** appear on cover. (1943) *Collection of Harold Jacobs.* $40

45

Sprinkled among the serious dramas were a generous allotment of wartime musicals and zany comedies. Award-winning *Yankee Doodle Dandy*, *Meet Me in St. Louis*, *Anchors Aweigh*, and *This Is the Army* kept audiences entertained, and the funny movies of Bud Abbott and Lou Costello and the popular "Road" pictures of Hope, Crosby, and Lamour kept them laughing. Spiritually uplifting films such as *The Song of Bernadette* and *Going My Way* vied with the shocking realism of a man's soul destroyed by alcoholism in *The Lost Weekend*.

The "Road" Pictures

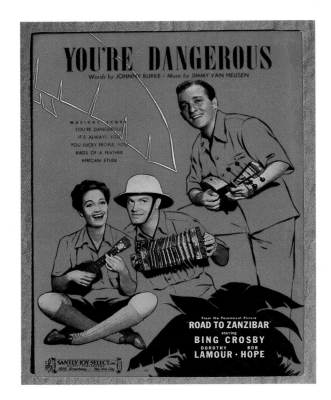

You're Dangerous
Road to Zanzibar followed the success of the first "road" picture. This time **Hope** and **Crosby** loosened up with witty asides and ad-libs. Bing Crosby introduced wonderful songs by Johnny Burke and Jimmy Van Heusen, Bob Hope was at his hilarious best wrestling a gorilla, and **Dorothy Lamour** provided the glamour. (1941) $25

Too Romantic
Road to Singapore was the first of the famous "road" pictures co-starring **Bing Crosby, Dorothy Lamour,** and **Bob Hope.** The threesome created a certain movie magic in an amusing story peppered with Hope's wisecracks, Crosby's singing, and Lamour's beauty. So popular was the movie that it led to a whole series of sequels in the same vein. (1940) $5 *($15)*

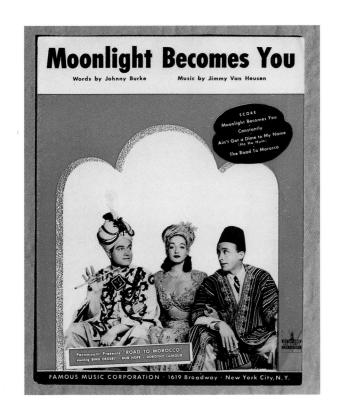

Moonlight Becomes You
The third time out, **Crosby, Hope,** and **Lamour** were off on the *Road to Morocco*, again with a Burke/Van Heusen score, including this romantic hit song that was crooned by Bing Crosby to Dorothy Lamour. Lighthearted and funny with the usual Hope and Crosby competitive repartee and gags, the film was a welcome respite for the American public from the grim reality of a World War. (1942) $4

Welcome to My Dream
Road to Utopia was one of the most hilarious of the "road" pictures, with **Dorothy Lamour** and **Bob Hope** portraying an old married couple reminiscing about adventures in the Klondike with friend, **Bing Crosby.** The movie was basically a flashback of the Klondike days, but ended with a great gag showing the Hope and Lamour baby as the spitting image of old friend Bing! Songs were again by Johnny Burke and Jimmy Van Heusen. (1945) $6

But Beautiful
The astonishing popularity of the "road" movies continued with this fifth in the series, *Road to Rio*. The charismatic threesome, **Hope, Crosby,** and **Lamour** again put over a basically mediocre plot with their usual flair and with wonderful songs written by the successful Burke/Van Heusen combination. (1947) $4

The Merry-Go-Runaround
After a five year lapse, *Road to Bali* appeared, the first "road" picture in Technicolor. The consummate professionals, **Hope, Crosby,** and **Lamour,** again provided good music and plenty of laughs, but the magic was beginning to wane. One more "road" picture, *The Road to Hong Kong*, was made in 1962, with Joan Collins replacing Dorothy Lamour (who was given a token cameo appearance in the film), after which the road came to a dead end for the series. (1952) $8

Film Noir Movies

Film noir is a French term that describes a certain type of "black movie" with a sinister theme that became prevalent in the 1940s, carrying over to the 1950s. It was characterized by its dark and somber mood, shadowy villains, and jaded hard-drinking, cigarette-smoking heroes. Footsteps echoing on dark, rain-slickened streets reflecting neon signs outside dingy cafes, and an underworld of unsavory characters and brittle dames were photographed with creative lighting and camera angles that emphasized the overall moodiness. Examples of the genre that generated sheet music were the movies *Casablanca, To Have and Have Not, The Postman Always Rings Twice, The Lady from Shanghai, Laura, Fallen Angel, The Woman in the Window, Gilda, Hangover Square, Spellbound, The Strange Love of Martha Ivers, Road House, Kiss of Death, Body and Soul, Dead Reckoning, Dark Passage, In a Lonely Place,* and *Kiss Me Deadly.*

I Hadn't Anyone Till You
In a Lonely Place was a *film noir* starring **Humphrey Bogart** as a neurotic Hollywood writer who is wrongly accused of murdering a hatcheck girl. **Gloria Grahame** played his romantic interest. Song was written in 1938 by Ray Noble. (1950) $8 *($33)*

Margot
Cover star **Faith Domergue** played a psychopathic murderess in *Where Danger Lives*, a mood movie that co-starred **Robert Mitchum** as a sympathetic doctor who is duped into thinking he was the murderer. Song by Ray Carter (W) and Roy Webb (M). (1950) $35

Put the Blame on Mame
Rita Hayworth, seductive in a strapless black satin gown, became Hollywood's "Love Goddess" after her performance in *Gilda* with Glenn Ford and George Macready as the other sides of a strange triangle of twisted relationships. Song was written for the film by Allan Roberts and Doris Fisher. (1946) $10

Slowly
Alice Faye, Dana Andrews, and **Linda Darnell,** left to right, shared billing in *Fallen Angel*, a *film noir* piece with Andrews cast as a devious press agent who becomes a murder suspect. This movie wound up Alice Faye's film career except for isolated appearances in the 1960s and 1970s. (1945) *$4*

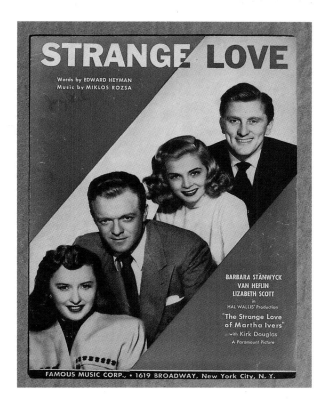

Strange Love
Kirk Douglas in his film debut played the disillusioned husband of murderess **Barbara Stanwyck** in *The Strange Love of Martha Ivers* with strong support from **Van Heflin** and **Lizabeth Scott.** On cover, left to right, are Stanwyck, Heflin, Scott, and Douglas. Theme song was written by Edward Heyman (W) and Miklos Rozsa (M). (1946) $7

Don't Call It Love
The classic *film noir*, *I Walk Alone*, starred **Burt Lancaster** as an ex-con who seeks revenge on his double-crossing gangster friend, played by **Kirk Douglas.** Sultry **Lizabeth Scott** is the femme fatale they both want. Song was written by Ned Washington (W) and Allie Wrubel (M). (1947) $6

She's Funny That Way
Sparks flew in *The Postman Always Rings Twice* as clandestine lovers **Lana Turner** and **John Garfield** conspire to murder her husband. This song was written by Richard Whiting (W) and Neil Morét (M) in 1928. (1946) $20

Again
Richard Widmark was well cast as a sadistic road house owner who winds up dead at the hands of saloon singer **Ida Lupino.** Miss Lupino introduced this hit song by Dorcas Cochran (W) and Lionel Newman (M) in the movie *Road House*. (1948) $4

Time Alone Will Tell
Betty Grable was the No. 1 Pin-Up Girl of World War II servicemen, and 20th Century-Fox capitalized on her popularity with the sparkling Technicolor musical *Pin-Up Girl*. **Martha Raye** and **Joe E. Brown,** seen on cover, provided the comedy, and **Charlie Spivak**'s orchestra played the Big Band sound in an entertaining movie with a timely U.S.O setting. (1944) $8

My Wonderful One Let's Dance
Two Girls on Broadway was a remake of *Broadway Melody*, this time around starring **Lana Turner** (left) and **Joan Blondell** (right) as two Broadway show girls whose sister act is threatened by **George Murphy.** (1940) $30

So-o-o-o-o in Love
If one **Danny Kaye** is good, two is even better. He played twins in *Wonder Man*, a clever movie that gave him plenty of opportunity to display his multiple talents. Virginia Mayo is the pretty lady on the cover. (1945) $6 *($12)*

His Rocking Horse Ran Away
And the Angels Sing co-starred **Betty Hutton** and **Dorothy Lamour** in this musical treat about a sister act with bandleader **Fred MacMurray** as the fly in the ointment. Great songs by Johnny Burke (W) and Jimmy Van Heusen (M) included this clever ditty sung with rowdy enthusiasm by Betty Hutton. (1944) $4

Come Closer to Me
Easy to Wed co-starred **Van Johnson** with his favorite swimming star **Esther Williams.** This movie had the added delight of **Lucille Ball** at her comic best, along with **Keenan Wynn.** Also on cover are organist **Ethel Smith** and **singer Carlos Ramirez** who sang this song in the movie. (1945) $4

Let the Rest of the World Go By
June Haver starred opposite **Dick Haymes,** who portrayed Irish-American songwriter Ernest R. Ball in *Irish Eyes Are Smiling*, a song-filled Technicolor extravaganza also showcasing the dry wit of **Monty Woolley.** (1944) $4

This Is Madness
Alan Ladd appeared in a tale of intrigue in *Calcutta* with co-stars **Gail Russell** and **William Bendix.** In searching for his buddy's killer Ladd becomes mired in deep trouble with jewel smugglers and bad guys. (1947) *Collection of Harold Jacobs.* $10

Spellbound
Gregory Peck, as a confused amnesiac who believes he's a murderer, co-starred with **Ingrid Bergman** as his psychiatrist in Alfred Hitchcock's suspenseful melodrama *Spellbound*. The taut thriller received three Academy Award nominations and won the Best Music Score award for Miklos Rozsa. (1945) $5

I Think of You
Holiday in Mexico was an entertaining and visually attractive musical starring **Walter Pidgeon** (top) as **Jane Powell**'s father. Teenagers Jane and **Roddy McDowell** (below Pidgeon) are in cahoots to match Dad up with beautiful **Ilona Massey**. Pianist **Jose Iturbi** and bandleader **Xavier Cugat** supplied the music. (1946) $6

As Years Go By
Katharine Hepburn played Clara Schumann in *Song of Love*, a movie based on the life of composer Robert Schumann, played by **Paul Henreid**. **Robert Walker** as Johannes Brahms was a friend of the family who admired Clara from afar. Charles Tobias and Peter De Rose adapted this song from a Brahms Hungarian Dance. (1947) $6

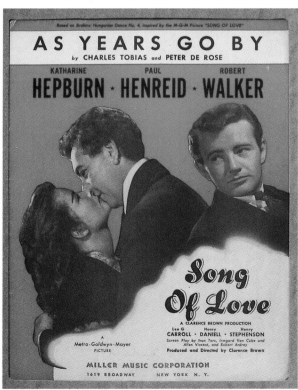

Betty Grable at Twentieth Century-Fox headed a parade of musical talent that included Alice Faye, Don Ameche, Carmen Miranda, Jack Haley, Charlotte Greenwood, and June Haver in brilliant Technicolor productions that were a pleasure for the eyes as well as the ears. Busby Berkeley lent his choreographic skills to stunning production numbers in *The Gang's All Here* with songs by Leo Robin (W) and Harry Warren (M)—"The Lady in the Tutti Frutti Hat," the "Polka Dot Polka," and "A Journey to a Star." Other pleasing Betty Grable musicals in the 1940s were set in glamorous locales—*Down Argentine Way, Moon Over Miami, That Night in Rio, Song of the Islands, Springtime in the Rockies*, and *Coney Island*.

Twentieth Century-Fox also gave us wholesome family musicals, some of which revived old songs from early Tin Pan Alley—movies like *State Fair, The Dolly Sisters, Centennial Summer, Greenwich Village*, and *Hello, Frisco, Hello*.

Is That Good?
Two pretty sisters, Betty Grable and Carole Landis, search for rich husbands in the entertaining 20th Century-Fox musical *Moon Over Miami*. Cast included (from top) **Betty Grable, Don Ameche, Robert Cummings, Charlotte Greenwood, Jack Haley,** and **Carole Landis.** Songs were written by Leo Robin (W) and Ralph Rainger (M). (1941) $10

Movie biographies of composers were also popular fare in the 1940s, with the double whammy of good music combined with a life story frequently embellished beyond total accuracy. George Gershwin was depicted in *Rhapsody in Blue*, George M. Cohan in *Yankee Doodle Dandy*, Cole Porter in *Night and Day*, Irving Berlin in *This Is the Army*, Richard Rodgers and Lorenz Hart in *Words and Music*, and Jerome Kern in *Till the Clouds Roll By*. Classical composers were represented as well—Chopin in *A Song to Remember*, Rimsky-Korsakoff in *Song of Scheherezade*, Brahms and Schumann in *Song of Love*.

Columbia Studios brought Rita Hayworth to the fore in the 1940s musicals *You'll Never Get Rich* and *You Were Never Lovelier* with Fred Astaire, *Cover Girl* with Gene Kelly, *Tonight and Every Night* with Lee Bowman, and *Down to Earth* with Larry Parks.

Ann Miller tap-danced her heart out in such B-movie events as *Reveille with Beverly*; *What's Buzzin' Cousin*; *Jam Session*; *Hey, Rookie*; *Eadie Was a Lady*; *Carolina Blues*; *The Thrill of Brazil*; and *Eve Knew Her Apples*. Larry Parks struck sparks in *The Jolson Story* and *Jolson Sings Again*. Pretty Janet Blair appeared in *Something to Shout About* and *Tars and Spars*. Columbia was also responsible for a number of 1940 B-musicals featuring its roster of entertainers like Jinx Falkenburg, Joan Woodbury, Judy Canova, Jean Porter, Adele Jergens, Leslie Brooks, and Jane Frazee in amiable, if unmemorable, diversions.

I Surrender Dear
Sweetheart of the Fleet was a wartime comedy with cover beauties **Jinx Falkenburg** (left) and **Joan Woodbury** (right) in a thin, if amusing, plot about a U.S.O. show in which they lip-sync the songs while the real singers, who are on the plain side, do the actual singing off-stage. This 1931 song was a huge hit for Bing Crosby in the 1930s. (1942) $8

Anywhere
Stunning **Rita Hayworth** played an entertainer in a London nightclub opposite pilot **Lee Bowman** in Columbia's wartime movie musical *Tonight and Every Night*. Songs were by Sammy Cahn (W) and Jule Styne (M). (1945) $5

Ac-cent-tchu-ate the Positive
Bing Crosby sang this great Johnny Mercer/Harold Arlen song in *Here Come the Waves*, a bright wartime musical co-starring **Betty Hutton** playing twin WAVES, one of whom gets Bing. The other twin gets **Sonny Tufts**, the grinning sailor at bottom. (1944) $3

Bing Crosby and Betty Hutton were major luminaries in Paramount's musicals of the 1940s. Bing was big with his "Road" pictures as well as other major hits: *Rhythm on the River*, *Birth of the Blues*, *Dixie*, *Holiday Inn*, *Blue Skies*, *Here Come the Waves*, and *The Emperor Waltz*. Betty Hutton sang her way through *The Fleet's In*, *Star Spangled Rhythm*, *Happy Go Lucky*, *And the Angels Sing*, *Incendiary Blonde*, and *The Perils of Pauline*.

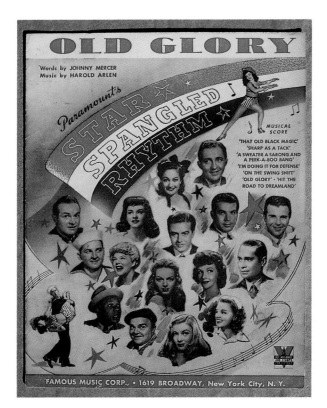

Old Glory
Paramount's top stars turned out for *Star Spangled Rhythm*, a wartime musical with a thin plot about sailor Eddie Bracken on leave who impresses his shipmates with a star-studded variety show at the Hollywood studio where his Dad works. Johnny Mercer (W) and Harold Arlen (M) wrote the song. (1942) $4

At RKO studios, Danny Kaye was a top star of the 1940s with one hit after another including *Up in Arms*, *Wonder Man*, *The Kid from Brooklyn*, *The Secret Life of Walter Mitty*, and *A Song Is Born*. Frank Sinatra was introduced in his first starring role in *Higher and Higher* followed by *Step Lively*. And Fred Astaire sang and danced his way through *The Sky's the Limit*.

The Music Stopped
Frank Sinatra pleased his legion of teenage fans with his first major role in *Higher and Higher*, an entertaining musical showcasing his fine singing. Co-stars were **Michele Morgan, Jack Haley,** and **Marcy McGuire.** Harold Adamson (W) and Jimmy McHugh (M) wrote the songs, several of which were best-selling records for Frank. (1943) $4

Because of serious war-time tensions, Warner Brothers declared a moratorium on musicals, and few were made during the 1940s. *Blues in the Night* was notable in 1941. Musical biographies *Yankee Doodle Dandy*, *Rhapsody in Blue*, and *Night and Day* were joined by *Shine on Harvest Moon* about Tin Pan Alley songwriters Nora Bayes and Jack Norworth, and *My Wild Irish Rose* about Irish composer Chauncey Olcott. Other musicals with a patriotic theme were: *This Is the Army*, *Thank Your Lucky Stars*, and *Hollywood Canteen*. *The Desert Song* was remade with a new anti-Nazi twist.

Hollywood Canteen
The *Hollywood Canteen* was a real-life haven for World War II servicemen where they could get a cup of coffee or a friendly ear from their favorite movie star. The all-star lineup in this Warner Brothers musical included **Bette Davis, John Garfield, Joan Crawford, Barbara Stanwyck Jane Wyman,** and countless others. (1944) $7

A group of light musicals starred various combinations of Jack Carson, Janis Paige, Dennis Morgan, Martha Vickers, Dorothy Malone, and Don DeFore—*The Time, The Place, and the Girl*; *Two Guys from Texas;* and *One Sunday Afternoon*. *Romance on the High Seas* introduced a fresh new personality in band-singer Doris Day followed by *My Dream Is Yours* and *It's a Great Feeling*.

Abbott and Costello did their thing in musical comedies *Buck Privates*, *In the Navy*, *Keep 'Em Flying*, *Ride 'Em Cowboy*, *Pardon My Sarong*, *Hit the Ice*, and *In Society*. The ubiquitous all-star wartime musical *Follow the Boys* was an offering, and the Andrews Sisters were top-starred in *Moonlight and Cactus*. Towards the end of the decade Donald O'Connor came into his own in the pleasant musicals *Feudin', Fussin' and A-Fightin'*, *Are You With It?*, and *Yes Sir, That's My Baby*.

It's Magic
Captivating **Doris Day** was a talented band singer when she was discovered by composer Jule Styne who heard her sing at a house party. She was offered a starring role in *Romance on the High Seas*, and the rest is history. On cover, left to right, are **Don DeFore, Miss Day, Jack Carson,** and **Janis Paige.** (1948) $5

A Little Imagination
Donald O'Connor loses his job and joins a carnival where he has ample opportunity to display his multiple talents, singing and dancing with co-star **Olga San Juan** in *Are You With It?* Other members of the cast included Broadway performer **Lew Parker** (left) and peppy **Martha Stewart.** (1948) $6

Universal Studios released a few Deanna Durbin movies in the 1940s—not really full-fledged musicals, but she had a few songs in each—*Nice Girl?*, *Spring Parade*, *It Started with Eve*, *The Amazing Mrs. Holliday*, *Hers to Hold*, *His Butler's Sister*, *Christmas Holiday*, *Lady on a Train*, *Because of Him*, *Something in the Wind*, and *Up in Central Park*.

Thank You America
Deanna Durbin, lovelier than ever at the ripe old age of 20, left the world of juvenile roles behind when she starred in Universal Studio's *Nice Girl?* In the movie she had a crush on attractive older man, Franchot Tone, but finally came to her senses and settled for Robert Stack. (1941) $7

Susan Hayward & Bette Davis

The 1950s
★ ★ ★ ★ ★

Doris Day & Gordon MacRae

Cary Grant & Leslie Caron

James Cagney

Bing Crosby & Danny Kaye

William Holden

Gary Cooper

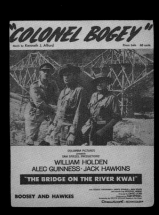

CHAPTER 5: THE 1950S AND BEYOND

Good movies continued to be made in the 1950s, the 1960s, and on up to the present time, and good collectible sheet music was issued in connection with these movies. But the demise of Hollywood's Golden Age was imminent when a revolutionary new entertainment medium found its way into the homes of America in the early 1950s. Television—vital, timely, and limitlessly entertaining—was luring the public away from the movie theaters in droves. Anti-trust actions in the late 1940s had divested major studios of some of their integrated holdings, and this also contributed to the breakdown of the old studio system.

Male Superstars

Many veterans of the 1930s and 1940s continued to star in movies. Superstars Fred Astaire, Humphrey Bogart, Gary Cooper, Bing Crosby, Clark Gable, James Stewart, Spencer Tracy, and John Wayne were still strong at the box office. Now they were joined by such talented actors as Kirk Douglas, Marlon Brando, William Holden, Charlton Heston, Robert Mitchum, and Elvis Presley.

The Bad and the Beautiful
Kirk Douglas played an ambitious Hollywood producer in *The Bad and the Beautiful*, who stops at nothing to get ahead. His convincing performance brought him an Oscar nomination for Best Actor, but he lost out to Gary Cooper in *High Noon*. Strong support came from co-stars **Lana Turner**, Dick Powell, Walter Pidgeon, and Gloria Grahame who copped an Academy Award for Best Supporting Actress. David Raksin wrote the title song. (1952) $7

The Wild One
Marlon Brando was praised for his role in *The Wild One* as the leader of a gang of tough motorcyclists who invade a small town and terrorize the citizens. Also in the cast was **Mary Murphy** who managed to soften his heart. Theme song piano solo was composed by Leith Stevens. (1953) *Collection of Harold Jacobs.* $25

Moonglow
William Holden played an itinerant drifter who stirs up the women-folk at the town's Labor Day celebration in *Picnic*, co-starring with **Kim Novak** and supporting actresses Rosalind Russell and Betty Field. (1956) $4

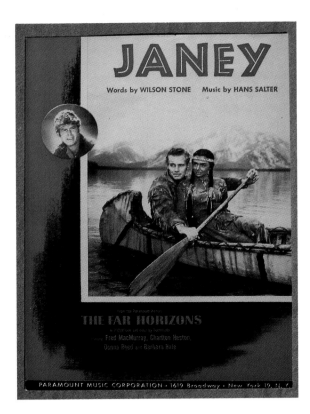

Janey
The Far Horizons was Hollywood's version of the Lewis and Clark expedition to the Pacific Northwest in 1804–1806. **Charlton Heston** played William Clark, and **Donna Reed** was the Indian guide Sacajawea. **Fred MacMurray** co-starred as Meriwether Lewis. (1955) $8

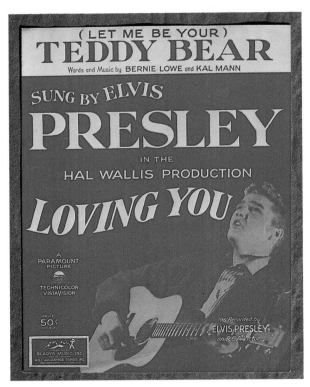

Teddy Bear
Elvis Presley's enormous talent burst from the screen in *Loving You*, a story that somewhat paralleled his own life. He played a country boy who is discovered and promoted into big time show business. This was Elvis's second movie, and his fantastic singing and charismatic screen personality gave his career a big boost. This song was a No. 1 hit record for Presley, and lots of girls wanted him for their "teddy bear." (1957) *Collection of James Nelson Brown.* $25

Ballad of Thunder Road
Robert Mitchum played a Kentucky moonshiner in the action-packed movie *Thunder Road*, also starring his 19-year-old son Jim Mitchum and singer **Keely Smith**. The screenplay was based on an original story by Mitchum Sr., and he also helped write the theme song. (1958) $20

Female Superstars

Although mature male stars were still well represented on covers, aging female stars were generally being replaced by younger women. Female stars such as Ava and Rita and Lana were joined by superstars Grace Kelly, Doris Day, Elizabeth Taylor, Debbie Reynolds, Audrey Hepburn, Natalie Wood, and Marilyn Monroe in the ranks of popularity. Sheet music with covers of certain stars such as James Dean, Rock Hudson, Marilyn Monroe, and Elvis Presley are prime collectible items because of the cultish interest by other memorabilia and nostalgia collectors.

Swingin' Down the Lane
I'll See You in My Dreams starred **Doris Day** as Grace LeBoy, a name well known to sheet music collectors as the partner of songwriter Gus Kahn in his early professional career. **Danny Thomas** played Kahn in this romantic movie that was praised for its fine musical numbers. (1952) $5

Right:

Hold My Hand
Susan Slept Here starred sparkling **Debbie Reynolds** as a precocious 18-year-old delinquent placed in the care of worldly **Dick Powell** with whom she falls in love. Don Cornell sang this song on the movie sound track and also popularized it on a recording. (1954) $5

A Place in the Sun
Beautiful **Elizabeth Taylor** played **Montgomery Clift**'s love interest in *A Place in the Sun*, based on the true story of Chester Gillette, convicted of murdering his erstwhile sweetheart when she tells him she's pregnant. The powerful movie brought Clift an Oscar nomination for Best Actor, but Humphrey Bogart took the prize for *The African Queen*. The film still won six Oscars including one for Franz Waxman's Best Score. (1951) $20

Love in the Afternoon
Audrey Hepburn played a young music student who falls in love with older man **Gary Cooper** in the sophisticated comedy *Love in the Afternoon*. Theme song was written by Johnny Mercer (W) and Matty Malneck (M). (1957) $6

Right:

A Very Precious Love
Gene Kelly as a theatrical producer co-starred with **Natalie Wood**, a young Jewish heroine who seeks fame and fortune in *Marjorie Morningstar*. Miss Wood was greatly admired as a child actress, and, as a beautiful young woman, moved smoothly into adult roles. (1958) $7

1950s Musicals

Metro-Goldwyn-Mayer continued to dominate the movie musical field in the 1950s with a strong lineup including *Annie Get Your Gun* with Betty Hutton; *The Toast of New Orleans, Because You're Mine,* and *The Great Caruso* with Mario Lanza; *Three Little Words, The Belle of New York, Royal Wedding,* and *Silk Stockings* with Fred Astaire; *Duchess of Idaho, Skirts Ahoy!, Pagan Love Song, Jupiter's Darling,* and *Dangerous When Wet* with Esther Williams; *Show Boat, Lovely to Look At,* and *Kiss Me Kate* with Kathryn Grayson; *Summer Stock* with Judy Garland; *Seven Brides for Seven Brothers* and *Hit the Deck* with Jane Powell; *Rose Marie* with Howard Keel; *Love Me or Leave Me* with Doris Day; *Guys and Dolls* and *High Society* with Frank Sinatra; *Jailhouse Rock* with Elvis Presley; and *Singin' in the Rain, Les Girls,* and the amazing *An American in Paris* with Gene Kelly.

Vincent Minnelli continued his fine directorial work on *An American in Paris*, Oscar winner for Best Picture in 1951. Other hits were *The Band Wagon, Brigadoon, Kismet,* and his crowning achievement, *Gigi*, winner of ten Academy Awards in 1958 including one for Best Picture and Best Director.

If I Loved You
Rodgers and Hammerstein's hit show *Carousel* was brought to the screen with its timeless songs performed by **Gordon MacRae** and **Shirley Jones.** (1956) $4

Wunderbar
Kiss Me Kate was an adaptation of Cole Porter's Broadway success co-starring **Howard Keel** and **Kathryn Grayson.** The dazzling score insured the popularity of this outstanding musical with many sparkling production numbers including "Too Darn Hot" with leggy Ann Miller burning up the screen. (1953) $4

Some Enchanted Evening
Handsome **Rossano Brazzi** mouthed the words to singer Giorgio Tozzi's passionate rendition of this famous song in the screen adaptation of Rodgers and Hammerstein's *South Pacific*. **Mitzi Gaynor** played spirited Nellie Forbush who fell in love with French planter Brazzi. (1958) $4

Twentieth Century-Fox made some good musicals too, including *I'll Get By* and *The Girl Next Door* with June Haver; *My Blue Heaven, Wabash Avenue, Call Me Mister,* and *Meet Me After the Show* with Betty Grable; *On the Riviera* with Danny Kaye; *Golden Girl* and *South Pacific* with Mitzi Gaynor; *Stars and Stripes Forever* with Clifton Webb; *With a Song in My Heart* with Susan Hayward; *Call Me Madam* and *There's No Business Like Show Business* with Ethel Merman; *Gentlemen Prefer Blondes* and *How to Marry a Millionaire* with Marilyn Monroe; *Daddy Long Legs* with Fred Astaire; *The Best Things in Life Are Free, Oklahoma,* and *Carousel* with Gordon MacRae; *The King and I* with Deborah Kerr; and *Say One for Me* with Bing Crosby.

Paramount came through with a few good musicals in the 1950s—the best ones starring old reliables Bing and Fred. *Mr. Music, White Christmas,* and *Anything Goes* with Bing Crosby; *Let's Dance* with Betty Hutton and Fred Astaire, and *Funny Face* with Audrey Hepburn and Astaire. Elvis Presley made a splash in *Loving You.*

Warner Brothers' musical movies of the 1950s were notable for the work of Doris Day—*On Moonlight Bay, Lullaby of Broadway, I'll See You in My Dreams, By the Light of the Silvery Moon, Calamity Jane,* and *Young at Heart,* and for the blockbuster hit *A Star Is Born* with Judy Garland.

Many of the best musicals in the 1950s and 1960s were adaptations of hit Broadway shows, and songs were reissued with movie star pictures on the covers. Some of the best were *Kiss Me Kate, Oklahoma, Carousel, The King and I, The Pajama Game, South Pacific, The Music Man, My Fair Lady,* and *The Sound of Music.*

Left:
A Little Girl from Little Rock
Jane Russell and **Marilyn Monroe** exuded glamour and sex appeal in the 20th Century-Fox offering *Gentlemen Prefer Blondes,* a frothy confection adapted from the Broadway musical. Monroe as Lorelei was a standout with her rendition of the Leo Robin/Jule Styne number "Diamonds Are a Girl's Best Friend." (1953) $15 *($35)*

I Could Have Danced All Night
My Fair Lady was a blockbuster film from Warner Brothers that won eight out of the twelve categories for which it was Oscar-nominated including Best Movie. **Rex Harrison** won Best Actor for his role of Henry Higgins, but **Audrey Hepburn** who played Eliza Doolittle was passed over for Julie Andrews who originally played the Hepburn part on Broadway. Andrews won Best Actress for her role in *Mary Poppins.* (1964) $4

The Lonely Goatherd
Rodgers and Hammerstein's hit Broadway musical *The Sound of Music* became an award winning movie when brought to the screen. **Julie Andrews**, governess to a wealthy Austrian widower's family, falls in love and becomes a baroness in the true life story. The movie won five Oscars including Best Picture and Best Score Adaptation by Irwin Kostal. (1965) $5

WINGS

Love Theme of the
Paramount Picture
"WINGS"

Lyric by
Ballard Macdonald
Music by
J. S. Zamecnik

ESTABLISHED THROUGHOUT THE WORLD
SAM FOX PUB. CO.
CLEVELAND   NEW YORK
LONDON · PARIS · BERLIN · MELBOURNE
Representatives in other important Centers

The category of Academy Award winning songs is a popular offshoot of movie sheet music collecting. Many of our most gifted songwriters contributed to movie music, and prize-winning songs have the double value of fine music and interesting movie-related covers. Most songs are still easy enough to find, and are not inordinately expensive. The prospect of owning all the songs in the Oscar category is not as remote as it is in other categories. Some collectors try to amass all the nominated songs as well as the winners.

The Oscar is a small gold-plated statuette that is the symbol of superlative achievement in Hollywood. It is voted annually as an award of merit by members of the Academy of Motion Picture Arts and Sciences, and is the most coveted award in the motion picture industry. Each category is voted upon by Academy members most closely involved, and the award of an Oscar is recognized the world over as a distinction of great honor.

Academy Award night causes a great stir of excitement in the United States and abroad, as the annual presentation show is televised to the continents of the world via satellite. Celebrities are greeted and interviewed as they arrive in limousines for the show, and crowds of the curious gather, eager to catch a glimpse of their favorite stars.

Early Academy Award Winners 1927-1929

The first Oscar presentation at the Academy Awards ceremony of 1927-1928 went to Emil Jannings for Best Actor in the movies *The Way of All Flesh* and *The Last Command*. Janet Gaynor won the Best Actress award for her cumulative performances in three films, *7th Heaven*, *Street Angel*, and *Sunrise*. *Wings* was voted the outstanding picture of the year.

Diane
Janet Gaynor and **Charles Farrell** appear on the cover of the famous love waltz from *Seventh Heaven*, a silent movie with a synchronized musical score. Miss Gaynor won the first Academy Award ever given for Best Actress, and the movie also copped a Best Director award for Frank Borzage. (WM) Lew Pollack and Erno Rapée. (1927) $4

Sunrise and You
Janet Gaynor starred in the widely admired F. W. Murnau movie *Sunrise*, that won Oscars for its artistic quality and its beautiful cinematography. Handsome **George O'Brien** was praised for his sensitive portrayal of Gaynor's confused husband. A romantic leading man in silents, he later became a popular Western star in 1930s talkies. (WM) Arthur A. Penn. (1928) $25

Opposite page:
1927-28 Best Picture, *Wings*
The two million dollar movie *Wings* won the first Academy Award for Best Picture. Both Richard Arlen and **Charles "Buddy" Rogers** played dashing airmen in love with **Clara Bow**, a seductive ambulance nurse. Gary Cooper also had a small part in the film, and later became one of Miss Bow's widely publicized romantic interests. (W) Ballard Macdonald, (M) J. S. Zamecnik. (1927) $25

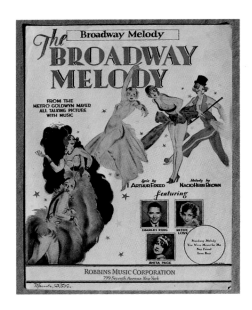

Broadway Melody
The Broadway Melody was the first movie musical to win the newly instituted Academy Award. It featured the hit songs "You Were Meant For Me," "Broadway Melody," and "The Wedding of the Painted Doll" by Nacio Herb Brown and Arthur Freed. (1929) $4

Angela Mia (My Angel)
The romantic team of **Janet Gaynor** and **Charles Farrell** were paired again in *Street Angel*, a Fox movie praised for its excellent cinematography by Ernest Palmer. Composer Erno Rapée and lyricist Lew Pollack followed their hit songs "Diane" and "Charmaine" with this lovely theme song from the movie. (1928) $3

All the winning films were silent movies, but recognition in the form of a special award was given to Warner Brothers for producing *The Jazz Singer*, the landmark first talking picture that revolutionized the movie industry. Charlie Chaplin also received a special award for acting, writing, directing, and producing *The Circus*.

Awards were not yet given for the best song from a movie, but theme songs from all the prize winning movies were top sheet music sellers. The theme song from *7th Heaven* was the very popular love waltz "Diane" by Erno Rapée and Lew Pollack. "Angela Mia" also by Rapée and Pollack was the theme from *Street Angel*. Both song sheet covers have pictures of the stars Janet Gaynor and Charles Farrell embracing. "Sunrise and You" by Arthur A. Penn was the musical theme from *Sunrise* with a cover picture of Janet Gaynor and George O'Brien.

Best Picture Academy Award in 1929 went to the first original movie musical *The Broadway Melody*. It was M-G-M's first "talkie," and curious audiences filled theaters across the country. As a promotional gimmick, uniformed pages were stationed in theater lobbies selling sheet music and recordings from the movie to the eager public.

Coquette
Mary Pickford was voted Best Actress in 1929 for her role in *Coquette*, her first talking picture. She played a Southern flirt with saucy bobbed hair who perjures herself to save her father. The movie's theme song was written by Irving Berlin. (1928) $4

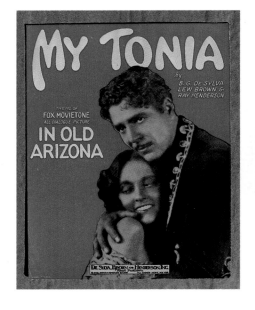

My Tonia
Good-looking **Warner Baxter** won the 1929 award for Best Actor for his role as an outlaw in *In Old Arizona*, also nominated for Best Picture. This first outdoor talking film pleased Western fans with its gunfights and cattle drives, and did well at the box office. Baxter appears with **Dorothy Burgess** on the cover. (1928) $4

Thirty Years of Academy Award Winning Songs

1934. The Continental
In 1934 the Best Song Category was added, and this song from *The Gay Divorcee* was the first winner. **Ginger Rogers** and **Fred Astaire** appear on cover. (W) Herbert Magidson, (M) Con Conrad. $8

1937. Sweet Leilani
Winner from movie *Waikiki Wedding* was sung in **Bing Crosby**'s inimitable style to co-star **Shirley Ross**. (WM) Harry Owens. $5

Left:
1936. The Way You Look Tonight
This winner was performed by **Fred Astaire** in the movie *Swing Time*. He dances with **Ginger Rogers** on the cover. (W) Dorothy Fields, (M) Jerome Kern. $5

1935. Lullaby of Broadway
Dick Powell and Wini Shaw sang this winning song in *Gold Diggers of 1935.* Starlets on cover. (W) Al Dubin, (M) Harry Warren. $5

Right:
1938. Thanks for the Memory
Winner from the movie *The Big Broadcast of 1938* was sung by **Bob Hope** and **Shirley Ross**. Popular song became Hope's theme song over the years. (WM) Leo Robin and Ralph Rainger. $4

Left:

1939. Over the Rainbow Winner from *The Wizard of Oz* was sung by **Judy Garland.** Her co-stars **Frank Morgan, Ray Bolger, Bert Lahr,** and **Jack Haley** also appear on cover. (W) E. Y. Harburg, (M) Harold Arlen. $15

Right:

1942. White Christmas This winner from *Holiday Inn* has become an all-time favorite and perennial best-seller. **Bing Crosby** introduced the song in the movie, seen on the cover with co-stars **Marjorie Reynolds, Fred Astaire,** and **Virginia Dale.** (WM) Irving Berlin. $3

1941. The Last Time I Saw Paris **Ann Sothern** sang this winner by Oscar Hammerstein 2nd (W) and Jerome Kern (M) in *Lady Be Good,* with dancer **Eleanor Powell** on the cover. This award caused some consternation within the Academy, as the song was already a hit when used in the movie. The Academy amended its rule so that a song, to be nominated for an Oscar, must be sung for the first time in the movie. $8

Left:

1940. When You Wish Upon a Star Jiminy Cricket sang this winner in the animated movie *Pinocchio* with the voice of Cliff Edwards. Disney drawing of Jiminy Cricket and Pinocchio decorates the cover. (W) Ned Washington, (M) Leigh Harline. $10

Right:

1943 You'll Never Know This winner was sung by sultry-eyed, husky-voiced **Alice Faye** in the movie *Hello, Frisco, Hello.* **John Payne** was the love interest, and supporting players **Jack Oakie** and **Lynn Bari** added to the cast. (W) Mack Gordon, (M) Harry Warren. $3

Left:

1944. *Swinging on a Star*
This charming winner was sung by **Bing Crosby** in the movie *Going My Way*. Crosby at the piano, with **Frank McHugh** standing to his right, is surrounded by boy singers. The film won Academy Awards for Best Picture, Best Actor (Crosby), Best Supporting Actor (Barry Fitzgerald), and Best Writer/Director Leo McCarey, who won two awards. (W) Johnny Burke, (M) Jimmy Van Heusen. $3

Right:

1946. *On the Atchison, Topeka and the Santa Fe*
A lively rendition by **Judy Garland** of this rollicking song in *The Harvey Girls* helped it win an Oscar. (W) Johnny Mercer, (M) Harry Warren. $6

Below:

1945. *It Might As Well Be Spring*
Winner from movie *State Fair* was sung by Louanne Hogan, who dubbed the singing for **Jeanne Crain,** right. **Dick Haymes** and **Vivian Blaine** are also on the cover. (W) Oscar Hammerstein 2nd, (M) Richard Rodgers. $3

1947. *Zip-a-Dee-Doo-Dah*
Winner for Walt Disney's animated movie *Song of the South* featured James Baskette as Uncle Remus, who received a special Oscar for singing this song to Disney's cartoon animals in the movie. (W) Ray Gilbert, (M) Allie Wrubel. $5

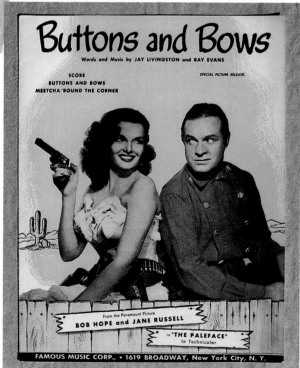

Right:

1948. *Buttons and Bows*
Bob Hope introduced this winning song in *The Paleface*, a hit movie that co-starred voluptuous **Jane Russell.** (WM) Jay Livingston and Ray Evans. $4

1959. High Hopes
This winner was a cute song from the movie *A Hole in the Head* sung by **Frank Sinatra** and **Eddie Hodges,** the boy he is holding on the cover. Other members of the cast were (left) **Carolyn Jones,** (right) **Thelma Ritter, Eleanor Parker, Edward G. Robinson,** and **Keenan Wynn.** (W) Sammy Cahn, (M) James Van Heusen. $4

1961. Moon River
This winner was the haunting refrain sung by Audrey Hepburn in *Breakfast at Tiffany's.* Cover drawing shows **Audrey Hepburn** as the enchanting character Holly Golightly, who she portrayed in the film. (W) Johnny Mercer, (M) Henry Mancini. $4

1962. Days of Wine and Roses
This winner from the *Days of Wine and Roses* co-starred **Jack Lemmon** and **Lee Remick** as a married couple with drinking problems. The nostalgic song contrasts the tender romance of the young couple at the beginning with the depths of degradation wrought by overindulgence at the end. (W) Johnny Mercer,(M) Henry Mancini. $4

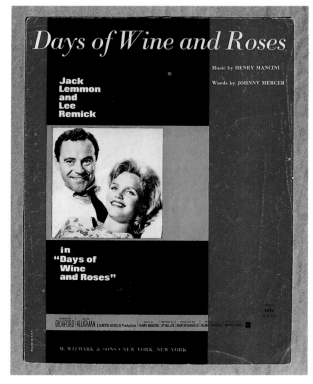

1960. Never on Sunday
 This winner from the movie *Never on Sunday* became an international favorite. Greek film star **Melina Mercouri** introduced the song in the film. (W) Billy Towne, (M) Manos Hadjidakis. $4

1963. Call Me Irresponsible
Cover star **Jackie Gleason** sang this Oscar winning song in the movie *Papa's Delicate Condition*, a comedy based on memoirs of silent screen star Corinne Griffith about her childhood. (W) Sammy Cahn, (M) James Van Heusen. $4

Additional Academy Award Winners:

1964 "Chim Chim Cher-ee" from *Mary Poppins*. (WM) Richard M. Sherman and Robert B. Sherman.

1965 "The Shadow of Your Smile" from *The Sandpiper*. (W) Paul Francis Webster; (M) Johnny Mandel.

1966 "Born Free" from *Born Free*. (W) Don Black; (M) John Barry.

1967 "Talk to the Animals" from *Doctor Dolittle*. (WM) Leslie Bricusse.

1968 "The Windmills of Your Mind" from *The Thomas Crown Affair*. (W) Alan and Marilyn Bergman; (M) Michel Legrand.

1969 "Raindrops Keep Fallin' on My Head" from *Butch Cassidy and the Sundance Kid*. (W) Hal David; (M) Burt Bacharach.

1970 "For All We Know" from *Lovers and Other Strangers*. (W) Robb Wilson and Arthur James; (M) Fred Karlin.

1971 "Theme from Shaft" from *Shaft*. (WM) Isaac Hayes.

1972 "The Morning After" from *The Poseidon Adventure*. (WM) Al Kasha and Joel Hirschhorn.

1973 "The Way We Were" from *The Way We Were*. (W) Alan and Marilyn Bergman; (M) Marvin Hamlisch.

1974 "We May Never Love Like This Again" from *The Towering Inferno*. (WM) Al Kasha and Joel Hirschhorn.

1975 "I'm Easy" from *Nashville*. (WM) Keith Carradine.

1976 "Evergreen" from *A Star Is Born*. (W) Paul Williams; (M) Barbra Streisand.

1977 "You Light Up My Life" from *You Light Up My Life*. (WM) Joseph Brooks.

1978 "Last Dance" from *Thank God It's Friday*. (WM) Paul Jabara.

1979 "It Goes Like It Goes" from *Norma Rae*. (W) Norman Gimbel; (M) David Shire.

1980 "Fame" from *Fame*. (W) Dean Pitchford; (M) Michael Gore.

1981 "Arthur's Theme (Best That You Can Do)" from *Arthur*. (WM) Burt Bacharach, Carole Bayer Sager, Christopher Cross, and Peter Allen.

1982 "Up Where We Belong" from *An Officer and a Gentleman*. (W) Will Jennings; (M) Jack Nitzsche and Buffy Sainte-Marie.

1983 "Flashdance. . . What a Feeling" from *Flashdance*. (W) Keith Forsey and Irene Cara; (M) Giorgio Moroder.

1984 "I Just Called to Say I Love You" from *The Woman in Red*. (WM) Stevie Wonder.

1985 "Say You, Say Me" from *White Nights*. (WM) Lionel Richie.

1986 "Take My Breath Away" from *Top Gun*. (W) Tom Whitlock; (M) Giorgio Morodor.

1987 "(I've Had) The Time of My Life" from *Dirty Dancing*. (W) Franke Previte; (M) Frankie Previte, John DeNicola, and Donald Markowitz.

1988 "Let the River Run" from *Working Girl*. (WM) Carly Simon.

1989 "Under the Sea" from *The Little Mermaid*. (W) Howard Ashman; (M) Alan Menken.

1990 "Sooner or Later (I Always Get My Man)" from *Dick Tracy*. (WM) Stephen Sondheim.

1991 "Beauty and the Beast" from *Beauty and the Beast*. (W) Howard Ashman; (M) Alan Menken.

1992 "A Whole New World" from *Aladdin*. (W) Tim Rice; (M) Alan Menken.

1993 "Streets of Philadelphia" from *Philadelphia*. (WM) Bruce Springsteen.

1994 "Can You Feel the Love Tonight" from *The Lion King*. (W) Tim Rice; (M) Elton John.

1995 "Colors of the Wind" from *Pocahontas*. (W) Steven Schwartz; (M) Alan Menken.

1996 "You Must Love Me" from *Evita*. (W) Tim Rice; (M) Andrew Lloyd Webber.

1997 "My Heart Will Go On" from *Titanic*. (W) Will Jennings; (M) James Horner.

The most commonly collected sheet music has movie star photos on the cover. Cinema sheet music was a great way to publicize a film, and hardly a movie was released without its attendant song. Following are thumbnail sketches of important Hollywood stars listed alphabetically, along with a list of movies in which they appeared for which sheet music was released. Regrettably, some favorite stars were omitted when no appropriate sheet music was available, and such omission is in no way a reflection on a star's popularity or ability.

Silent stars generally are not included here, since, they are profiled in a previous book, *From Footlights to "The Flickers."* Some stars whose careers straddled the sound breakthrough have been included—Norma Shearer, Greta Garbo, Joan Crawford, Ronald Colman, Janet Gaynor, among others. Space constraints preclude listing the song titles as some movies, especially musicals, had many songs in their productions. Songs from each movie generally all had the same cover, with a few exceptions.

Abbott and Costello. This popular comedy team made a string of laugh hits in the 1940s. Bud Abbott (1895-1974), thin and humorless, played the fast-talking straight man to chubby Lou Costello's (1908-1959) bumbling comedy. One of their most famous routines, the priceless "Who's on First?," is enshrined on a plaque in the Baseball Hall of Fame.

ABBOTT AND COSTELLO MOVIE COVERS: *Buck Privates,* 1941. *In the Navy,* 1941. *Keep 'Em Flying,* 1941. *Ride 'Em Cowboy,* 1942. *Rio Rita,* 1942. *Hit the Ice,* 1943. *It Ain't Hay,* 1943. *In Society,* 1944. *Lost in a Harem,* 1944. *Bud Abbott and Lou Costello in Hollywood,* 1945. *Here Come the Co-eds,* 1945. *The Naughty Nineties,* 1945. *Jack and the Beanstalk,* 1952.

My Dreams Are Getting Better All The Time
In Society was an entertaining farce highlighted by **Abbott** and **Costello**'s antics as clumsy plumbers at a weekend society party. **Marion Hutton,** the blonde on the cover, introduced this song in the movie. $15

Opposite page:
As Time Goes By
The *film noir* classic World War II movie *Casablanca* starred **Humphrey Bogart** as a nightclub owner opposite underground leader **Paul Henreid** and his wife **Ingrid Bergman.** With everything right about it, the movie won Oscars for Best Picture, Director, and Screenplay. Dooley Wilson sang this 1931 Herman Hupfeld song in the film. (1942) $12 *($27)*

Long Before You Came Along
The 1927 Broadway musical *Rio Rita* was updated for World War II with **Abbott** and **Costello** working on a ranch that is overrun with Nazi spies. E. Y. Harburg wrote the words and Harold Arlen, the music, for this song warbled by **Kathryn Grayson** and **John Carroll.** *Collection of Harold Jacobs.* $30

June Allyson (born 1923). With her sweet girl-next-door wholesome aura peppered with a kittenish sexiness, Miss Allyson became a popular leading lady in Hollywood. She started out in Broadway musicals where she was discovered by Hollywood dancing and singing in *Best Foot Forward* in the early 1940s. After successfully repeating her Broadway role on the screen, she became a favorite performer in movies of the 1940s and 1950s, equally at ease in musical comedy or dramatic roles. In later years she became a spokeswoman for television commercials.

ALLYSON MOVIE COVERS: *Music for Millions*, 1944. *Two Girls and a Sailor*, 1944. *Her Highness and the Bellboy*, 1945. *The Secret Heart*, 1946. *Till the Clouds Roll By*, 1946. *Two Sisters from Boston*, 1946. *Good News*, 1947. *Words and Music*, 1948. *Remains to be Seen*, 1953. *The Glenn Miller Story*, 1954. *Woman's World*, 1954. *The McConnell Story*, 1955. *The Shrike*, 1955. *Strategic Air Command*, 1955. *The Opposite Sex*, 1956. *You Can't Run Away from It*, 1956. *Interlude*, 1957.

Don Ameche (1908-1993). A popular leading man at Twentieth Century-Fox in the 1930s and 1940s, Don Ameche was a frequent co-star of Alice Faye, Betty Grable, and Sonja Henie. He made a phenomenal comeback at age 77, winning a Best Supporting Actor Academy Award for his role in *Cocoon* in 1985.

AMECHE MOVIE COVERS: *One in a Million*, 1936. *Love Under Fire*, 1937. *You Can't Have Everything*, 1937. *Alexander's Ragtime Band*, 1938. *Happy Landing*, 1938. *In Old Chicago*, 1938. *Josette*, 1938. *Midnight*, 1939. *Swanee River*, 1939. *The Three Musketeers*, 1939. *Down Argentine Way*, 1940. *Lillian Russell*, 1940. *The Feminine Touch*, 1941. *Moon over Miami*, 1941. *That Night in Rio*, 1941. *Something to Shout About*, 1943. *Greenwich Village*, 1944. *So Goes My Love*, 1946. *Sleep My Love*, 1948. *Slightly French*, 1949.

Voila
This lively musical version of *The Three Musketeers* starred **Don Ameche** as a singing D'Artagnan with the zany **Ritz Brothers** posing as musketeers. $8

Sweet and Lovely
In *Two Girls and a Sailor*, cute **June Allyson** (right) vied with **Gloria DeHaven** (left) for handsome sailor **Van Johnson.** This sparkling M-G-M musical had a great lineup of performers—the **Harry James** orchestra with singer **Helen Forrest,** Jose Iturbi, Jimmy Durante, Gracie Allen, Lena Horne, and Xavier Cugat. $4

The World Is Mine
June Allyson played **James Stewart**'s wife in *Strategic Air Command*, a drama about the inner workings of SAC and its development of America's atom-bomb carrying planes. $7 *($33)*

They Met In Rio
Don Ameche played dual roles in the entertaining musical *That Night in Rio* opposite lovely **Alice Faye. Carmen Miranda** (right), as the jealous girlfriend, was outstanding in her numbers singing "Chica Chica Boom Chic" and "I Yi Yi Yi Yi." $15

Julie Andrews (born 1935). As a pretty young singer from England, she made a splash on Broadway as Eliza Doolittle in *My Fair Lady* in 1956. Her Hollywood debut was in the movie *Mary Poppins* in 1964, for which she won an Academy Award. She also enchanted the public the following year with her portrayal of Maria von Trapp in *The Sound of Music*, after which she attempted to change her image with more worldly roles.

ANDREWS MOVIE COVERS: *The Americanization of Emily*, 1964. *Mary Poppins*, 1964. *The Sound of Music*, 1965. *Hawaii*, 1966. *Torn Curtain*, 1966. *Thoroughly Modern Millie*, 1967. *Star!* 1968. *Darling Lili*, 1970.

Chim Chim Cher-ee
Julie Andrews portrayed a magical English nanny in the charming Disney movie *Mary Poppins*, with **Dick Van Dyke** as Bert, the singing/dancing chimney sweep. Richard M. Sherman and Robert B. Sherman won Oscars for best music score and best song performed by Andrews and Van Dyke in the movie. $5

Fred Astaire (1899-1987). With his sister Adele, he dazzled theater audiences in New York and London for many years until their dancing partnership dissolved upon her marriage in the 1930s. He went on to Hollywood where he was successfully paired with Ginger Rogers in ten entertaining musical films in which he sang and danced and charmed the movie-going public.

For the next 30 years he continued his brilliant career starring in a string of fine musicals with lovely leading ladies, including Rita Hayworth, Eleanor Powell, Judy Garland, Vera-Ellen, Cyd Charisse, and Leslie Caron. The 1940s saw him co-starring with Bing Crosby in the perennial Christmas favorite *Holiday Inn* with its wonderful Irving Berlin songs. Mr. Astaire received a special Academy Award in 1949 "for his unique artistry and his contributions to the technique of musical pictures."

ASTAIRE MOVIE COVERS: *Flying Down to Rio*, 1933. *The Gay Divorcée*, 1934. *Roberta*, 1935. *Top Hat*, 1935. *Follow the Fleet*, 1936. *Swing Time*, 1936. *Shall We Dance*, 1937. *A Damsel in Distress*, 1937. *Carefree*, 1938. *The Story of Vernon and Irene Castle*, 1939. *Broadway Melody of 1940*. *Second Chorus*, 1940. *You'll Never Get Rich*, 1941. *Holiday Inn*, 1942. *You Were Never Lovelier*, 1942. *The Sky's the Limit*, 1943. *Yolanda and the Thief*, 1945. *Blue Skies*, 1946. *Ziegfeld Follies*, 1946. *Easter Parade*, 1948. *The Barkleys of Broadway*, 1949. *Let's Dance*, 1950. *Royal Wedding*, 1950. *Three Little Words*, 1950. *The Belle of New York*, 1951. *The Band Wagon*, 1953. *Daddy Long Legs*, 1955. *Funny Face*, 1957. *Silk Stockings*, 1957. *On the Beach*, 1959. *The Pleasure of His Company*, 1961. *The Notorious Landlady*, 1962. *Finian's Rainbow*, 1968.

Star!
Legendary musical comedy star Gertrude Lawrence was the subject of *Star!*, with **Julie Andrews** portraying Lawrence. The movie was praised for its fine production numbers of music by the Gershwins, Noel Coward, Kurt Weill, Cole Porter, and others. Sammy Cahn (W) and James Van Heusen (M) wrote the title song. $4

A Foggy Day
Charming Gershwin songs highlighted the RKO movie *Damsel in Distress* co-starring **Fred Astaire** as an American dancer wooing English aristocrat **Joan Fontaine.** Capable support came from **George Burns** and **Gracie Allen,** seen at right. Choreographer Hermes Pan won an Oscar for his "Fun House" number in the movie. $5

I'm Building Up to an Awful Let-Down
Talented **Mr. Astaire** was not only a superlative actor, singer, and dancer, but also a capable composer as evidenced by this song he wrote with words by Johnny Mercer. (1938) $15

Wyomin', 1942. *Stardust on the Sage*, 1942. *Sioux City Sue*, 1946. *The Last Round-up*, 1947. *Strawberry Roan*, 1948. *Rim of the Canyon*, 1949. *Sons of New Mexico*, 1950. *Texans Never Cry*, 1951. *The Old West*, 1952. *On Top of Old Smoky*, 1953.

Dearly Beloved
Glamorous **Rita Hayworth** and charming **Fred Astaire** co-starred in the Columbia movie *You Were Never Lovelier* with a rich film score by Jerome Kern and lyricist Johnny Mercer including the songs "I'm Old Fashioned" and "Shorty George." Also seen on the cover are **Xavier Cugat** and **Adolphe Menjou.** $5

Waltzing Matilda
Fred Astaire capped off the decade of the 1950s with a straight non-musical role in *On the Beach* for which he received critical accolades for his dramatic acting. The movie told the grim story of survivors of a World War III nuclear war who face certain death when radioactive drift reaches them in Australia. Also on cover are co-stars **Gregory Peck, Ava Gardner, Anthony Perkins,** and **Donna Anderson.** $12

My Cross Eyed Gal
After a successful first appearance in the Western movie *In Old Santa Fe*, **Gene Autry** landed the leading role in the 13 chapter serial *The Phantom Empire*. Autry wrote the words for this song, with music by Jimmy Long. $15 *($50)*

Gene Autry (born 1907). Autry was a pleasing cowboy singer and songwriter who abandoned a career as a railroad telegrapher for a career in show business. With his horse, Champion, and his loyal sidekick, gravel-voiced character actor Smiley Burnett, he made dozens of Hollywood westerns entertaining legions of fans for almost 20 years.

AUTRY MOVIE COVERS: *Jack Ahoy*, 1933. *In Old Santa Fe*, 1934. *Melody Trail*, 1935. *The Phantom Empire*, 1935. *Sagebrush Troubadour*, 1935. *The Singing Vagabond*, 1935. *Tumbling Tumbleweeds*, 1935. *Comin' Round the Mountain*, 1936. *Guns and Guitars*, 1936. *Oh, Susanna*, 1936. *Red River Valley*, 1936. *The Singing Cowboy*, 1936. *The Big Show*, 1937. *Boots and Saddles*, 1937. *Git Along Little Dogies*, 1937. *Gold Mine in the Sky*, 1938. *The Man from Music Mountain*, 1938. *The Old Barn Dance*, 1938. *Public Cowboy Number One*, 1938. *Rhythm of the Saddle*, 1938. *Ride Ranger Ride*, 1938. *Round Up Time in Texas*, 1938. *The Singing Outlaw*, 1938. *Western Jamboree*, 1938. *Blue Montana Skies*, 1939. *Home on the Prairie*, 1939. *In Old Monterey*, 1939. *Mountain Rhythm*, 1939. *South of the Border*, 1939. *Washington Cowboy*, 1939. *Melody Ranch*, 1940. *Prairie Moon*, 1940. *Rancho Grande*, 1940. *Shooting High*, 1940. *Back in the Saddle*, 1941. *Down Mexico Way*, 1941. *Ridin' on a Rainbow*, 1941. *Under Fiesta Stars*, 1941. *A Gay Ranchero*, 1942. *Heart of the Rio Grande*, 1942. *Home in*

Nevertheless
M-G-M's movie *Three Little Words* was a musical biography of two gifted songwriters, Bert Kalmar and Harry Ruby, played respectively by **Fred Astaire** and **Red Skelton. Vera-Ellen** was Astaire's dance partner, and **Arlene Dahl,** lower right, played Ruby's wife. Andre Previn's score was nominated for an Oscar. $4

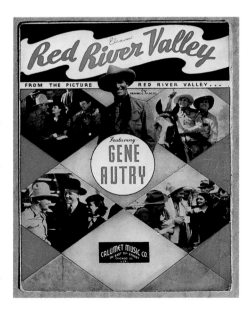

Red River Valley
Red River Valley co-starred **Gene Autry** with his longtime friend and sidekick, **Smiley Burnett,** seen together on cover photo, top left. That's Smiley playing the guitar as Gene romances the gal. $5

Lew Ayres (born 1908). Though he studied medicine at the University of Arizona, he opted for a show business career. He was a nightclub musician adept at banjo, guitar, and piano when he was discovered by Hollywood. In 1930 he attracted favorable attention as the sensitive young German soldier in *All Quiet on the Western Front*. He is also known for his believable characterization of young Dr. Kildare in the popular series of nine *Kildare* films that co-starred Lionel Barrymore as the crusty Dr. Gillespie. During World War II, Ayres alienated his public when he refused to fight, registering as a conscientious objector. Though he volunteered for non-combatant medical duties, his career after the war never recaptured its early impetus, though he had two strong successes in *The Dark Mirror* and *Johnny Belinda*.

AYRES MOVIE COVERS: *All Quiet on the Western Front*, 1930. *My Weakness*, 1933. *She Learned About Sailors*, 1934. *Lottery Lover*, 1935. *These Glamour Girls*, 1939.

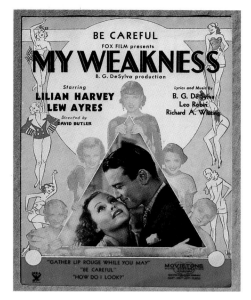

Be Careful
Young **Lew Ayres**'s movies in the 1930s were frequently frivolous affairs like the romantic Fox film *My Weakness*, in which he co-starred with international film star **Lilian Harvey.** $6

How Little We Know
The movie *To Have and Have Not* was loosely based on a Hemingway story, and 19-year-old **Lauren Bacall** made screen history in a seductive role opposite **Humphrey Bogart.** This song by Johnny Mercer (W) and Hoagy Carmichael (M) was sung by Carmichael in the movie. $8 *($26)*

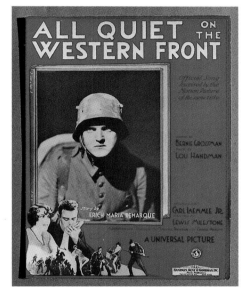

All Quiet on the Western Front
A very young **Lew Ayres** played a German soldier fighting during World War I in *All Quiet on the Western Front*, a movie based on Erich Maria Remarque's novel about the wastefulness of war. The powerful film won Academy Awards for Best Picture and Best Director. The title song was composed by Lou Handman with words by Bernie Grossman. *Collection of Harold Jacobs.* $35

Lauren Bacall (born 1924). "Bogey's Baby" was a beautiful young actress on Broadway and a striking model and cover girl when discovered by Hollywood in 1943. She sparkled in her first movie *To Have and Have Not*, and her suggestive phrase, "If you want anything, all you have to do is whistle," scorched the screen and lit a fire in the heart of her co-star Humphrey Bogart, whom she later married. After his death she returned to the stage, eventually winning Tony Awards for *Applause* (1970) and *Woman of the Year* (1981). Her wry comedy role as Barbra Streisand's mother in the 1996 movie *The Mirror Has Two Faces* brought her an Academy Award nomination for Best Supporting Actress.

BACALL MOVIE COVERS: *To Have and Have Not*, 1945. *Dark Passage*, 1947. *How to Marry a Millionaire*, 1953. *Woman's World*, 1954. *Designing Woman*, 1957. *Written on the Wind*, 1957. *The Gift of Love*, 1958. *Northwest Frontier*, 1959. *Harper*, 1966. *Murder on the Orient Express*, 1974. *The Shootist*, 1976.

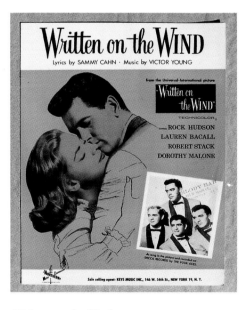

Written on the Wind
Written on the Wind starred **Lauren Bacall** as a young wife struggling to make her marriage work, while **Rock Hudson** (on cover) loved her from afar. Robert Stack was magnificent as her rich, spoiled, alcoholic husband, and Dorothy Malone won an Oscar for her role as Stack's nymphomaniac sister. Theme song was written by Sammy Cahn (W) and Victor Young (M). $10

Lucille Ball (1911-1989). This lovely vivacious redheaded show girl starred in numerous entertaining Hollywood films before going on to greater fame as an inspired comedienne on *I Love Lucy*, a hit television series that ran from 1951 to 1957 and co-starred her then husband, band-leader Desi Arnaz.

BALL MOVIE COVERS: *Dance, Girl, Dance*, 1940. *Too Many Girls*, 1940. *Seven Days Leave*, 1942. *Best Foot Forward*, 1943. *Meet the People*, 1944. *Easy to Wed*, 1946. *Two Smart People*, 1946. *Ziegfeld Follies*, 1946. *Easy Living*, 1949. *Sorrowful Jones*, 1949. *Fancy Pants*, 1950. *Forever Darling*, 1956. *The Facts of Life*, 1960. *Yours Mine and Ours*, 1968. *Mame*, 1974.

Home Cookin'
Lucille Ball was at her best playing a rich American girl opposite **Bob Hope** as a bumbling English butler in *Fancy Pants*, a hilarious comedy culminating in a lively fox hunt. Jay Livingston and Ray Evans wrote the song. $5

Forever Darling
Madcap **Lucille Ball** and **Desi Arnaz,** her real life husband, play a married couple in the zany comedy *Forever Darling*, with **James Mason** as the angel who comes to earth to help them save their faltering marriage. $5 *($27)*

Anne Baxter (1923-1985). This competent actress won an Academy Award for Best Supporting Actress for *The Razor's Edge* in 1946, and another nomination in 1950 for her strong portrayal of a scheming actress in *All About Eve*. She startled Hollywood when she and her husband opted to live on a primitive cattle station in the Australian outback, a colorful experience that she described in her 1956 autobiographical book, *Intermission, A True Story*.

BAXTER MOVIE COVERS: *The North Star*, 1943. *The Razor's Edge*, 1946. *Blaze of Noon*, 1947. *You're My Everything*, 1949. *The Blue Gardenia*, 1953. *I Confess*, 1953. *Carnival Story*, 1954. *Bedevilled*, 1955. *Three Violent People*, 1956. *Chase a Crooked Shadow*, 1958. *A Walk on the Wild Side*, 1962.

Blue Gardenia
The Blue Gardenia was a murder mystery with **Anne Baxter** wrongly accused of the crime. **Nat King Cole** sang the theme song by Bob Russell and Lester Lee on the movie sound track. $7

Mam'selle
Anne Baxter was outstanding in a drab role as an alcoholic in *The Razor's Edge*, based on the W. Somerset Maugham book. The cast included (left to right) **Herbert Marshall, John Payne, Tyrone Power, Gene Tierney, Anne Baxter,** and **Clifton Webb.** $4

Wallace Beery (1885-1949). Beery was around a long time, starting in silent comedy shorts, and moving smoothly into sound pictures. He was a talented versatile actor who proved his mettle by winning an Oscar as a rough-spoken prizefighter with a heart of gold in *The Champ*, with child actor Jackie Cooper. He ultimately became one of Hollywood's most popular stars.

BEERY MOVIE COVERS: *Beggars of Life*, 1928. *Dinner at Eight*, 1933. *Viva Villa*, 1934. *O'Shaughnessy's Boy*, 1935.

Joan Bennett (1910-1990). She descended from an acting family and carried on the tradition, slipping smoothly into starring roles while still in her teens, playing opposite Ronald Colman in *Bulldog Drummond*. She was at her best in femme fatale roles—sexy, greedy, manipulative women—but was also effective playing the mother of Elizabeth Taylor in *Father of the Bride* opposite Spencer Tracy. In later years she did TV soap opera work on "Dark Shadows."

BENNETT MOVIE COVERS: *Maybe It's Love*, 1930. *Careless Lady*, 1932. *Little Women*, 1933. *Mississippi*, 1935. *Two for Tonight*, 1935. *The Texans*, 1938. *Vogues of 1938*, 1937. *The House Across the Bay*, 1940. *Woman in the Window*, 1944. *Nob Hill*, 1945. *We're No Angels*, 1955.

Ingrid Bergman (1915-1982). She was a Swedish import who came to Hollywood in 1939 to star in *Intermezzo*, her first American movie. As a popular dramatic leading lady, she starred in a number of prestigious films in the 1940s, notably in *Casablanca* with Humphrey Bogart, and her Academy Award winning role in *Gaslight*. After a scandal in 1949 involving an extramarital affair with Roberto Rossellini, she was blacklisted from American movies for several years. She made a comeback in 1956 starring in *Anastasia*, for which she won the 1956 Best Actress Oscar. She subsequently won a third award for her supporting role in *Murder on the Orient Express*.

BERGMAN MOVIE COVERS: *Intermezzo*, 1939. *Casablanca*, 1943. *For Whom the Bell Tolls*, 1943. *The Bells of St. Mary's*, 1945. *Saratoga Trunk*, 1945. *Spellbound*, 1945. *Arch of Triumph*, 1948. *Under Capricorn*, 1949. *Anastasia*, 1956. *Indiscreet*, 1954. *The Inn of the Sixth Happiness*, 1958. *Goodbye Again*, 1961. *The Yellow Rolls Royce*, 1964. *Cactus Flower*, 1969. *A Walk in the Spring Rain*, 1970. *From the Mixed-Up Files of Mrs. Basil E. Frankweiler*, 1973. *Murder on the Orient Express*, 1974. *A Matter of Time*, 1976.

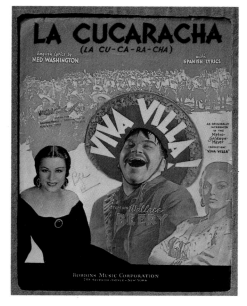

La Cucaracha
One of **Wallace Beery**'s most memorable roles was Pancho Villa in the M-G-M movie *Viva Villa!*, a lively action film set during the Mexican Revolution, and filmed on location in Mexico. **Fay Wray** was his co-star who was horse-whipped for rejecting his advances in the movie. $7

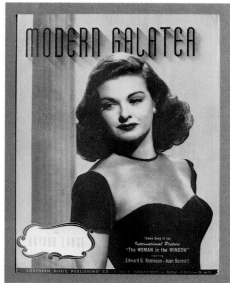

Modern Galatea
The Woman in the Window was a suspenseful *film noir* tale about a middle-aged professor, played by Edward G. Robinson, who falls in love with gorgeous **Joan Bennett**, and commits a murder in a moment of passion. This is very rare sheet music of high value. *Collection of Harold Jacobs.* $300

As Long As I Live
Ingrid Bergman played a New Orleans Creole who carried on with cowboy gambler, **Gary Cooper,** in *Saratoga Trunk*, a movie version of Edna Ferber's novel. Song was written by Charles Tobias (W) and Max Steiner (M). $7

That Old Feeling
Beautiful brunette **Joan Bennett** was a blonde in her earlier movies. She is seen here with **Warner Baxter** on the cover of *Vogues of 1938*, a lavish Technicolor musical featuring gorgeous models wearing sumptuous designer gowns. Producer Walter Wanger was Miss Bennett's third husband, the one who went to jail for shooting Bennett's agent, Jennings Lang, in a jealous rage. $5

Long After Tonight
As a nightclub singer in pre-war Paris, **Ingrid Bergman** sang this song in *Arch of Triumph*. Her co-stars in the heavy drama were Charles Boyer and Charles Laughton. $6

Anastasia
In her Hollywood comeback **Ingrid Bergman** was outstanding as the supposedly missing daughter of a Russian czar in *Anastasia*. Strong support came from **Helen Hayes** and **Yul Brynner**. Theme song was written by Paul Francis Webster (W) and Alfred Newman (M).$6

Ann Blyth (born 1928). She began her show business career as a radio singer and from there moved into opera, the Broadway stage, and then the movies. At age 15 she made her first Hollywood film, and was nominated as Best Supporting Actress two years later for her role as Joan Crawford's spoiled rotten daughter in *Mildred Pierce*. She also starred in several musicals before her early retirement from the screen in 1957.

BLYTH MOVIE COVERS: *Chip Off the Old Block*, 1944. *The Merry Monahans*, 1944. *Mr. Peabody and the Mermaid*, 1948. *Top o' the Morning*, 1949. *Our Very Own*, 1950. *The Great Caruso*, 1951. *Katie Did It*, 1951. *One Minute to Zero*, 1952. *The World in His Arms*, 1952. *The Student Prince*,1954. *The Buster Keaton Story*, 1957. *The Helen Morgan Story*, 1957.

Because
The Great Caruso was chiefly a vehicle for the fiery singer **Mario Lanza**, but **Ann Blyth** contributed to the musical production as Caruso's beautiful wife who sang "The Loveliest Night of the Year." Lanza, as Caruso, sang this 1902 song in the movie. $4

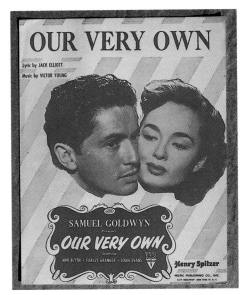

Our Very Own
Samuel Goldwyn's production of *Our Very Own* starred **Ann Blyth** as a young high school girl who is dismayed to find out she is adopted. **Farley Granger** was her boyfriend in the film, and eleven-year-old Natalie Wood and Joan Evans played her younger sisters. $5

Humphrey Bogart (1899-1957). As gangster Duke Mantee in the Broadway play *The Petrified Forest*, Bogart caught the attention of Hollywood. He was subsequently cast in the same role in the movie. He continued to play gangsters for a few years, then advanced to roles with more depth, culminating in his winning of the Academy Award for his performance as the salty captain in *The African Queen* in 1951.

Some movie sheet music covers from the 1940s have become classic collectibles because of their strong association with a popular movie. Humphrey Bogart and Ingrid Bergman on the cover of "As Time Goes By" from the movie *Casablanca* is one such cover that has become much sought after by sentimentalists. Other Bogart films have followed suit, and covers with "Bogey" and Lauren Bacall are very popular, not only with sheet music collectors but with Bogart cultists as well.

BOGART MOVIE COVERS: *San Quentin*, 1937. *Swing Your Lady*, 1938. *The Roaring Twenties*, 1939. *All Through the Night*, 1942. *Casablanca*, 1943. *Thank Your Lucky Stars*, 1943. *Passage to Marseilles*, 1944. *To*

Have and Have Not, 1945. *Dark Passage,* 1947. *Dead Reckoning,* 1947. *In a Lonely Place,* 1950. *The African Queen,* 1952. *The Barefoot Contessa,* 1954. *The Caine Mutiny,* 1954. *Sabrina,* 1954. *We're No Angels,* 1955.

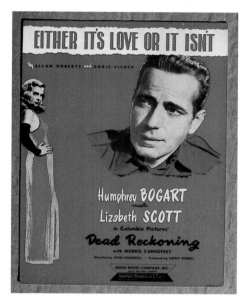

Either It's Love or It Isn't
Humphrey Bogart played a tough World War II veteran who gets involved with a bunch of bad guys and a beautiful girl, while trying to solve his Army buddy's murder. Sultry **Lizabeth Scott** sang this song in the *film noir* movie *Dead Reckoning.* $8

Sabrina
Humphrey Bogart played a lighter role as a rich businessman who vies with his brother, **William Holden,** for the love of the chauffeur's daughter, **Audrey Hepburn,** in the entertaining movie *Sabrina.* $10 *($46)*

Charles Boyer (1897-1978). He was a French actor with limpid "bedroom eyes" and a strong deep voice that caressed like velvet. He became a popular romantic lead in Hollywood and co-starred with some of Hollywood's top leading ladies. Mr. Boyer was nominated as Best Actor in 1944, losing out to popular Bing Crosby in *Going My Way.* He continued acting well into his seventies, but in a fit of despondency over his wife's death, he took his own life with an overdose of barbiturates.

BOYER MOVIE COVERS: *Caravan,* 1934. *Algiers,* 1938. *Love Affair,* 1939. *Hold Back the Dawn,* 1941. *Tales of Manhattan,* 1942. *Arch of Triumph,* 1948. *The Happy Time,* 1952. *Thunder in the East,* 1953. *Fanny,* 1961. *Is Paris Burning,* 1966. *Madwoman of Chaillot,* 1969.

Wishing
Charles Boyer and **Irene Dunne** were perfectly cast as a romantic couple in *Love Affair,* a sentimental movie with a happy ending, later remade as *An Affair to Remember.* Miss Dunne sang this popular song by Buddy De Sylva in the movie. $4

A Sinner Kissed an Angel
In *Hold Back the Dawn,* **Charles Boyer** won critical praise for his performance as the illegal alien who wanted to marry demure schoolteacher **Olivia de Havilland,** in order to obtain citizenship. **Paulette Goddard** (left) was in the able supporting cast. In an interesting case of sibling rivalry, Miss de Havilland lost the Oscar to her sister, Joan Fontaine, who won for *Suspicion.* $7

Caine Mutiny Theme
As skipper of the *Caine,* **Humphrey Bogart** was outstanding as the paranoic Captain Queeg, whose weird behavior over missing strawberries in the mess hall precipitates a mutiny. Strong support came from **Jose Ferrer, Van Johnson,** and **Fred MacMurray.** *The Caine Mutiny* received lots of Oscar nominations, but no awards due to the heavy competition that year. $8

C'est La Vie
Charles Boyer went down in film history as the crooked Pepe Le Moko, who is lured out of hiding in the Casbah section of Algiers by luscious **Hedy Lamarr** in her American film debut. *Algiers* is the movie in which he supposedly said, "Come wiz me to ze Casbah," a haunting phrase long associated with him. *Collection of Robert Johnson.* $150 *($200)*

Marlon Brando (born 1924). As a young actor on Broadway, he first attracted critical praise portraying the brutal, uncouth Stanley Kowalski in *A Streetcar Named Desire*. He made his movie debut in 1950 playing a paraplegic in *The Men*, and subsequently received several Academy Award nominations for his dramatic work, eventually winning Best Actor awards for *On the Waterfront* (1954) and *The Godfather* (1972).

BRANDO MOVIE COVERS: *The Men*, 1950. *The Wild One*, 1953. *On the Waterfront*, 1954. *Désirée*, 1954. *Guys and Dolls*, 1955. *Sayonara*, 1957. *One Eyed Jacks*, 1961. *Morituri*, 1965. *The Chase*, 1966. *Last Tango in Paris*, 1973. *The Missouri Breaks*, 1976.

James Cagney (1899-1986). This popular star started out in movies in 1931, playing a cocky gangster in *Public Enemy*, a role that he played so well that he was typecast for several years thereafter. He was also a brilliant dancer and capable singer and his great talent was rewarded with an Academy Award for his role as George M. Cohan in *Yankee Doodle Dandy* in 1942.

CAGNEY MOVIE COVERS: *Footlight Parade*, 1933. *Here Comes the Navy*, 1934. *Something to Sing About*, 1937. *Angels with Dirty Faces*, 1938. *The Oklahoma Kid*, 1939. *The Roaring Twenties*, 1939. *Torrid Zone* 1940. *The Strawberry Blonde*, 1941. *Captains of the Clouds*, 1942. *Yankee Doodle Dandy*, 1942. *Johnny Come Lately*, 1943. *West Point Story*, 1950. *What Price Glory*, 1952. *Love Me or Leave Me*, 1955. *Run for Cover*, 1954. *The Seven Little Foys*, 1955. *Never Steal Anything Small*, 1959.

A Woman in Love
In an interesting stretch proving his versatility, **Marlon Brando** played a convincing lead in the musical film *Guys and Dolls*. Principal players in the movie were (left to right) **Brando, Jean Simmons, Frank Sinatra,** and **Vivian Blaine.** Frank Sinatra sang this Frank Loesser song in the film. $5

On the Waterfront
Marlon Brando won his first Academy Award for Best Actor in *On the Waterfront*, with the movie itself taking a total of eight awards. It was a powerful indictment of union politics at the New York docks, and Brando is outstanding as he sorts his way through good and evil with the help of co-star **Eva Marie Saint,** who won the Best Supporting Actress Oscar. Title song was written by John Latouche (W) and Leonard Bernstein (M), who also wrote the score. *Collection of Harold Jacobs.* $40

Mi Caballero
James Cagney, as a plantation foreman in Central America, co-starred for the eighth time with **Pat O'Brien**, who played the plantation owner in *Torrid Zone*. Luscious **Ann Sheridan** (well-concealed on the sheet music cover behind the tree trunk) was the love interest. *Collection of Harold Jacobs.* $40

One Eyed Jacks
Marlon Brando not only acted in the absorbing Western movie *One Eyed Jacks*, but he also directed it. He was compared with Erich von Stroheim for his expansive vision that took the movie way over budget with its protracted shooting schedule and extravagant amount of film footage. $15

By the Kissing Rock
In the backstage musical *The West Point Story*, **James Cagney** played a Broadway director who stages a musical revue at West Point. He was ably assisted by **Doris Day** and **Gordon MacRae** (top), **Virginia Mayo,** and **Gene Nelson** (bottom). Songs by Sammy Cahn (W) and Jule Styne (M). $5

Bless 'em All
Cocky devil-may-care **James Cagney** joined the Canadian Air Force and became a hero under fire in *Captains of the Clouds*. His heroics were applauded by co-star, lovely **Brenda Marshall.** Words and music for this song were written by Jimmy Hughes, Frank Lake, and Al Stillman. The movie score was composed by Max Steiner. $25

Maurice Chevalier (1888-1972). A one-time French cabaret singer, Chevalier became a popular leading man in Paramount movies of the 1930s starring in a slew of light romantic films. Later in the 1950s, he made a comeback playing elderly character roles, always with his debonair charm and grace. He was given a Special Academy Award in 1958 "for his contributions to the world of entertainment for more than half a century."

CHEVALIER MOVIE COVERS: *Innocents of Paris,* 1929. *The Love Parade,* 1929. *The Big Pond,* 1930. *Paramount on Parade,* 1930. *Playboy of Paris,* 1930. *The Smiling Lieutenant,* 1931. *Love Me Tonight,* 1932. *One Hour with You,* 1932. *A Bedtime Story,* 1933. *The Way to Love,* 1933. *The Merry Widow,* 1934. *Folies Bergère de Paris,* 1935. *Break the News,* 1936. *Love in the Afternoon,* 1957. *A Breath of Scandal,* 1960. *Can-Can,* 1960. *Fanny,* 1961. *In Search of the Castaways,* 1962.

While Hearts Are Singing
Maurice Chevalier, at his most charming, starred in Paramount's *The Smiling Lieutenant,* a movie adaptation of the Oscar Straus operetta *A Waltz Dream.* $5

Claudette Colbert (1903-1996). Paris born, she came to New York with her parents at age six. She drifted into acting on the stage, and made her movie debut in the silent movie, *For the Love of Mike,* in New York in 1927. The advent of sound found Ms. Colbert much in demand with her bilingual skills, perfect English, and saucy good looks. She was at her best playing sophisticated comedy roles, winning a Best Actress Academy Award in 1934 for *It Happened One Night.* She continued acting into the 1950s, and had quite a fling appearing in the stage play *The Marriage-Go-Round* for 450 performances with Charles Boyer in 1958.

COLBERT MOVIE COVERS: *The Big Pond,* 1930. *Young Man of Manhattan,* 1930. *I Cover the Waterfront,* 1933. *Torch Singer,*

In the Park in Paree
Cute **Baby LeRoy** stole the picture from **Maurice Chevalier** without even trying. *A Bedtime Story* involves an abandoned baby who puts a crimp in Parisian playboy Chevalier's sophisticated life style. Songs were by Leo Robin (W) and Ralph Rainger (M). $4

1933. *The Bride Comes Home,* 1935. *The Gilded Lily,* 1935. *I Met Him in Paris,* 1937. *Midnight,* 1939. *Zaza,* 1939. *Arise My Love,* 1940. *Practically Yours,* 1944. *Since You Went Away,* 1944. *The Secret Heart,* 1946. *Tomorrow Is Forever,* 1946. *The Egg and I,* 1947. *Sleep My Love,* 1948. *Texas Lady,* 1955.

Give Me Liberty or Give Me Love
Claudette Colbert played a nightclub singer in *Torch Singer,* and she did her own singing of this Robin and Rainger song in the movie. Seen with her on cover are, left to right, **David Manners** and **Ricardo Cortez.** $4

Tomorrow Is Forever
In the poignant drama *Tomorrow Is Forever*, **Claudette Colbert** played a grief-stricken war widow, whose husband (Orson Welles) returned from the war, crippled, disfigured, and unrecognized, to find she has remarried. This pretty theme song was written by Charles Tobias (W) and Max Steiner (M). $6

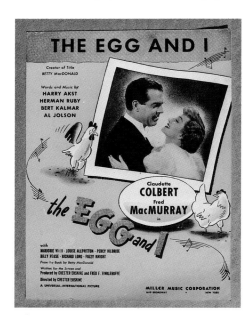

The Egg and I
Claudette Colbert was perfectly cast as a city girl who marries **Fred MacMurray** and moves to a chicken farm in *The Egg and I*, a thoroughly entertaining movie based on Betty McDonald's best-selling book. $6

Ronald Colman (1891-1958). At the top of the heap in silent movies, Colman was one of the rare breed who surmounted the transfer to the sound era. He was a major star in the 1920s, a handsome gentlemanly actor with a beautiful speaking voice and a slightly British accent that was a major asset in talking pictures. What is surprising is that he didn't win an Academy Award until 1948 for his dual role in *A Double Life*.

COLMAN MOVIE COVERS: *The White Sister*, 1923. *A Thief in Paradise*, 1925. *Beau Geste*, 1926. *The Magic Flame*, 1927. *Bulldog Drummond*, 1929. *Condemned*, 1929. *Lost Horizon*, 1937. *Kismet* 1944.

There's the One for Me
Ronald Colman, who was big in silent movies, survived the change to sound movies by virtue of his mellifluous voice and debonair good looks. In his talking debut, he played the title role in the melodrama *Bulldog Drummond,* for which he received an Academy Award nomination. $18

Sean Connery (born 1930). Scottish born young Sean Connery was a high school dropout who knocked around at various jobs before landing a role in the chorus of the London production of *South Pacific*. He continued amassing acting experience playing small parts in movies and on television. His big break came when he was chosen for the role of James Bond in the first Bond movie *Dr. No*, and the rest is history.

CONNERY MOVIE COVERS: *Darby O'Gill and the Little People*, 1959. *Dr. No*, 1962. *From Russia with Love*, 1963. *Goldfinger*, 1964. *Marnie*, 1964. *Thunderball*, 1965. *You Only Live Twice*, 1967. *Shalako*, 1968. *Diamonds Are Forever*, 1971. *Murder on the Orient Express*, 1974. *The Man Who Would Be King*, 1975. *Wrong Is Right*, 1982. *The Untouchables*, 1987. *Presidio*, 1988.

Lost Horizon
Ronald Colman, as Robert Conway, found his utopian dream in the Shangri-La of *Lost Horizon*, an ambitious film based on James Hilton's novel, and directed brilliantly by Frank Capra. Dimitri Tiomkin's music score was nominated for an Oscar, and he also wrote this theme song with words by Gus Kahn. *Collection of James Nelson Brown.* $100

Marnie
Sean Connery played the sympathetic employer who falls in love with **Tippi Hedren**, a compulsive young kleptomaniac, in the Alfred Hitchcock psychodrama *Marnie*. Theme song was written by Bernard Herrmann, Peter Jason, and Gloria Shayne. $10

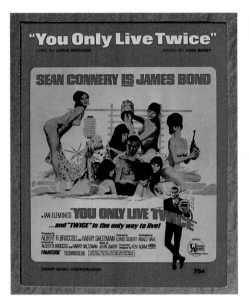

You Only Live Twice
Sean Connery made *You Only Live Twice* in Japan surrounded by exotic Japanese beauties. This was his fifth movie starring the indestructible James Bond saving the world from destruction. $5

Farewell to Arms
Gary Cooper as a World War I ambulance driver and a luminous **Helen Hayes** as an English nurse were highly praised for their work in *A Farewell to Arms* based on Ernest Hemingway's best-selling novel. This lovely theme song was written by Allie Wrubel (W) and Abner Silver (M). $5

A Love Like This
Writer Ernest Hemingway insisted he had **Gary Cooper** in mind when he wrote *For Whom the Bell Tolls*, and Cooper was great as an American mercenary during the Spanish Civil War who blows up a strategic bridge. **Ingrid Bergman** was effective as his co-star. The film was nominated for all the top Academy Awards, but only took one, that of Best Supporting Actress by Katina Paxinou. $12

Gary Cooper (1901-1961). Cooper started out in silent movies as a cowboy extra in Westerns. With his appealing strong silent type aura and his tall handsome good looks, he easily made the transition to talkies. From the 1940s, he is remembered for two of his greatest roles, that of Lou Gehrig in *The Pride of the Yankees* (1942), and *Sergeant York* (1941) for which he won his first Academy Award. Cooper won a second Best Actor Oscar in 1952 for his role in *High Noon*.

COOPER MOVIE COVERS: *Beau Sabreur*, 1928. *The First Kiss*, 1928. *The Shopworn Angel*, 1929. *The Wolf Song*, 1929. *Morocco*, 1930. *Paramount on Parade*, 1930. *A Farewell to Arms*, 1932. *Design for Living*, 1933. *Operator 13*, 1934. *Desire*, 1936. *Mr. Deeds Goes to Town*, 1936. *Souls at Sea*, 1937. *The Cowboy and the Lady*, 1938. *The Pride of the Yankees*, 1942. *For Whom the Bell Tolls*, 1943. *Casanova Brown*, 1944. *Along Came Jones*, 1945. *Saratoga Trunk*, 1945. *Task Force*, 1949. *High Noon*, 1952. *Blowing Wild*, 1953. *Return to Paradise*, 1953. *Vera Cruz*, 1954. *Friendly Persuasion*, 1956. *Love in the Afternoon*, 1957. *The Hanging Tree*, 1959. *They Came to Cordura*, 1959.

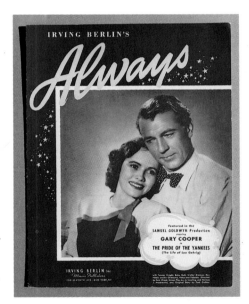

Always
The Pride of the Yankees was Lou Gehrig, New York Yankee first baseman, played by **Gary Cooper**, with **Teresa Wright** as his brave, devoted wife Eleanor. Despite suffering from an incurable disease, Gehrig was an inspiration to the country when he counted his blessings and said to his fans, "...Today I consider myself the luckiest man on the face of the earth." *Collection of Harold Jacobs.* $15

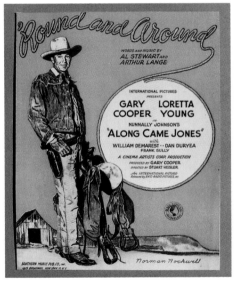

'Round and Around
Lean, laconic, and lanky, **Gary Cooper** starred as mild-mannered Melody Jones in the humorous Western movie *Along Came Jones*. His co-star was Loretta Young, who could shoot a gun better than he could. The song was by Al Stewart and Arthur Lange, and the arresting cover drawing of Cooper was by Norman Rockwell. This is an extremely rare piece. *Collection of Robert Johnson.* $200 *($350)*

Joseph Cotten (1905-1994). His acting career began under the aegis of Orson Welles's Mercury Theater. After appearing successfully on the New York stage, he was brought to Hollywood by Welles for important roles in *Citizen Kane*, *The Magnificent Ambersons*, and *Journey Into Fear*. Other memorable roles were as the psychopathic murderer in the Hitchcock thriller *Shadow of a Doubt*, and the romantic artist in *Portrait of Jennie*.

COTTEN MOVIE COVERS: *Hers to Hold*, 1943. *Since You Went Away* 1944. *I'll Be Seeing You*, 1945. *Love Letters*, 1945. *Duel in the Sun*, 1946. *Portrait of Jennie*, 1948. *The Third Man*, 1949. *Under Capricorn*, 1949. *September Affair*, 1950. *The Steel Trap*, 1952. *Niagara*,1953. *Hush...Hush,Sweet Charlotte*, 1965.

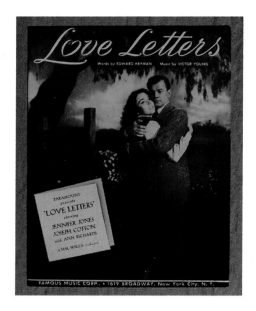

Love Letters
Joseph Cotten brought great sincerity to his role as the man who restores amnesiac **Jennifer Jones**'s memory in the sentimental movie *Love Letters*. The beautiful theme song by Edward Heyman (W) and Victor Young (M) deserves special commendation. $4

Jeanne Crain (born 1925). As a 16-year-old beauty contest winner and a successful cover girl and model, she was snapped up by Hollywood to make movies. Her peak Hollywood years as an actress were during the 1940s and 1950s, during which she had a busy private life as the mother of seven children.

CRAIN MOVIE COVERS: *Winged Victory*, 1944. *State Fair*, 1945. *Centennial Summer*, 1946. *Margie*, 1946. *You Were Meant for Me*, 1948. *Cheaper by the Dozen*, 1950. *Duel in the Jungle*, 1954. *Gentlemen Marry Brunettes*, 1955. *Man Without a Star*, 1955. *The Second Greatest Sex*, 1955. *The Joker Is Wild*, 1957.

The Harry Lime Theme
Joseph Cotten portrayed a writer searching for his old friend, the mysterious Harry Lime (Orson Welles), in the taut suspense movie *The Third Man*. The film was colored by the haunting zither music composed by Anton Karas. $6

Margie
Jeanne Crain was perfectly cast as a high school senior with a crush on her French teacher. The movie featured many nostalgic 1920s songs including this title song with words by Benny Davis and music by Con Conrad and J. Russel Robinson. On cover, left to right, are **Alan Young, Glenn Langan, Jeanne Crain,** and **Lynn Bari.** $8

Joan Crawford (1908-1977). Crawford was a major silent star who portrayed vivacious Charleston-dancing flappers in 1920s movies. In school she never went past the fifth grade, but with innate intelligence taught herself what she needed to know to get ahead. She became the shopgirl's idol in her early movies, frequently portraying one herself. As one of the fortunate actresses who made the successful transition from silents to talkies, she eventually won the 1945 Oscar for Best Actress in *Mildred Pierce*.

CRAWFORD MOVIE COVERS: *Pretty Ladies*, 1925. *Our Dancing Daughters*, 1928. *The Duke Steps Out*, 1929. *Hollywood Revue*, 1929. *Our Modern Maidens*, 1929. *Untamed*, 1929. *Montana Moon*, 1930. *The Laughing Sinners*, 1931. *Possessed*, 1931. *Dancing Lady*, 1933. *Sadie McKee*, 1934. *Love on the Run*, 1936. *The Bride Wore Red*, 1937. *Mannequin*, 1937. *Ice Follies of 1939*. *Hollywood Canteen*, 1944. *Humoresque*, 1946. *Daisy Kenyon*, 1947. *Flamingo Road*, 1949. *Sudden Fear*, 1952. *Torch Song*, 1953. *Johnny Guitar*, 1954. *Female on the Beach*, 1955. *What Ever Happened to Baby Jane?*, 1962.

When You Wore a Tulip
Jeanne Crain is one of the dozen Gilbreth children in the charming movie *Cheaper By the Dozen*. **Clifton Webb** stole the movie as a strict but loving father, who is always there for his brood, including escorting his daughter to her high school prom. $8

Chant of the Jungle
Untamed was **Joan Crawford**'s first all talking movie. She played an oil heiress from the tropics named Bingo, who fights for the love of poor boy Robert Montgomery. She sang this theme song by Arthur Freed (W) and Nacio Herb Brown (M) in the movie. $4

Always and Always
Joan Crawford, as a poor tenement girl, played opposite rich tycoon Spencer Tracy in *Mannequin,* the only movie they made together. Crawford sang this song by Chet Forrest and Bob Wright (W) and Edward Ward (M) in the movie.$8

Afraid
Joan Crawford, in a powerful bit of emoting, comes unglued on the cover of this song from *Sudden Fear.* The movie thriller co-starred Jack Palance as her husband, who is plotting to kill her. Song was written by Jack Brooks (W) and Elmer Bernstein (M). *Collection of Harold Jacobs.* $60

Bing Crosby (1904-1977). Possessor of a wonderful baritone voice and with a pleasant relaxed manner, Crosby was America's most popular crooner in the 1930s. He sang on his own radio show, recorded many hit songs that flooded the airwaves, and starred in a raft of entertaining movie musicals. With vast amounts of sheet music to his credit, Crosby is a collecting category all by himself. The twenty-plus movies in which he starred in the 1930s had over a hundred songs published. Folios that featured collections of songs sung by Crosby were also big sellers.

Crosby teamed with Bob Hope and Dorothy Lamour in a series of successful "Road" pictures with numerous song covers featuring the three. He remained a superstar throughout his entire career. "White Christmas," sung by Crosby in *Holiday Inn,* won an Academy Award for best song in 1942, and became a perennial holiday classic. "Swinging on a Star" from *Going My Way* garnered the coveted award in 1944. Other Academy nominations for best song that were featured in Crosby movies were: "Accentuate the Positive" from *Here Come the Waves,* "Aren't You Glad You're You" from *The Bells of St. Mary's,* and "You Keep Coming Back Like a Song" from *Blue Skies.*

Bing Crosby proved himself a capable dramatic actor in *Going My Way,* playing a Catholic priest in a role that won for him the Acad-emy Award that year. He played another serious part as an alcoholic actor in *The Country Girl* in 1954, but it was for his lighter roles and relaxed manner that he is best remembered.

CROSBY MOVIE COVERS: *The Big Broadcast,* 1932. *College Humor,* 1933. *Going Hollywood,* 1933. *Too Much Harmony,* 1933. *Here Is My Heart,* 1934. *She Loves Me Not,* 1934. *We're Not Dressing,* 1934. *The Big Broadcast of 1936.* *Mississippi,* 1935. *Two for Tonight,* 1935. *Anything Goes,* 1936. *Pennies from Heaven,* 1936. *Rhythm on the Range,* 1936. *Double or Nothing,* 1937. *Waikiki Wedding,* 1937. *Doctor Rhythm,* 1938. *Sing You Sinners,* 1938 *(a.k.a. The Unholy Beebes).* *East Side of Heaven,* 1939. *The Star Maker,* 1939. *Paris Honeymoon,* 1939. *If I Had My Way,* 1940. *Rhythm on the River,* 1940. *Road to Singapore,* 1940. *Birth of the Blues,* 1941. *Road to Zanzibar,* 1941. *Holiday Inn,*1942. *Road to Morocco,* 1942. *Star Spangled Rhythm,* 1942. *Dixie,* 1943. *Going My Way,* 1944. *Here Come the Waves,* 1944. *The Bells of St. Mary's,* 1945. *Duffy's Tavern,* 1945. *Out of This World,* 1945. *Road to Utopia,* 1945. *Blue Skies,* 1946. *Road to Rio,* 1947. *Variety Girl,* 1947. *Welcome Stranger,* 1947. *The Emperor Waltz,* 1948. *A Connecticut Yankee in King Arthur's Court,* 1949. *Top o' the Morning,* 1949. *Mr. Music,* 1950. *Riding High,* 1950. *You Can Change the World,* 1950. *Here Comes the Groom,* 1951. *Just for You,* 1952. *Road to Bali,* 1952. *Little Boy Lost,* 1953. *White Christmas,* 1954. *The Country Girl,* 1954. *Anything Goes,* 1956. *High Society,* 1956. *Man on Fire,* 1957. *Say One for Me,* 1959. *High Time,* 1960. *Robin and the Seven Hoods,* 1964.

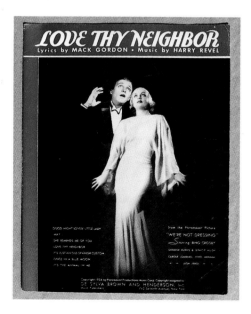

Love Thy Neighbor
Carole Lombard plays a rich girl who is shipwrecked on a desert island with **Bing Crosby** as the marooned sailor who takes care of her in *We're Not Dressing.* Lots of great songs written by Mack Gordon (W) and Harry Revel (M) were performed by Bing. $5

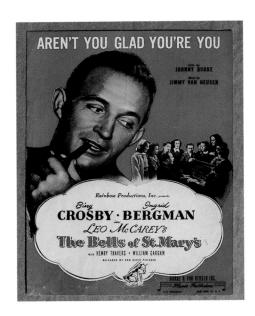

Aren't You Glad You're You
The Bells of St. Mary's was a sequel to the popular movie *Going My Way*, again starring **Bing Crosby** as the laid-back priest Father O'Malley. **Ingrid Bergman** (in small group at piano) played Sister Superior. This hit song was written by Johnny Burke (W) and Jimmy Van Heusen (M). $4

You Keep Coming Back Like a Song
The brilliant combination of **Bing Crosby, Fred Astaire,** and the music of Irving Berlin guaranteed the success of *Blue Skies*. At least 20 Berlin songs were featured including this new one that Bing warbled in the movie. The girl in the piece was **Joan Caulfield.** $4

Tony Curtis (born 1925). This tough street kid grew up in the Bronx, served in the Navy during World War II, and was wounded on Guam. Out of the service, he studied acting in New York, and broke into movies in 1949, moving rapidly up to star status. He was equally good at period swashbucklers, light comedies, and solid drama. His performance in *The Defiant Ones* earned him a Best Actor Academy Award nomination in 1958.

CURTIS MOVIE COVERS: *Forbidden*, 1953. *Houdini*, 1953. *So This Is Paris*, 1954. *Six Bridges to Cross*, 1955. *The Rawhide Years*, 1956. *Sweet Smell of Success*, 1957. *Kings Go Forth*, 1958. *The Perfect Furlough*, 1959. *The Great Imposter*, 1961. *The Rat Race*, 1960. *Who Was That Lady?* 1960. *The Outsider*, 1962. *Taras Bulba*, 1962. *Forty Pounds of Trouble*, 1963. *Goodbye Charlie* , 1964. *Sex and the Single Girl*, 1964. *Arrivederci Baby*, 1966. *Not with My Wife, You Don't*, 1966. *Don't Make Waves*, 1967.

The Rat Race
Tony Curtis co-starred with **Debbie Reynolds** in *The Rat Race*, a charming romance of a musician and dance hall girl set in New York City. Elmer Bernstein wrote the score and arranged the movie theme for piano solo. $5

Linda Darnell (1921-1965). An exotic brunette beauty, Ms. Darnell was a popular star of 1940 movies. Insiders considered her an adequate if not outstanding actress with a pleasing personality and exquisite good looks that carried her to the top. She died at quite a young age in a disastrous house fire while watching one of her old movies on television.

DARNELL MOVIE COVERS: *Star Dust*, 1940. *Blood and Sand*, 1941. *Rise and Shine*, 1941. *It Happened Tomorrow*, 1944. *Summer Storm* 1944. *Sweet and Lowdown*, 1944. *Fallen Angel*, 1945. *The Great John L.*, 1945. *Hangover Square*, 1945. *Centennial Summer* 1946. *Forever Amber*, 1947. *Second Chance*, 1953. *This Is My Love*, 1954. *Zero Hour*, 1957. *Black Spurs*, 1965.

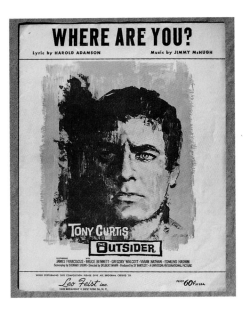

Where Are You?
In *The Outsider*, **Tony Curtis** portrayed the true life story of Ira Hayes, a Pima Indian, who was one of the heroic flag-raisers on Mount Suribachi during World War II. $6

Secrets in the Moonlight
The movie *Star Dust* was based on **Linda Darnell**'s own life story as a young Hollywood contract player who searches for stardom. **John Payne** played her devoted boyfriend in the movie. Ironically this was the movie she was watching on TV when the house caught fire and she was fatally burned. $8

Marion Davies (1897-1961). A struggling Broadway chorus girl, Marion Davies got her big break in the *Ziegfeld Follies of 1916*. She made her Hollywood screen debut the following year in *Runaway Romany*. As the protégée of millionaire newspaper tycoon William Randolph Hearst, she was launched on a fabulous screen career that was aided by the publicity campaign mounted in Hearst newspapers. Pretty and talented with an affinity for comedy roles, she managed to rise above the innocuous heroine roles that Hearst foisted upon her. She starred in both silent movies and talkies and retired from the screen in 1937.

DAVIES MOVIE COVERS: *The Belle of New York*, 1919. *The Dark Star*, 1919. *When Knighthood Was in Flower*, 1922. *Little Old New York*, 1923. *Lights of Old Broadway*, 1925. *The Red Mill*, 1927. *Marianne*, 1929. *The Florodora Girl*, 1930. *Blondie of the Follies*, 1932. *Going Hollywood*, 1933. *Peg O' My Heart*, 1933. *Operator 13*, 1934. *Page Miss Glory*, 1935. *Cain and Mabel*, 1936. *Hearts Divided*, 1936.

Sweetheart Darlin'
Marion Davies was praised for her performance as a light-hearted Irish lass in *Peg O' My Heart*, in which she both sang and danced. **Onslow Stevens**, lower left, was her leading man. $4

I'll Sing You a Thousand Love Songs
Clark Gable played a heavyweight champion boxer opposite **Marion Davies** as a musical comedy star in *Cain and Mabel*. The musical numbers in the movie were written by Al Dubin and Harry Warren. $5 (*$11*)

All for You
Hangover Square was a gothic study of a mad musician portrayed by **Laird Cregar** (left), an actor of great potential who died shortly after making this movie at age 28. **Linda Darnell** played the girl he loved, and **George Sanders** (right) played a sympathetic psychologist. *Collection of Harold Jacobs.* $20

Bette Davis (1908-1989). More striking than beautiful, and the possessor of a distinctive voice, Bette Davis dominated the screen in all of her movies, and was one of Hollywood's most prominent and effective actresses. She won Academy Awards for *Dangerous* (1935) and *Jezebel* (1938). Her popularity continued into the 1940s and 1950s, and her covers are first rate collectibles—much in demand.

In the 1960s Davis moved into character roles playing Susan Hayward's mother in *Where Love Has Gone*, and portraying Apple Annie in *Pocketful of Miracles*. More typically, the sixties saw her pursuing the horror film genre in *Whatever Happened to Baby Jane?* and *Hush ... Hush, Sweet Charlotte*.

DAVIS MOVIE COVERS: *Fashions of 1934. Kid Galahad*, 1937. *Jezebel*, 1938. *Dark Victory*, 1939. *The Great Lie*, 1941. *Now Voyager*, 1942. *Old Acquaintance*, 1943. *Thank Your Lucky Stars*, 1943. *Hollywood Canteen*, 1944. *Payment on Demand*, 1951. *Pocketful of Miracles*, 1961. *Whatever Happened to Baby Jane?* 1962. *Where Love Has Gone*, 1964. *Hush...Hush, Sweet Charlotte*, 1965. *Death on the Nile*, 1978.

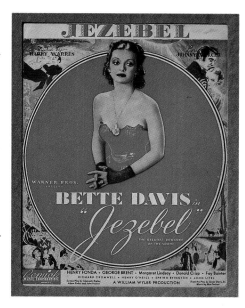

Jezebel
Despite her demure expression on the cover, **Bette Davis** was at her scenery chewing best as a scheming Southern belle in *Jezebel*, a role that brought her an Academy Award as Best Actress. Fay Bainter also won the prized Oscar for her Best Supporting role of Aunt Belle. Title song was written by Johnny Mercer (W) and Harry Warren (M). $60

Oh Give Me Time for Tenderness
Bette Davis played a spoiled heiress who gallantly faces certain death from an inoperable brain tumor in *Dark Victory*. **George Brent** portrayed the brain specialist who falls in love and marries her to share what little time is left. This poignant song was written by Elsie Janis (W) and Edmund Goulding (M), with the lush romantic film score composed by the great Max Steiner. *Collection of Harold Jacobs.* $50 ($82)

Old Acquaintance
In *Old Acquaintance* **Bette Davis** and **Miriam Hopkins** grow from childhood friends to adult rivals with Hopkins playing the bitch and Davis as the long-suffering heroine. Rumors have it that the two stars continued their rivalry offscreen as well as on. $5

Doris Day (born 1924). Her bright-eyed, well-scrubbed, freckle-faced good looks, sparkling personality, and beautiful singing voice made her a favorite with audiences. She was a top recording star when she entered the movies towards the end of the 1940s. Where she became a superstar, characterized in many roles as a naive virginal type. One of her biggest song hits was "Secret Love," the Oscar winning song from *Calamity Jane*.

DAY MOVIE COVERS: *Romance on the High Seas*, 1948. *My Dream Is Yours*, 1949. *It's a Great Feeling*, 1949. *Tea for Two*, 1950. *West Point Story*, 1950. *I'll See You in My Dreams*, 1951. *Lullaby of Broadway*, 1951. *On Moonlight Bay*, 1951. *April in Paris*, 1952. *By the Light of the Silvery Moon*, 1953. *Calamity Jane*, 1953. *Lucky Me*, 1954. *Love Me or Leave Me*, 1955. *Young at Heart*, 1955. *Julie*, 1956. *The Man Who Knew Too Much*, 1956. *The Pajama Game*, 1957. *Teacher's Pet*, 1958. *The Tunnel of Love*, 1958. *It Happened to Jane*, 1959 (a.k.a. *Twinkle and Shine*). *Pillow Talk*, 1959. *Midnight Lace*, 1960. *Please Don't Eat the Daisies*, 1960. *Jumbo*, 1962. *Lover Come Back*, 1962. *Move Over, Darling*, 1963. *The Thrill of It All*, 1963. *Send Me No Flowers*, 1964. *Do Not Disturb*, 1965. *Caprice*, 1967. *The Ballad of Josie*, 1968. *Where Were You When the Lights Went Out?*, 1968.

It Can't Be Wrong
Bette Davis received an Oscar nomination for her superb performance as a New England spinster in *Now, Voyager*, but lost out to Greer Garson's *Mrs. Miniver*. Max Steiner was the fortunate recipient of the award for his sensitive score. This romantic song evokes images of actor **Paul Henried** as he lovingly lights two cigarettes, and Davis's memorable closing line, "Oh, Jerry, don't let's ask for the moon ... we have the stars." $6

Hush...Hush, Sweet Charlotte
Hush...Hush, Sweet Charlotte was a psychological exercise in *film noir*, with **Bette Davis** driven almost insane by the devious plot hatched by **Olivia de Havilland** and **Joseph Cotten.** Al Martino sang the Mack David/Frank De Vol title song on the sound track. $8

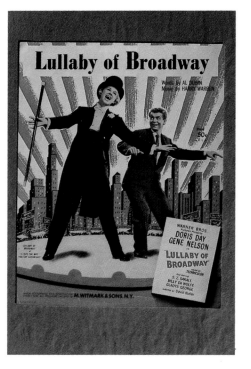

Lullaby of Broadway
Doris Day played a musical comedy star in *Lullaby of Broadway* at her best singing plenty of wonderful standard songs. **Gene Nelson** was her singing/dancing co-star. The title song was written in 1935 by Al Dubin (W) and Harry Warren (M). $5

Moonlight Bay
The charming movie *On Moonlight Bay* co-starred **Doris Day** and **Gordon MacRae** as young lovers, both with beautiful voices. Lots of singing and great old tunes like this title song written by Edward Madden (W) and Percy Wenrich (M) in 1907 added to the overall nostalgic mood. $6

Teacher's Pet
Clark Gable, as a newspaperman working on a story, becomes **Doris Day**'s best pupil in the popular movie *Teacher's Pet*. **Mamie Van Doren** is the sexy blonde on the cover of the Joe Lubin title song performed by Doris in the movie. Gig Young almost stole the picture as second lead, whose performance was recognized with an Academy Award nomination for Best Supporting Actor. $25 *($48)*

James Dean (1931-1955). With only a few movies to his credit before his untimely death in an auto crash at age 24, James Dean's outstanding acting ability was recognized with two Academy Award nominations—for *East of Eden* in 1955 and *Giant* in 1956. He has since become a cult idol and his memory is cherished by his fans who avidly collect Dean memorabilia.

DEAN MOVIE COVERS: *Rebel Without a Cause,* 1955. *Giant,* 1956. *The James Dean Story,* 1957.

Secret Doorway
James Dean dominated the screen in his portrayal of a wild, misunderstood teenager in *Rebel Without a Cause,* an acclaimed movie commentary on the problems of contemporary youth. **Natalie Wood** burst the bounds of awkward adolescence and was effective as Dean's young girlfriend in a role that showed her budding maturity. Song was written by Mack Discant (W) and Leonard Rosenman (M). *Collection of Harold Jacobs.* $50

Olivia de Havilland (born 1916). She started out in movies playing sweet helpless young heroines in the 1930s, ending the decade with an acclaimed performance as Melanie in *Gone With the Wind*. She subsequently garnered Best Actress Oscars for the movies *To Each His Own* and *The Heiress*.

DE HAVILLAND MOVIE COVERS: *Hard to Get,* 1938. *Along the Santa Fe Trail,* 1940. *Hold Back the Dawn,* 1941. *The Strawberry Blonde,* 1941. *Princess O'Rourke,* 1943. *Thank Your Lucky Stars,* 1943. *To Each His Own,* 1946. *The Heiress,* 1949. *Not As a Stranger,* 1955. *The Proud Rebel,* 1958. *The Light in the Piazza,* 1962. *Hush...Hush, Sweet Charlotte,* 1964.

Giant
The epic motion picture *Giant* starred **James Dean** as Jett Rink, a young farmhand who discovers oil in Texas and becomes a millionaire. Dean died before the film's release, and he received a posthumous Oscar nomination for Best Actor. The picture received several nominations and won the Best Director award for George Stevens. Also on cover are co-stars **Elizabeth Taylor** and **Rock Hudson**. $15 *($42)*

Good-Bye Little Girl, Good-Bye
Olivia de Havilland was the girl **James Cagney** married in *The Strawberry Blonde,* and Rita Hayworth was the girl he thought he loved. Will D. Cobb (W) and Gus Edwards (M) wrote the 1904 song that perfectly suited the Gay Nineties' period movie. $6

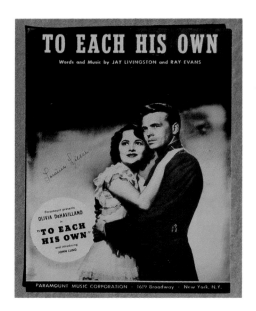

To Each His Own
Olivia de Havilland won the Best Actress Academy Award playing an unwed mother who gives up her baby and watches from the sidelines as he grows to adulthood. **John Lund** was her co-star. The theme song by Jay Livingston and Ray Evans became a hit record for Eddy Howard. $4

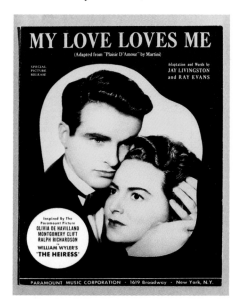

My Love Loves Me
Olivia de Havilland won an Oscar for her portrayal of a dowdy spinster of means, who is pursued by an attractive fortune hunter, played by **Montgomery Clift**. The distinguished music score by composer Aaron Copland also received an Oscar. Jay Livingston and Ray Evans wrote this song. *Collection of Harold Jacobs.* $40

Marlene Dietrich (1901-1992). The sheet music covers of legendary Marlene Dietrich are top-drawer collectibles. "See What the Boys in the Back Room Will Have," from *Destry Rides Again* with its fine close-up picture of Marlene Dietrich and James Stewart has sold at auction for a startling $125. She remained an enticing star into the 1940s and 1950s, and maintained her glamorous mystique until her death.

DIETRICH MOVIE COVERS: *I Kiss Your Hand Madame*, 1929. *The Blue Angel*, 1930. *Morocco*, 1930. *Three Loves*, 1931. *Blonde Venus*, 1932. *Song of Songs*, 1933. *The Devil Is a Woman*, 1935. *Desire*, 1936. *Angel*, 1937. *Destry Rides Again*, 1939. *Seven Sinners*, 1940. *The Lady Is Willing*, 1942. *Kismet*, 1944. *Golden Earrings*, 1947. *A Foreign Affair*, 1948. *Stage Fright*, 1950. *Rancho Notorious*, 1952. *The Monte Carlo Story*, 1957. *Witness for the Prosecution*, 1957. *Judgment at Nuremberg*, 1961.

Falling In Love Again
Marlene Dietrich became an international film star after starring as Lola-Lola, a sexy cabaret singer, in *The Blue Angel*. **Emil Jannings**, also on cover, played an introverted professor who was obsessed with her. This Frederick Hollander song was sung by Dietrich in the movie and also on records. $30 *($45)*

Then It Isn't Love
Marlene Dietrich was at her most beautiful in *The Devil Is a Woman*, a period movie set in 1890 Spain with sumptuous sets and costumes. She played a seductress who destroyed men for fun. Leo Robin and Ralph Rainger wrote the song. $150

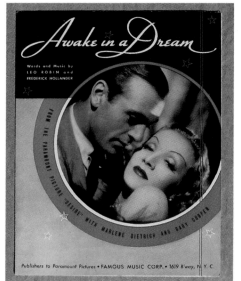

Awake in a Dream
As a glamorous jewel thief, **Marlene Dietrich** played opposite **Gary Cooper** in the stylish movie *Desire*. She sang this title song by Leo Robin and Frederick Hollander in the movie. $25 *($52)*

You've Got That Look
Marlene Dietrich was sensational as the saloon singer Frenchy in *Destry Rides Again*—a perfect foil for co-star **James Stewart** who played a sheriff's deputy uneasy with guns who proves his mettle at the end. Marlene was totally in command, singing with suggestive gusto and indulging in a remarkable hair-pulling contest with Una Merkel. *Collection of Harold Jacobs.* $50

Irene Dunne (1898-1990). Her professional career as a singer started in Ziegfeld's road show production of *Show Boat* in 1929. She was soon lured to Hollywood where her versatility enabled her to play a wide range of parts, both comedy and melodrama. No matter what she played, she always projected an aura of sweet dignity. She was nominated twice for Best Actress Oscar, in *Love Affair* (1939) and *I Remember Mama* (1948).

DUNNE MOVIE COVERS: *Consolation Marriage*, 1931. *Back Street*, 1932. *Stingaree*, 1934. *Roberta*, 1935. *Sweet Adeline*, 1935. *Show Boat*, 1936. *High Wide and Handsome*, 1937. *Joy of Living*, 1938. *Love Affair*, 1939. *Penny Serenade*, 1941. *Unfinished Business*, 1941. *A Guy Named Joe*, 1943. *Life with Father*, 1947. *Never a Dull Moment*, 1950. *You Can Change the World*, 1950.

Tonight Is Mine
In *Stingaree*, **Irene Dunne,** as an Australian opera singer, had an opportunity to show off her vocal talents. She played opposite **Richard Dix,** a dashing bandit who improbably carries her off on a white horse. $5

Kirk Douglas (born 1916). As a young man, he worked on the Broadway stage. After service in the U.S. Navy, he entered movies in the 1940s. He went on to become a first-rate star after his stunning portrayal of a corrupt boxer in the 1949 movie *Champion*. Mr. Douglas has starred in more than 50 films, and also branched out into production and directing. The many honors he amassed during his career include the Presidential Medal of Honor for his work as U.S. goodwill ambassador, the American Film Institute's coveted Lifetime Achievement Award, the Chevalier of the Legion of Honor from France, and three Oscar nominations—for *Champion, Lust for Life*, and *The Bad and the Beautiful*. In his later years, he has become a successful author.

DOUGLAS MOVIE COVERS: *The Strange Love of Martha Ivers*, 1946. *I Walk Alone*, 1947. *Young Man With a Horn*, 1950. *The Bad and the Beautiful*, 1952. *The Big Sky*, 1952. *20,000 Leagues Under the Sea*, 1954. *The Indian Fighter*, 1955. *Man Without a Star*, 1955. *The Racers*, 1955. *Gunfight at the O.K. Corral*, 1957. *The Vikings*, 1958. *Strangers When We Meet*, 1960. *The Last Sunset*, 1961. *Town Without Pity*, 1961. *Two Weeks in Another Town*, 1962. *The Hook*, 1963. *Seven Days in May*, 1964. *The Heroes of Telemark*, 1965. *Cast a Giant Shadow*, 1966. *Is Paris Burning?* 1966. *The War Wagon*, 1967. *The Way West*, 1967. *The Brotherhood*, 1968. *Tough Guys*, 1986.

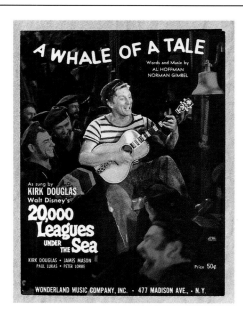

A Whale of a Tale
Kirk Douglas, shown here singing and strumming a guitar, played a salty whaler in *20,000 Leagues Under the Sea*. Walt Disney spared no expense bringing the Jules Verne sci-fi story to the screen with James Mason as Captain Nemo and convincing backup support from Paul Lukas and Peter Lorre. $10

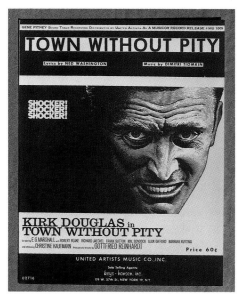

Town Without Pity
Town Without Pity was a courtroom drama with **Kirk Douglas** playing a lawyer defending four GIs who are accused of raping a local German girl. The title song by Ned Washington (W) and Dimitri Tiomkin (M) was sung on the movie sound track by Gene Pitney who also had a hit record. $8

Bill
Irene Dunne as Magnolia joined some of the great talents from the stage production who recreated their Broadway roles in this version of *Show Boat*. **Helen Morgan** (right) sang her heart out as a convincing Julie, and **Paul Robeson** (below Morgan) gave a masterful rendition of "Ol' Man River." Other stars were **Charles Winninger** as a lovable Cap'n Andy, and **Allan Jones** as Ravenal. $8

You Were Meant for Me
Irene Dunne and **Cary Grant** were a charming young married couple who have to cope with the death of their adopted daughter in the sentimental movie *Penny Serenade*. The story was effectively told in song—to phonograph records played by Miss Dunne, each song evoking a tender memory. *Collection of James Nelson Brown.* $75

Deanna Durbin (born 1921). Sweet and pretty with a lovely singing voice, young Miss Durbin started out in movies when she was 15, and went on to become a world famous movie star. She and Mickey Rooney shared a special Academy Award in 1938 for "bringing to the screen the spirit and personification of youth." Miss Durbin matured into a beautiful young woman, and maintained her popularity into the late 1940s, starring as a romantic lead in a number of films until she inexplicably retired when only 27 years old.

DURBIN MOVIE COVERS: *Three Smart Girls*, 1936. *100 Men and a Girl*, 1937. *Mad About Music*, 1938. *That Certain Age*, 1938. *First Love*, 1939. *Three Smart Girls Grow Up*, 1939. *It's a Date*, 1940. *Spring Parade*, 1940. *It Started with Eve*, 1941. *Nice Girl*, 1941. *The Amazing Mrs. Holliday*, 1943. *Hers to Hold*, 1943. *His Butler's Sister*, 1943. *Christmas Holiday*, 1944. *Can't Help Singing*, 1944.

Lady on a Train, 1945. *Because of Him*, 1946. *I'll Be Yours*, 1947. *Something in the Wind*, 1947. *Up in Central Park*, 1948.

My Own
In *That Certain Age*, **Deanna Durbin** played a young girl with a crush on an older man, coming to her senses at the end of the movie. Songs included this big hit sung by Deanna, and written by Harold Adamson (W) and Jimmy McHugh (M). $6

In the Spirit of the Moment
Deanna Durbin, in a lighter role, played an ambitious singer hoping to get her big break working as a maid for a famous composer. She had ample opportunity to sing in *His Butler's Sister*—classical arias as well as this song by Bernie Grossman and Walter Jurman. $7

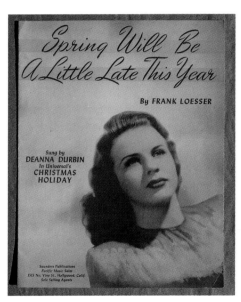

Spring Will Be a Little Late This Year
This beautiful ballad by Frank Loesser was sung by a delightfully grown-up **Deanna Durbin** who, in a change of character, portrayed a worldly nightclub singer in the Universal movie *Christmas Holiday*. $8

96

Clint Eastwood (born 1930). This California boy cut his acting teeth in the TV western *Rawhide* in the late 1950s. He hit the big time in the 1960s as the cool, mysterious "Man with No Name" hero of three movies made in Italy that came to be known as "spaghetti Westerns." The Oscar winning *Unforgiven*, in 1992, won him the additional honor of Best Director. A solid citizen, active in politics, he was the one-time mayor of Carmel, California.

EASTWOOD MOVIE COVERS: *The Good, the Bad, and the Ugly*, 1966. *Hang 'Em High*, 1968. *Paint Your Wagon*, 1969. *Where Eagles Dare*, 1969. *Kelly's Heroes*, 1970. *Play Misty for Me*, 1971. *The Eiger Sanction*, 1975. *Every Which Way but Loose*, 1978. *Bronco Billy*, 1980. *Sudden Impact*, 1980.

Nelson Eddy (1901-1967). His fine operatic voice and blonde good looks stood him in good stead as a singing hero at M-G-M. He was teamed with Jeanette MacDonald in numerous screen operettas, and they became the top romantic duo in motion pictures billed as "America's Singing Sweethearts."

EDDY MOVIE COVERS: *Naughty Marietta*, 1935. *Rose Marie*, 1936. *Maytime*, 1937. *Rosalie*, 1937. *The Girl of the Golden West*, 1938. *Sweethearts*, 1938. *Balalaika*, 1939. *Let Freedom Ring*, 1939. *Bitter Sweet*, 1940. *New Moon*, 1940. *The Chocolate Soldier*, 1941. *I Married an Angel*, 1942. *Phantom of the Opera*, 1943. *Knickerbocker Holiday*, 1944. *Northwest Outpost*, 1947.

Lullaby of the Bells
This first talkie version of *Phantom of the Opera* starred **Nelson Eddy** with a new young co-star, singer **Susanna Foster.** But the top acting honors went to Claude Rains as the tragic disfigured composer who haunts the Paris Opera house. $6

Hang 'em High
Steely-eyed **Clint Eastwood** survived an attempted lynching in the Western movie *Hang 'em High*, and sets out to avenge himself on the nine men who tried to hang him. Dominic Frontiere wrote the theme music. $10

At the Balalaika
Balalaika was a stage hit brought to the screen co-starring **Nelson Eddy** as a Russian prince and **Ilona Massey** as a talented cafe singer. They fall in love but are parted by the Russian Revolution, reuniting years later in Paris. Miss Massey sang this song in the movie, assisted by the Russian Art Choir. $5

Alice Faye (1915-1998). With a mellow singing voice and melting big blue eyes, Alice Faye was a Broadway chorine when she was discovered by Rudy Vallee. He gave her a start singing with his band and promoted her in movies. She became the reigning queen of Twentieth Century-Fox musicals until the mid-1940s when she retired from films but for a few isolated appearances. Despite her retirement she continued to have a faithful following of fan clubs around the world who mourned her passing in 1998.

Right:
Hold My Hand
George White's Scandals of 1934 was **Alice Faye**'s first movie, made under the sponsorship of **Rudy Vallee** over the protests of George White himself. With her sparkling blonde good looks and lovely singing voice, she soon became one of Fox studio's top stars. British printing. $6

The First Thing You Know
Hollywood's film version of the 1951 hit Broadway show *Paint Your Wagon* co-starred (left to right) **Lee Marvin, Jean Seberg,** and **Clint Eastwood.** Andre Previn composed music for additional songs not in the Broadway show including this song with words by Alan Jay Lerner. $7

FAYE MOVIE COVERS: *George White's Scandals of 1934. Now I'll Tell, 1934. She Learned About Sailors, 1934. 365 Nights in Hollywood, 1934. Every Night at Eight, 1935. George White's Scandals of 1935. King of Burlesque, 1935. Music Is Magic, 1935. Poor Little Rich Girl, 1936. Sing Baby Sing, 1936. Stowaway, 1936. On the Avenue, 1937. Wake Up and Live, 1937. You're a Sweetheart, 1937. You Can't Have Everything, 1937. Alexander's Ragtime Band, 1938. In Old Chicago, 1938. Sally, Irene and Mary, 1938. Barricade, 1939. Rose of Washington Square, 1939. Tail Spin, 1939. Lillian Russell, 1940. Little Old New York, 1940. Tin Pan Alley, 1940. The Great American Broadcast, 1941. That Night in Rio, 1941. Weekend in Havana, 1941. Hello, Frisco, Hello, 1943. The Gang's All Here, 1943. Fallen Angel, 1945. The Magic of Lassie, 1978.*

W. C. Fields (1879-1946). He was known as a master comedian with a fine sense of timing and a probing sense of humor. Fields's distinctive style and unique voice and personality endeared him to fans throughout the world. He started his show business career in vaudeville as a juggler, and moved on to the *Ziegfeld Follies* and *George White's Scandals* before starring in the hit Broadway production *Poppy*. He wrote the screenplays for many of his films, and is famous for his hilarious ad-libs that never failed to delight his fans, even to this day.

FIELDS MOVIE COVERS: *The Old Fashioned Way, 1934. The Man on the Flying Trapeze, 1935. Poppy, 1936. Big Broadcast of 1938. My Little Chickadee, 1940. Song of the Open Road, 1944. Sensations of 1945.*

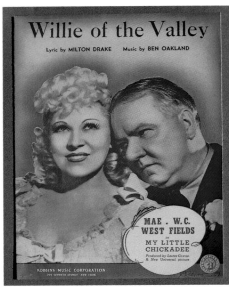

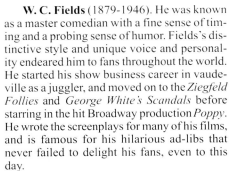

Willie of the Valley
With **W. C. Fields** and **Mae West** co-starring in *My Little Chickadee*, its success was guaranteed. The witty twosome wrote most of their own dialogue, and the script abounds with clever one-liners and subtle double entendres. This rarely found song from the movie was written by Milton Drake (W) and Ben Oakland (M). *Collection of Harold Jacobs.* $150

Too Much in Love
Although the movie *Song of the Open Road* was mainly a showcase for talented young **Jane Powell**, it included a cast of stellar acts, like **Edgar Bergen** and his wooden dummy **Charlie McCarthy**, the **Sammy Kaye Orchestra**, and **W. C. Fields**. $7

Sing, Baby, Sing
Alice Faye had another chance to show off her talents in *Sing, Baby Sing*, playing a nightclub entertainer who struggles to advance her career. The movie also featured the **Ritz Brothers** and **Adolphe Menjou**. This song, a British edition, was written by Jack Yellen (W) and Lew Pollack (M). $6

Blue Lovebird
Lillian Russell was a perfect vehicle for **Alice Faye**. As the famous musical star in the screen biography, she co-starred with **Don Ameche** who played Miss Russell's first husband. Many old-time songs were featured in elaborate stage settings, and Miss Faye wore her sumptuous gowns with characteristic poise. $8

Errol Flynn (1909-1959). He was at his best playing a dashing adventurer in 1930s costume films. Tall, handsome, and charming, he became one of Hollywood's most notorious Casanovas. In real life, his hedonistic life style culminated in a statutory rape charge involving two teenage girls in 1942. Though he was acquitted, he continued his life of excess and died at age fifty.

FLYNN MOVIE COVERS: *Along the Santa Fe Trail, 1940. Thank Your Lucky Stars, 1943. Uncertain Glory, 1944. San Antonio, 1945. Never Say Goodbye, 1946. Escape Me Never, 1947. Montana, 1950. Lilacs in the Spring, 1954. King's Rhapsody, 1955. The Sun Also Rises, 1957. The Roots of Heaven, 1958.*

Henry Fonda (1905-1982). Tall and lean with a direct and plain-spoken manner, Henry Fonda exuded the qualities of an American farm boy—first on the Broadway stage and later in movies. He was equally effective in dramatic roles in *Young Mr. Lincoln* and *The Grapes of Wrath* or in comedy parts in *The Lady Eve* and *The Male Animal*. In World War II he enlisted in the Navy, serving with distinction and earning the rank of Lieutenant, a Bronze Star, and a Presidential Citation. Fonda appeared in 87 films and 21 plays in a brilliant career that brought him a Lifetime Achievement Award by the American Film Institute in 1978 and an Academy Award for his last movie *On Golden Pond* in 1981.

HENRY FONDA MOVIE COVERS: *The Moon's Our Home*, 1936. *You Only Live Once*, 1937. *Blockade*, 1938. *Spawn of the North*, 1938. *Tales of Manhattan*, 1942. *Daisy Kenyon*, 1947. *The Long Night*, 1947. *Mister Roberts*, 1955. *War and Peace*, 1956. *The Tin Star*, 1957. *The Man Who Understood Women*, 1959. *A Big Hand for a Little Lady*, 1966. *Stranger on the Run*, 1967. *Yours Mine and Ours*, 1968. *Once Upon a Time in the West*, 1969. *Sometimes a Great Notion*, 1971. *On Golden Pond*, 1982.

A Thousand Dreams of You
You Only Live Once starred **Henry Fonda** as an innocent man wrongly sent to prison who takes up a life of crime when released. **Sylvia Sidney** was his sympathetic wife. This sentimental song was written by Paul Webster (W) and Louis Alter (M). $12

Farewell
Henry Fonda recreated his stage role in the movie *Mister Roberts*, an entertaining comedy about the adventures of an officer on a World War II Navy cargo ship. Several recordings were made of this featured song from the movie written by Jack Brooks (W) and Eddie Lund (M). $5

Along the Santa Fe Trail
Errol Flynn portrayed Cavalry officer Jeb Stuart in Warner Brothers' interpretation of history in the movie *Along The Santa Fe Trail*. **Olivia de Havilland** was his love interest, and Ronald Reagan also contributed, playing the part of Stuart's West Point classmate, George Armstrong Custer. $5

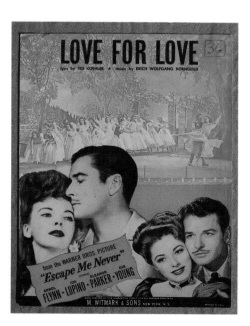

Love for Love
In *Escape Me Never*, **Errol Flynn** played a two-timing composer who took up with his brother's girlfriend, **Eleanor Parker. Gig Young** (right) played the brother, and **Ida Lupino** (left) was Flynn's long-suffering wife. This lovely song from the movie was written by Ted Koehler (W) and Erich Wolfgang Korngold (M) who also composed the superb score. $5

On Golden Pond
For his last movie role as a somewhat confused 80-year-old in *On Golden Pond*, **Henry Fonda** was awarded a Best Actor Academy Award. Sharing in the glory were **Katharine Hepburn** as his supportive wife who won the award for Best Actress, and **Jane Fonda**, his real-life daughter. *Collection of Roy Bishop.* $6

Jane Fonda (born 1937). Henry Fonda's daughter, Jane, was educated at Vassar College, dabbled in art in Paris, and did some modeling in New York before seriously studying acting at the Actors Studio. She made her first movie in 1960, and reached the pinnacle of success with an Academy Award for her role as a prostitute in *Klute* in 1971. She won a second Oscar for *Coming Home* in 1978. She is perhaps as well known for her political activism as she is for her movies, and received strong criticism for her antiwar stance during the Vietnam War.

JANE FONDA MOVIE COVERS: *Tall Story*, 1960. *The Chapman Report*, 1962. *Period of Adjustment*, 1962. *Walk on the Wild Side*, 1962. *In the Cool of the Day*, 1963. *Sunday in New York*, 1963. *Joy House*, 1964. *Any Wednesday*, 1966. *The Chase*, 1966. *Barefoot in the Park*, 1967. *Barbarella*, 1968. *They Shoot Horses, Don't They?* 1969. *Fun with Dick and Jane*, 1977. *California Suite*, 1978. *The Electric Horseman*, 1979. *On Golden Pond*, 1982. *Old Gringo*, 1989.

Barefoot in the Park
Jane Fonda played opposite **Robert Redford,** who repeated his Broadway success in *Barefoot in the Park.* The Neil Simon play made a hilarious movie and benefited from the performances of **Mildred Natwick** in her Broadway mother role and **Charles Boyer** as a colorful neighbor. Theme song was written by Johnny Mercer (W) and Neil Hefti (M). $7

Peter Fonda (born 1939). Another member of the famous Fonda family, Peter Fonda, is Henry's son and Jane's brother. He acted in college productions and on Broadway before making Hollywood films. *Easy Rider* was his first really successful movie, one in which he acted as well as produced and co-scripted. His career has not yet reached the mercurial heights of his other famous relatives, but he's still in there slugging. He recently received critical accolades and a Golden Globe award for his movie *Ulee's Gold* (1997).

PETER FONDA MOVIE COVERS: *Young Lovers*, 1964. *Easy Rider*, 1969. *Two People*, 1972. *Dirty Mary Crazy Larry*, 1974.

Time Will Tell
Peter Fonda played an Army deserter who meets and falls in love with **Lindsay Wagner**, a fashion model with a past in *Two People*. Love song by Richard Maltby Jr. (W) and David Shire (M) highlighted the emotions of the tormented couple. $8

Joan Fontaine (born 1917). A lovely blonde with an air of wide-eyed refinement, Joan Fontaine showed her versatility playing both shy and innocent heroines and experienced women of the world. She is Olivia de Havilland's sister, and she came into her own after being nominated for an Oscar for her outstanding acting in Alfred Hitchcock's *Rebecca* in 1940. She won the honor the following year as Best Actress in *Suspicion*. In private life she is admired for her many accomplishments—as an expert sports fisherman and golfer, a licensed pilot and champion balloonist, and a fine homemaker with a license in interior decorating and Cordon Bleu cooking credentials.

FONTAINE MOVIE COVERS: *Damsel in Distress*, 1937. *Music for Madame*, 1937. *The Duke of West Point*, 1938. *From This Day Forward*, 1946. *Ivy*, 1947. *The Emperor Waltz*, 1948. *Letter from an Unknown Woman*, 1948. *September Affair*, 1950. *Darling How Could

You, 1951. *Something to Live For*, 1952. *Casanova's Big Night*, 1954. *Beyond a Reasonable Doubt*, 1956. *A Certain Smile*, 1958. *Voyage to the Bottom of the Sea*, 1961.

Ivy
Joan Fontaine played a wicked conniving temptress in the melodramatic *Ivy*, looking her most gorgeous in lavish period hats and gowns. Hoagy Carmichael's theme song was introduced on the movie sound track, becoming quite popular, with recordings by Vic Damone, Jo Stafford, and Dick Haymes. $4

September Song
The romantic movie *September Affair* co-starred **Joan Fontaine** and **Joseph Cotten** as passengers listed as fatalities in a plane crash who manage to steal some precious moments of happiness together before returning to the real world. Walter Huston's 1938 version of this theme song on the sound track added a note of wistful nostalgia. $5

Dick Foran (1910-1979). This handsome Western hero was the son of a U.S. Senator. He started out as a band singer, and wound up in the movies as a top performer in B westerns. He endeared himself to this author when she was six years old, when she named him her favorite movie star. Foran appeared in nearly 100 movies through more than 30 years of steady work, and also performed on television.

FORAN MOVIE COVERS: *Moonlight on the Prairie*, 1935. *Song of the Saddle*, 1936. *Cherokee Strip*, 1937. *Winners of the West*, 1940. *Keep 'Em Flying*, 1941. *Ride 'Em Cowboy*, 1942.

Underneath a Western Sky
Good-looking **Dick Foran** played The Singing Kid in *Song of the Saddle*. Our hero avenges the murder of his father, and warbles a couple of tunes by Jack Scholl (W) and M. K. Jerome and Ted Fio Rito (M). *Collection of Harold Jacobs.* $30

Glenn Ford (born 1916). Young Ford started out acting in high school plays and West Coast dramatic companies, which led to a screen test at Columbia Pictures in 1939. He was snapped up by the studio and was a promising leading man until his career was interrupted by World War II. After his discharge from the Marine Corps, he resumed acting and became a solid, dependable leading man, striking fire with Rita Hayworth in *Gilda*, *The Loves of Carmen*, and *Affair in Trinidad*. His wide range included both drama and comedy roles.

FORD MOVIE COVERS: *So Ends Our Night*, 1941. *The Americano*, 1942. *The Loves of Carmen*, 1948. *Cry for Happy*, 1950. *Affair in Trinidad*, 1952. *The Green Glove*, 1952. *The Man from the Alamo*, 1953. *Human Desire*, 1954. *Blackboard Jungle*, 1955. *Interrupted Melody*, 1955. *3:10 to Yuma*, 1957. *Don't Go Near the Water*, 1957. *Cowboy*, 1958. *The Gazebo*, 1959. *It Started with a Kiss*, 1959. *Cimarron*, 1960. *Pocketful of Miracles*, 1961.

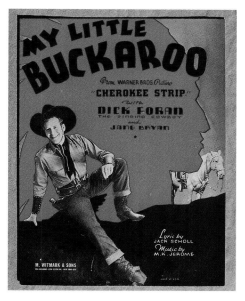

My Little Buckaroo
Dick Foran starred in *The Cherokee Strip*, an exciting Western set during the historic Oklahoma land rush. The plot involved his horse Smokey, which was lamed by the land-grabbing bad guys. Foran sang this song in the movie, later made into a hit record by Bing Crosby. $5

I've Been Kissed Before
After the success of *Gilda*, **Glenn Ford** was again cast opposite gorgeous **Rita Hayworth** creating electricity in the movie *Affair in Trinidad*, an espionage drama set in the tropics. This song by Bob Russell and Lester Lee was dubbed by Jo Ann Greer for Rita Hayworth in the movie. *Collection of Harold Jacobs .* $25

Experiment in Terror, 1962. *The Courtship of Eddie's Father*, 1963. *Love Is a Ball*, 1963. *Advance to the Rear*, 1964. *Fate Is the Hunter*, 1964. *Dear Heart*, 1965. *Is Paris Burning?*, 1966. *Heaven with a Gun*, 1984.

Clark Gable (1901-1960). Known as "The King" in Hollywood, Clark Gable was respected by the industry and by audiences alike. He played a rakish adventurer in most of his 1930 movies, and was very popular with the ladies. While riding the crest of his career af-

China Seas
Two of Hollywood's top box office stars, **Clark Gable** and **Jean Harlow**, co-starred in *China Seas*, ably assisted by a supporting cast that included Wallace Beery as a modern day pirate and Rosalind Russell as a hoity-toity lady. Theme song was written by Arthur Freed (W) and Nacio Herb Brown (M). $65

Dear Heart
The romantic movie *Dear Heart* co-starred **Glenn Ford** and **Geraldine Page** who meet and fall in love at a convention in New York City. The theme song by Jay Livingston and Ray Evans (W) and Henry Mancini (M) was a popular hit record for Andy Williams. $4

ter his success in *Gone With the Wind*, he suffered a tragic loss when his wife, Carole Lombard, was killed in a plane crash while returning from a war bond tour. A bereaved Gable joined the Air Force, and distinguished himself by flying several bombing missions over Germany. He returned to the screen in 1945, and theater marquees were emblazoned with "Gable's Back and Garson's Got Him" touting the movie *Adventure* starring Gable with Greer Garson. Gable's appeal didn't wane in his maturity. He still had a strong following of loyal fans despite his graying temples. Songs with his picture on the cover are much in demand.

GABLE MOVIE COVERS: *Possessed*, 1931. *Dancing Lady*, 1933. *Hold Your Man*, 1933. *China Seas*, 1935. *Mutiny on the Bounty*, 1935. *Cain and Mabel*, 1936. *San Francisco*, 1936. *Love on the Run*, 1936. *Saratoga*, 1937. *Gone With the Wind*, 1939. *Idiot's Delight*, 1939. *Adventure*, 1945. *The Hucksters*, 1947. *To Please a Lady*, 1950. *Across the Wide Missouri*, 1951. *Betrayed*, 1954. *The Tall Men*, 1955. *Soldier of Fortune*, 1955. *Band of Angels*, 1957. *Teacher's Pet*, 1958. *But Not for Me*, 1959. *It Started in Naples*, 1960. *The Misfits*, 1961.

Across the Wide Missouri
In the Western movie *Across the Wide Missouri*, **Clark Gable** was a trapper married to an Indian girl played by **Maria Elena Marques**. A strong supporting cast, plenty of action, and gorgeous Colorado scenery added to the package. The theme song was adapted from a folk song by Ervin Drake and Jimmy Shirl. $12

Gone
Clark Gable and **Joan Crawford** were frequent co-stars at M-G-M, and delighted audiences with the lighthearted movie *Love on the Run* that co-starred Franchot Tone, who was also pursuing Joan. Gus Kahn (W) and Franz Waxman (M) wrote the song. $8

Would You
San Francisco was a stunning movie highlighted by fantastic earthquake scenes and Oscar winning sound effects. An all-star cast that included **Clark Gable, Jeanette MacDonald,** and Spencer Tracy, and memorable singing by MacDonald made this a profitable movie for M-G-M. Song is by Freed and Brown. $8

Don't Tell Me
Clark Gable was the good guy in *The Hucksters*, an exposé of corruption in the advertising world. Lovely lady co-stars were **Ava Gardner** and **Deborah Kerr** in her movie debut. Sidney Greenstreet was a sinister big business egomaniac. $8

Band of Angels
The fine flick *Band of Angels* starred **Clark Gable** as a Southern gentleman, and **Yvonne De Carlo** as the daughter of a wealthy plantation owner who is stripped of her property and dignity when it is discovered she has Negro blood. **Sidney Poitier** was memorable as an educated slave. Max Steiner wrote the music. $8

Greta Garbo (1905-1990). A well-trained Swedish actress, she came to Hollywood in 1925, becoming one of M-G-M's most prestigious leading ladies. Though somewhat shy and withdrawn in real life, she came alive on the screen and projected an air of charismatic magnetism and restrained sensuality that captivated both male and female audiences. She was one of the few silent stars from Europe that moved successfully into talking pictures. A studio campaign ballyhooed her first talkie *Anna Christie* in 1930: "GARBO TALKS!" In a clear husky voice, her first spoken words were: "Give me a whiskey, ginger ale on the side ... and don't be stingy, baby." Audiences loved her.

Garbo's early retirement from motion pictures in 1941 caused consternation and disappointment. She became a semi-recluse, and her desire for privacy added to the aura of mystery that surrounded her. She was awarded an honorary Oscar in 1954 "for her unforgettable screen performances."

GARBO MOVIE COVERS: *Love*, 1927. *A Woman of Affairs*, 1928. *Wild Orchids*, 1929. *Romance*, 1930. *Camille*, 1936.

Wild Orchids
This theme song from M-G-M's *Wild Orchids* starred **Greta Garbo** as plantation owner Lewis Stone's unfaithful wife who gets involved with a handsome Javanese prince played by Nils Asther. Garbo excelled in silent movies, and moved smoothly into talking productions with her husky voice and piquant accent. $15

Song of the Barefoot Contessa
In *The Barefoot Contessa*, **Ava Gardner** portrayed a fiery Spanish slum girl who rose to the heights of Hollywood stardom and marriage to royalty. The story is told in flashback by Humphrey Bogart, her former director, who was perhaps a little in love with her himself. Edmund O'Brien won a Best Supporting Actor Oscar for his role as a cynical press agent. $10

Ava Gardner (1922-1990). Her luscious 18-year-old beauty caught the eye of Hollywood where she was screen-tested and signed up by M-G-M, who proceeded to groom her for stardom. After an ill-fated marriage to Mickey Rooney and a few lackluster movies, she finally broke through as a successful actress in the mid-1940s, notably in *The Killers* with newcomer Burt Lancaster. She was one of Hollywood's sex symbols all through the 1940s and 1950s, and developed into a creditable actress as well.

GARDNER MOVIE COVERS: *The Hucksters*, 1947. One *Touch of Venus*, 1948. *The Bribe*, 1949. *Pandora and the Flying Dutchman*, 1951. *Show Boat*, 1951. *The Barefoot Contessa*, 1954. *The Little Hut*, 1957. *The Sun Also Rises*, 1957. *On the Beach*, 1959. *55 Days at Peking*, 1963. *Seven Days in May*, 1964. *Earthquake*, 1974.

You Are Love
This 1951 screen version of Jerome Kern's monumental *Show Boat* co-starred lovely **Ava Gardner** as the ill-fated Julie, with **Kathryn Grayson** and **Howard Keel** supplying the duets and Joe E. Brown as a memorable Captain Andy. $6

Speak Low
The Kurt Weill stage musical *One Touch of Venus* was brought to the screen with **Ava Gardner** as the Greek statue who comes to life. This song from the original production by Ogden Nash (W) and Kurt Weill (M) was sung in the movie by Dick Haymes and Eileen Wilson dubbing for Ava Gardner. $4

How Am I to Know?
The fantasy movie *Pandora and the Flying Dutchman* co-starred **Ava Gardner** and James Mason in the title roles. Miss Gardner did her own singing in this movie, and also recorded the song. $10

John Garfield (1913-1952). A real-life tough guy, Garfield grew up on the streets of New York one step away from reform school. The turning point for him was his winning of a debating contest leading to a scholarship at acting school, and leading roles on Broadway. In his Hollywood movies he often played rebellious characters in trouble with the law, roles not too far removed from his own experiences. He was considered a competent, effective actor, with nominations for Best Supporting Actor in *Four Daughters* (1938) and for Best Actor in *Body and Soul* (1947). He had a wide following until he was blacklisted by the House Un-American Activities Committee for refusing to name friends that perhaps had Communist leanings. He died of a heart attack at age 39.

GARFIELD MOVIE COVERS: *Dust Be My Destiny*, 1939. *Saturday's Children*, 1940. *Thank Your Lucky Stars*, 1943. *Hollywood Canteen*, 1944. *Humoresque*, 1946. *The Postman Always Rings Twice*, 1946. *Body and Soul*, 1947. *Under My Skin*, 1950.

Dust Be My Destiny
John Garfield was well-cast in the sociological melodrama *Dust Be My Destiny*. He played an ex-convict from the other side of the tracks who is wrongly accused of murdering **Priscilla Lane**'s drunken father. Theme song was by M. K. Jerome and Jack Scholl (W) and Max Steiner (M). *Collection of Harold Jacobs*. $20

Body and Soul
John Garfield was nominated for a Best Actor Oscar for his role in *Body and Soul* as a boxer who almost took a dive in the big fight. **Lilli Palmer** (top) played the good girl, and **Hazel Brooks** (center) was the sexy show girl who tried to seduce him into corruption. The theme song was written in 1930 by Edward Heyman, Robert Sour, and Frank Eyton (W) and John Green (M). $7

Humoresque
John Garfield, as a young violinist from the ghetto, was sponsored by wealthy patroness **Joan Crawford.** When he deserted her for his music, she walked into the sea, never to return. The virtuoso violin playing was by Isaac Stern who cleverly dubbed the solos through a hole cut into the elbow of Garfield's coat. Music by composer Anton Dvorak has words by William Nameiw. $8

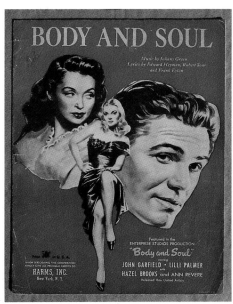

Judy Garland (1922-1969). Judy's most memorable role was Dorothy in *The Wizard of Oz* singing "Over the Rainbow," the song that will forever be associated with her. It brought her world renown, and a special miniature Academy Award for her outstanding performance as a screen juvenile in 1939. She was teamed up with Mickey Rooney in the 1930s in the first of many successful juvenile productions that showcased their extraordinary talents. She really hit her stride in the 1940s, moving from lighthearted teenager roles to parts that called for more maturity. Her musicals for M-G-M were top money makers.

Judy Garland entered the 1950s co-starring with Gene Kelly in the hit musical *Summer Stock*, which yielded many fine songs with them on the cover. She was nominated for a Best Actress Academy Award for her stirring performance in the remake of *A Star Is Born* in 1954. Other memorable dramatic performances were in *Judgment at Nuremberg* and *A Child Is Waiting*. She died of an accidental overdose of sleeping pills at age 47.

GARLAND MOVIE COVERS: *Two Hearts in Harmony*, 1935. *Thoroughbreds Don't Cry*, 1937. *Broadway Melody of* 1938. *Everybody Sing*, 1938. *Listen Darling*, 1938. *Love Finds Andy Hardy*, 1938. *Babes in Arms*, 1939. *The Wizard of Oz*, 1939. *Andy Hardy Meets Debutante*, 1940. *Little Nellie Kelly*, 1940. *Strike Up the Band*, 1940. *Babes on Broadway*, 1941. *Ziegfeld Girl*, 1941. *For Me and My Gal*, 1942. *Girl Crazy*, 1943. *Presenting Lily Mars*, 1943. *Thousands Cheer*, 1943. *Meet Me in St. Louis*, 1944. *The Harvey Girls*, 1946. *Till the Clouds Roll By*, 1946. *Easter Parade*, 1948. *The Pirate*, 1948. *Words and Mu-*

You Made Me Love You
Fifteen-year-old **Judy Garland**'s dynamism and talent exploded on the screen in *Broadway Melody of 1938*, when she sang a touching preamble to this well-known 1913 song to a photo (at right) of her movie screen idol, Clark Gable. $80

sic, 1948. *In the Good Old Summertime*, 1949. *Summer Stock*, 1950. *A Star Is Born*, 1954. *Judgment at Nuremberg*, 1961. *Gay Purr-ee*, 1962. *A Child Is Waiting*, 1963. *I Could Go on Singing*, 1963.

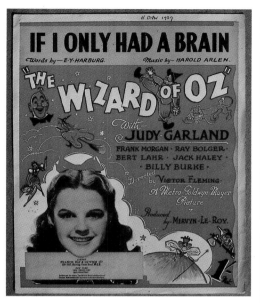

If I Only Had a Brain
Judy Garland achieved immortality in *The Wizard of Oz*, in a role originally intended for Shirley Temple. Ray Bolger as the Scarecrow sang this Harburg/Arlen song in the movie. Judy is seen here on a British edition of the song. $20

"Dear Mr. Gable, I am writing this to you, and I hope that you will read it so you'll know. My heart beats like a hammer, and I stutter and I stammer, every time I see you at the picture show. I guess I'm just another fan of yours, and I thought I'd write and tell you so."

Wonderful One
Handsome **Clark Gable** was reportedly pleased with Judy Garland's declaration of affection in "You Made Me Love You." He grins rakishly from the cover of a song from *To Please a Lady*. Gable played a racing driver in the movie, and **Barbara Stanwyck** was a tough reporter who falls in love with him. $6

It Only Happens When I Dance with You
Judy Garland as a struggling young hoofer is drafted by **Fred Astaire** as his dancing partner to make **Ann Miller** jealous. The whole thing backfires when Judy falls for Fred. Johnny Green and Roger Eden won an Oscar for Best Musical Score, though most of the songs were by Irving Berlin. $5

Drummer Boy
Judy Garland and **Mickey Rooney** teamed up in the delightful movie musical *Strike Up the Band* with Rooney as the leader of a high school band, and Judy belting out several songs. They were backed up by Paul Whiteman and his orchestra with the whole affair directed by Busby Berkeley. $10

James Garner (born 1928). A high school dropout who later fought with distinction with the Army in Korea, James Garner was wounded in action and awarded a Purple Heart. After his discharge he bounced around at various jobs, and with his good looks and winning personality was soon modeling swim trunks, and playing small parts on TV shows and in the movies. His name became a household word when he starred in the long-running *Maverick* series on TV, leading to a career in films as a popular leading man.

GARNER MOVIE COVERS: *Boys' Night Out*, 1962. *The Great Escape*, 1963. *Move Over Darling*, 1963. *The Thrill of It All*, 1963. *The Wheeler Dealers*, 1963. *The Americanization of Emily*, 1964. *Thirty-Six Hours*, 1964. *The Art of Love*, 1965. *Duel at Diablo*, 1966. *Grand Prix*, 1966. *How Sweet It Is*, 1968. *Marlowe*, 1969.

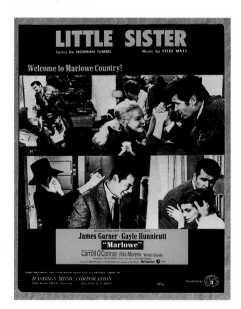

Little Sister
James Garner starred in *Marlowe* as Philip Marlowe, a hard-boiled detective created by mystery author Raymond Chandler. The plot was based on Chandler's story, *The Little Sister*, from whence came the song title. Scenes from the movie show Garner with **Gayle Hunnicutt** (top) and **Rita Moreno** (bottom). $5

Greer Garson (1908-1996). A London actress who came to Hollywood in 1934, Greer Garson made a splash in *Goodbye, Mr. Chips*, for which she received her first of many Academy Award nominations. Other nominated movies were *Blossoms in the Dust*, *Madame Curie*, *Mrs. Parkington*, *The Valley of Decision*, and *Sunrise at Campobello*. Without question her most important role was the brave English housewife, Mrs. Miniver, who weathered the Blitz bombings during World War II in a sympathetic and compassionate performance that finally brought her a well-deserved Oscar for Best Actress in 1942.

GARSON MOVIE COVERS: *Mrs. Miniver*, 1942. *Adventure*, 1945. *Desire Me*, 1947. *Julia Misbehaves*, 1948. *Strange Lady in Town*, 1955.

Strange Lady in Town
Greer Garson was the *Strange Lady in Town*, a doctor from Boston who takes her practice to 1880s Santa Fe, and attracts the amorous attentions of **Dana Andrews**. Title song by Ned Washington (W) and Dimitri Tiomkin (M) was introduced by Frankie Laine. $8

Norah Girl
Much advance publicity introduced the lavish production of *Adventure* with **Greer Garson** co-starred for the first and only time with **Clark Gable**, back from the war. She played a prim librarian, and he a wandering seaman. Song was by Fred Brennan (W) and Herbert Stothart (M). *Collection of James Nelson Brown*. $10.

Janet Gaynor (1906-1984). The first Academy Award ever given for Best Actress went to Janet Gaynor. She started out as a starstruck usherette in a Los Angeles theater before working as an extra in movies, moving up through the ranks to top stardom. She had a lengthy career in silent films in the 1920s, successfully traversing the bumpy road to the talkies in the 1930s, and dabbling a few times in television in the 1950s.

GAYNOR MOVIE COVERS: *Seventh Heaven*, 1927. *Sunrise*, 1927. *Four Devils*, 1928. *Street Angel*, 1928. *Christina*, 1929. *Sunny Side Up*, 1929. *Happy Days*, 1930. *High Society Blues*, 1930. *Delicious*, 1931. *Merely Mary Ann*, 1931. *Adorable*, 1933. *Paddy the Next Best Thing*, 1933. *State Fair*, 1933. *Carolina*, 1934. *Small Town Girl*, 1936. *A Star Is Born*, 1937. *The Young in Heart*, 1939.

Paulette Goddard (1905-1990). A former Ziegfeld girl named "Peaches" became the starlet Paulette Goddard in Hollywood. She was a beautiful vivacious girl with a sparkling smile, and exuded sex appeal. While married to Charlie Chaplin she appeared in two films with him—*Modern Times* and *The Great Dictator*. She became an important Paramount star in the 1940s, effective mainly in comedy roles, but always brightening the screen with her striking good looks and personality. In 1943 her acting ability was recognized with a Best Supporting Actress nomination for *So Proudly We Hail*.

GODDARD MOVIE COVERS: *The Young in Heart* 1938. *Second Chorus*, 1940. *Hold Back the Dawn*, 1941. *Pot o' Gold*, 1941. *The Forest Rangers*, 1942. *Reap the Wild Wind*, 1942. *Star Spangled Rhythm*, 1942. *Kitty*, 1945. *A Miracle Can Happen*, 1947. *Suddenly It's Spring*, 1947.

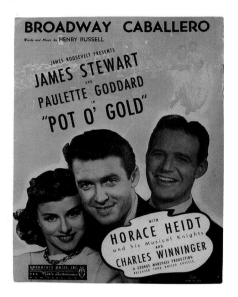

Broadway Caballero
Paulette Goddard and harmonica-playing **James Stewart** were two shining faces in the pleasant movie musical *Pot O' Gold*, with bandleader Horace Heidt and his Musical Knights providing the musical backup. $25

Delishious
This theme song cover shows **Janet Gaynor** as she appeared in the movie *Delicious* a romantic vehicle for her and frequent co-star Charles Farrell. George and Ira Gershwin wrote the song. $8

Jingle Jangle Jingle
Paulette Goddard plays a socialite who marries a ranger, **Fred MacMurray,** in *The Forest Rangers.* She manages to surmount her tenderfoot ways in feats of bravery during a spectacular forest fire, earning the admiration of all. This song by Frank Loesser (W) and Joseph J. Lilley (M) was introduced on the movie sound track, and went on to become a major hit recording. $4

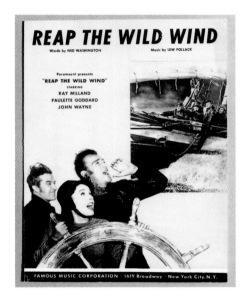

Reap the Wild Wind
The brilliant cast of *Reap the Wild Wind* included **Paulette Goddard,** torn between two men—**Ray Milland** and **John Wayne.** Cecil B. DeMille brought his epic vision to the movie, staging an underwater fight with a giant squid off the Florida Keys, and it paid off with an Oscar for Best Special Effects. *Collection of Harold Jacobs.* $40

Betty Grable (1916-1973). After starting out as a teenage chorus girl in the 1930s, Miss Grable left her mark in B musicals as an attractive singer and dancer. She moved up to major stardom in the 1940s, starring in many sparkling musicals. During World War II, she became the number one "pin-up girl" for American G.I.'s, smiling flirtatiously over her shoulder in her famous bathing suit picture. Though not a great singer, Grable delivered her songs in an inimitable plain and straightforward style that endeared her to movie-goers. After the demise of the movie musical in the mid-1950s, she did some stage work including the lead role in *Hello, Dolly!,* but died of lung cancer at age 56.

GRABLE MOVIE COVERS: *Palmy Days,* 1931. *Nitwits,* 1935. *Collegiate,* 1936. *This Way Please,* 1937. *Thrill of a Lifetime,* 1937. *College Swing,* 1938. *Give Me a Sailor,* 1938. *Down Argentine Way,* 1940. *Tin Pan Alley,* 1940. *Moon Over Miami,* 1941. *A Yank in the R.A.F.,* 1941. *I Wake Up Screaming,* 1941. *Footlight Serenade,* 1942. *Song of the Islands,* 1942. *Springtime in the Rockies,* 1942. *Coney Island,* 1943. *Sweet Rosie O'Grady,* 1943. *Pin-Up Girl,* 1944. *Diamond Horseshoe,* 1945. *The Dolly Sisters,* 1945. *Mother Wore Tights,* 1947. *The Shocking Miss Pilgrim,* 1947. *That Lady in Ermine,* 1948. *When My Baby Smiles at Me,* 1948. *The Beautiful Blonde from Bashful Bend,* 1949. *My Blue Heaven,* 1950. *Wabash Avenue,* 1950. *Call Me Mister,* 1951. *Meet Me After the Show,* 1951. *The Farmer Takes a Wife,* 1953. *How to Marry a Millionaire,* 1953. *How to Be Very Very Popular,* 1955. *Three for the Show,* 1955.

I'm Still Crazy for You
Betty Grable was pursued by both her handsome co-stars **John Payne** (left) and **Victor Mature** (right) in *Footlight Serenade.* As a dancer in a Broadway show, Grable had a couple of nice musical numbers in which to show off her talents. Leo Robin and Ralph Rainger wrote the songs. $20

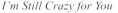

I Had the Craziest Dream
The gorgeous scenery included Lake Louise in the Canadian Rockies and **Betty Grable**'s famous legs in *Springtime in the Rockies.* On the cover, Grable dances with **Cesar Romero,** while her soon-to-be real life husband, **Harry James,** tootles his horn. This song was introduced in the movie by Helen Forrest, who ultimately had a No. 1 hit record with Harry James. $6

Who Threw the Overalls in Mistress Murphy's Chowder?
The turn-of-the-century locale is *Coney Island,* and **Betty Grable** played a saloon singer who learned the proper way to put over a song from co-star George Montgomery. This novelty song was written in 1899 by George L. Giefer. $10

For You, For Me, For Evermore
The Shocking Miss Pilgrim co-starred **Betty Grable** as a crusading suffragette in the 1870s with **Dick Haymes** as her love interest. The Gershwin songs in the movie were adapted posthumously from George Gershwin's manuscripts by Kay Swift and Ira Gershwin, with lyrics provided by Ira. $6

Love Song from "Houseboat"
Cary Grant hires **Sophia Loren** as his housekeeper to help him with his motherless children in the entertaining movie *Houseboat*. This song was written by Jay Livingston and Ray Evans. $6 *($10)*

Night and Day
Although *Night and Day*, based on the life of Cole Porter, had many of Porter's best songs performed by big stars, it was a critical disaster. But the public supported it, no doubt because of the calling card of **Cary Grant** playing the lead with **Alexis Smith** as his society wife. British edition. $5

Cary Grant (1904-1986). A perennial leading man, Cary Grant was handsome and debonair and exuded charm. He was born Archibald Leach in Bristol, England, and carried his unique accent throughout his life. He was equally adept in serious romantic roles or screwball comedies. Starting out in the 1930s, he maintained his handsome romantic charisma well into the 1960s. In 1969 he was given an honorary Oscar for his unique mastery of the art of screen acting with the respect and affection of his colleagues. In response to the standing ovation, Grant commented, "You're applauding my stamina," referring to his lengthy career as a romantic lead.

GRANT MOVIE COVERS: *Kiss and Make Up*, 1934. *Suzy*, 1936. *The Amazing Quest of Ernest Bliss*, 1936. *The Toast of New York*, 1937. *Topper*, 1937. *Penny Serenade*, 1941. *Night and Day*, 1946. *The Bachelor and the Bobby-Soxer*, 1947. *The Bishop's Wife*, 1947. *Mr. Blandings Builds His Dream House*, 1948. *Monkey Business*, 1952. *Dream Wife*, 1953. *To Catch a Thief*, 1955. *An Affair to Remember*, 1957. *Kiss Them for Me*, 1957. *Houseboat*, 1958. *Indiscreet*, 1958. *North by Northwest*, 1959. *The Grass Is Greener*, 1960. *Charade*, 1963. *Father Goose*, 1964. *Walk Don't Run*, 1966.

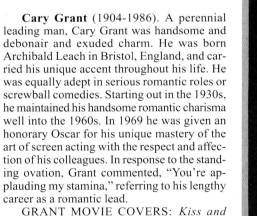

Lost April
Cary Grant was charming in *The Bishop's Wife*, as the angel who comes to earth at Christmas to help the Bishop (David Niven) and his wife (Loretta Young) raise money for their new church. Nat King Cole had a hit recording of this haunting theme song. $10

Kathryn Grayson (born 1922). With her pretty brunette coloring, lovely figure, and lilting soprano voice, specializing in coloratura arias, Miss Grayson entertained audiences in a series of Technicolor spectaculars. She was one of M-G-M's top singing stars in musicals of the 1940s and 1950s, holding her own with talented leading men Gene Kelly, Frank Sinatra, Howard Keel, and Mario Lanza.

GRAYSON MOVIE COVERS: *The Vanishing Virginian*, 1941. *Rio Rita*, 1942. *Seven Sweethearts*, 1942. *Thousands Cheer*, 1943. *Anchors Aweigh*, 1945. *Till the Clouds Roll By*, 1946. *Two Sisters from Boston*, 1946. *Ziegfeld Follies*, 1946. *It Happened in Brooklyn*, 1947. *The Kissing Bandit*, 1948. *That Midnight Kiss*, 1949. *The Toast of New Orleans*, 1950. *Show Boat*, 1951. *Lovely to Look At*, 1952. *The Desert Song*, 1953. *Kiss Me Kate*, 1953. *So This Is Love*, 1953. *The Vagabond King*, 1956.

Jean Harlow (1911-1937). She was a glamorous platinum blonde superstar of the 1930s who died prematurely at age 26. Her early roles as a vulgar, wise-cracking sex-pot were reviewed with disdain by critics, but in a few short years they changed their tune and praised her for her subtlety and comedic timing. She was at the peak of her career when she became ill during the filming of *Saratoga*, and died in the hospital from cerebral edema.

HARLOW MOVIE COVERS: *Dinner at Eight, 1933. Hold Your Man ,1933. The Girl from Missouri, 1934. China Seas, 1935. Reckless, 1935. Suzy, 1936. Saratoga, 1937.*

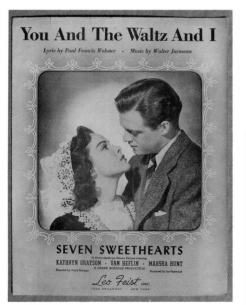

Hold Your Man
Jean Harlow and **Clark Gable** were effective together in *Hold Your Man*, each playing nefarious characters on the fringe of the law. Harlow gave a strong performance as a wise-cracking prison-bound gangster's moll. $8

Reckless
Jean Harlow played a chorus girl in *Reckless*, using a double for her singing and dancing scenes. The screenplay about her husband committing suicide drew a close parallel with Harlow's real life marriage to Paul Bern. *Collection of Harold Jacobs.* $100

Dinner at Eight
Jean Harlow shone as a social-climbing dame in the star-studded expensive M-G-M movie *Dinner at Eight*. The blockbuster cast included (top to bottom) **Marie Dressler, John Barrymore, Wallace Beery, Jean Harlow, Lionel Barrymore, Lee Tracy, Edmund Lowe,** and **Billie Burke**. $4

Be My Love
Lovely **Kathryn Grayson** co-starred with dynamic singer **Mario Lanza** in their second movie together, *The Toast of New Orleans*. Lanza played a New Orleans fisherman who is discovered and launched as an opera star. This song by Sammy Cahn (W) and Nicholas Brodszky (M) was Lanza's big hit in the movie, and became a top best-selling record as well. $5

You and the Waltz and I
Seven Sweethearts starred **Kathryn Grayson** as one of seven daughters of an old-fashioned Dutchman, who won't let any of the girls marry before the oldest does. **Van Heflin** was the leading man. Song was written by Paul Francis Webster (W) and Walter Jurmann (M). $8

The Horse With the Dreamy Eyes
Jean Harlow played the granddaughter of a wealthy horse breeder opposite **Clark Gable** as a big time bookie in *Saratoga*, a racing world comedy. Harlow became ill and died during the filming, and her stand-in Mary Dees filled in to complete the picture. Song was written by Bob Wright and Chet Forrest (W) and Walter Donaldson (M). *Collection of James Nelson Brown.* $75

Rex Harrison (1908-1990). He had a lengthy career on stage and screen both in England and the United States. Notable Hollywood successes were *Anna and the King of Siam* (1946), *The Ghost and Mrs. Muir* (1947), and *The Agony and the Ecstasy* (1965). His crowning achievement was as Professor Henry Higgins in the Broadway production of *My Fair Lady*, a role he repeated in the movie version for which he won an Academy Award.

HARRISON MOVIE COVERS: *Midnight Lace*, 1960. *The Happy Thieves*, 1962. *Cleopatra*, 1963. *My Fair Lady*, 1964. *The Yellow Rolls Royce*, 1964. *The Agony and the Ecstasy*, 1965. *Doctor Doolittle*, 1967. *A Flea in Her Ear*, 1968. *Staircase*, 1969.

After Today
Rex Harrison played the title role in *Doctor Doolittle*, a charming musical about an eccentric doctor in Victorian England who preferred animals to humans (not an entirely unwise choice). Songs for the production were by Leslie Bricusse including "Talk to the Animals," which garnered an Oscar for Best Song in 1967. $11

June Haver (born 1926). Miss Haver was an engaging singer and dancer who appeared on many sheet music covers. She left films in 1953, searching for her role in life as a nun in a convent. She later left the convent and married actor Fred MacMurray, but did not return to films.

HAVER MOVIE COVERS: *Irish Eyes Are Smiling*, 1944. *The Dolly Sisters*, 1945. *Where Do We Go from Here?* 1945. *Three Little Girls in Blue*, 1946. *Wake Up and Dream*, 1946. *I Wonder Who's Kissing Her Now*, 1947. *Look for the Silver Lining*, 1949. *Oh You Beautiful Doll*, 1949. *The Daughter of Rosie O'Grady*, 1950. *I'll Get By*, 1950. *The Girl Next Door*, 1953.

Susan Hayward (1918-1975). This pretty redhead started out in Hollywood as a starlet in shallow roles, but her talent was eventually rewarded with meatier parts. In 1947 she was nominated for an Oscar, but lost out to Loretta Young in *The Farmer's Daughter*. She became one of Hollywood's most important stars in the 1950s, eventually winning the coveted Academy Award in 1958 for her role in *I Want to Live*.

HAYWARD MOVIE COVERS: *Hit Parade of 1943*. *The Fighting Seabees*, 1944. *And Now Tomorrow*, 1944. *Canyon Passage*, 1946. *The Lost Moment*, 1947. *Smash Up* 1947. *The Saxon Charm*, 1948. *My Foolish Heart*, 1949. *Tulsa*, 1949. *With a Song in My Heart*, 1952. *I'll Cry Tomorrow*, 1955. *Soldier of Fortune*, 1955. *The Conqueror*, 1956. *Thunder in the Sun*, 1959. *The Marriage-Go-Round*, 1960. *Ada*, 1961. *Back Street*, 1961. *Where Love Has Gone*, 1964.

Life Can Be Beautiful
Susan Hayward was outstanding in *Smash Up* playing an insecure housewife with a drinking problem and an egotistical husband played by **Lee Bowman.** Her fine work was recognized with an Oscar nomination for Best Actress. Harold Adamson (W) and Jimmy McHugh (M) wrote this lovely song that highlighted the pathos of the movie. $6

I Wonder Who's Kissing Her Now
June Haver sparkled in *I Wonder Who's Kissing Her Now*, based on the life of vaudeville songwriter Joe Howard, played by Mark Stevens. Lots of good songs were featured, including this 1909 title song with words by Will M. Hough and Frank R. Adams and music ascribed to Joseph E. Howard but actually composed by Harold Orlob. $5

I Want You to Want Me
Oh, You Beautiful Doll was based on the life of songwriter Fred Fisher played by **S. Z. Sakall.** **June Haver** was his talented daughter, singing and dancing up a storm, with **Mark Stevens** as her love interest. Lots of good Fisher songs were used in the movie. $5

Here You Are
My Gal Sal was the story of songwriter Paul Dresser played by **Victor Mature** with **Rita Hayworth** cast as the love of his life. Set in the late 19th century, it used gorgeous costumes and sets, and wonderful songs by Paul Dresser. This song was written for the movie by Leo Robin (W) and Ralph Rainger (M). $20

With a Song in My Heart
Courageous singer Jane Froman was portrayed by **Susan Hayward** in a strong performance in the dramatic movie *With a Song in My Heart*. The title song was written by Rodgers and Hart in 1929 for the musical show *Spring Is Here*. Hayward's singing was dubbed by the real Jane Froman. Two different covers exist for this song, this being the more valuable of the two. $8

Happiness Is a Thing Called Joe
Susan Hayward did her own singing in *I'll Cry Tomorrow*, the life story of singer Lillian Roth who fell from stardom to skid row by way of the bottle. She won the Cannes Festival award for her fine acting, but was passed over in the Academy Awards. This cover song by E. Y. Harburg (W) and Harold Arlen (M) was one of the great torch songs performed in the film. $6

Rita Hayworth (1918-1987). Young Miss Hayworth was discovered in her teens dancing in a Mexican nightclub as Margarita Carmen Cansino. She was successfully groomed for stardom, changing both her name and appearance, and became Hollywood's newest love goddess in the 1940s, a favorite pin-up girl of American servicemen. Her tempestuous personal life included five marriages—including husbands Orson Welles, Aly Khan, and Dick Haymes.

HAYWORTH MOVIE COVERS: *Music in My Heart*, 1940. *Blood and Sand*, 1941. *You'll Never Get Rich*, 1941. *My Gal Sal*, 1942. *Tales of Manhattan*, 1942. *You Were Never Lovelier*, 1942. *Cover Girl*, 1944. *Tonight and Every Night*, 1945. *Gilda*, 1946. *Down to Earth*, 1947. *The Lady from Shanghai*, 1948. *The Loves of Carmen*, 1948. *Affair in Trinidad*, 1952. *Miss Sadie Thompson*, 1953. *Salome*, 1953. *Fire Down Below*, 1957. *Pal Joey*, 1957. *Separate Tables*, 1958. *They Came to Cordura*, 1959. *The Happy Thieves*, 1962.

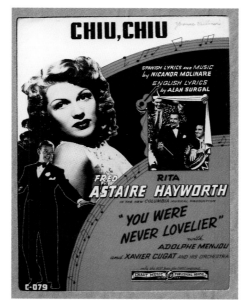

Chiu, Chiu
Rita Hayworth and **Fred Astaire** were sensational in their dance numbers in *You Were Never Lovelier*, a glamorous black and white movie set in Latin America. This song was played by **Xavier Cugat** and his orchestra with vocal by Lina Romay. $8 *($20)*

Sadie Thompson's Song (The Blue Pacific Blues)
Rita Hayworth was at her sultry best playing sexy Sadie Thompson, a woman of questionable virtue who is chased out of Honolulu by holier-than-thou Jose Ferrer. She dances some hot numbers, including this cover song which was dubbed for Miss Hayworth by Jo Ann Greer in the movie *Miss Sadie Thompson*. $6

Sonja Henie (1912-1969). A famous Norwegian athlete, Miss Henie was a figure-skating champion and winner of countless awards including Olympic gold medals in 1928, 1932, and 1936. She was a pretty little blonde with a sparkling smile and engaging personality, and was eventually lured to Hollywood to star in movies. She became very popular during the 1930s and into the 1940s in a series of entertaining movies that featured her incredible skating in lavish production numbers.

HENIE MOVIE COVERS: *One in a Million*, 1936. *Thin Ice*, 1937. *Happy Landing*, 1938. *My Lucky Star*, 1938. *Second Fiddle*, 1939. *Sun Valley Serenade*, 1941. *Iceland*, 1942. *Wintertime*, 1943. *It's a Pleasure*, 1945. *The Countess of Monte Cristo*, 1948. *Hello London*, 1958.

My Swiss Hilly Billy
Sonja Henie played a Swiss ski instructor in *Thin Ice* who falls in love with a handsome young man, Tyrone Power, who turns out to be a prince. Great skating sequences for Henie and songs by Sidney Mitchell (W) and Lew Pollack (M) enriched the film. $10

A Gypsy Told Me
The entertaining musical *Happy Landing* starred **Sonja Henie** as a Norwegian skater who makes it big in America. She also gets the guy, **Don Ameche,** and **Ethel Merman** and **Cesar Romero** get each other. $6

I Poured My Heart Into a Song
Sonja Henie and **Tyrone Power** are a charming couple in *Second Fiddle*, radiating health and good looks. He played a Hollywood publicist who discovers her in Minnesota and stars her in a major movie. Supporting players are **Rudy Vallee** and **Mary Healy.** Lots of skating numbers and Irving Berlin songs make for good entertainment. $8 *($16)*

The Unforgiven
Audrey Hepburn played a Native American passed off as a white girl in 1870s Texas, and **Burt Lancaster** was the rancher who took up her cause when her Indian tribe comes for her. Song for *The Unforgiven* was by Dimitri Tiomkin (M) and Ned Washington (W). $6

Audrey Hepburn (1929-1993). Tall and graceful with a fragile incandescent beauty, Audrey Hepburn became a major Hollywood film star in 1953, after her first role in *Roman Holiday* won her the coveted Academy Award for Best Actress. She subsequently was nominated four more times for her fine acting in the movies *Sabrina*, *The Nun's Story*, *Breakfast at Tiffany's*, and *Wait Until Dark*.

AUDREY HEPBURN MOVIE COVERS: *Sabrina*, 1954. *War and Peace*, 1956. *Funny Face*, 1957. *Love in the Afternoon*, 1957. *Green Mansions*, 1959. *The Unforgiven*, 1960. *Breakfast at Tiffany's*, 1961. *Charade*, 1963. *My Fair Lady*, 1964. *How to Steal a Million*, 1966. *Two for the Road*, 1967. *Wait Until Dark*, 1967. *They All Laughed*, 1981.

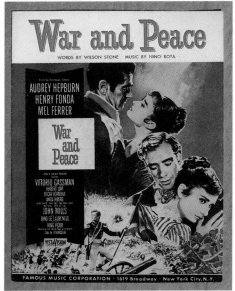

War and Peace
Audrey Hepburn was at her most luminous in a strong cast including **Henry Fonda** and **Mel Ferrer** in the epic movie *War and Peace*. This opulent production was praised for its spectacular battle scenes. Song by Wilson Stone (W) and Nino Rota (M). $8

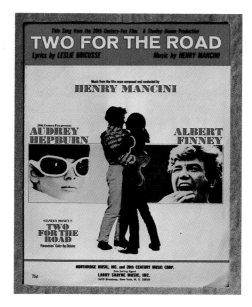

Two for the Road
Audrey Hepburn and **Albert Finney** co-starred in *Two for the Road*, as a young couple who struggle to save their 12-year faltering marriage. Henry Mancini composed the theme song with words by Leslie Bricusse. $5

Morning Glory
Katharine Hepburn won her first Academy Award for *Morning Glory*, as a passionate young New England girl who stops at nothing to become a top actress. Title theme song was written by Joe Young (W) and Max Steiner (M). $25

Believe in Me
Still lovely and highly respected in the 1950s, **Katharine Hepburn** was nominated for the Best Actress Academy Award for her role as a spinster schoolteacher on holiday in Venice in *Summertime*. Under the spell of the romantic city, she falls in love with a married Italian antique dealer played by **Rossano Brazzi.** Beautiful score by Icini was played throughout the film. $8

The Lion in Winter
As Eleanor of Aquitaine in *The Lion in Winter*, **Katharine Hepburn,** shared Oscar-winning honors with Barbra Streisand in *Funny Girl*. Hepburn's co-star was **Peter O'Toole** as Henry II, King of England. The movie received many nominations including Best Picture, and won for Best Screenplay by James Goldman and Best Original Score by John Barry, who wrote this theme song. $8

Katharine Hepburn (born 1907). This distinguished actress won her first of four Academy Awards for her role in *Morning Glory* in 1933. Youthfully radiant, she appears on the cover of the theme song from the movie. She won again for *Guess Who's Coming to Dinner, The Lion in Winter,* and *On Golden Pond*—awards that spanned almost 50 years of superlative acting. During her career she made nine successful movies with Spencer Tracy, with whom she shared a special rapport and congenial off-screen relationship.
KATHARINE HEPBURN MOVIE COVERS: *Little Women,* 1933. *Morning Glory,* 1933. *Alice Adams,* 1935. *Undercurrent,* 1946. *Song of Love,* 1947. *Adam's Rib,* 1949. *The African Queen,* 1951. *Summertime,* 1955. *The Rainmaker,* 1956. *Long Day's Journey into Night,* 1962. *Guess Who's Coming to Dinner,* 1967. *The Lion in Winter,* 1968. *The Mad-woman of Chaillot,* 1969. *On Golden Pond,* 1982.

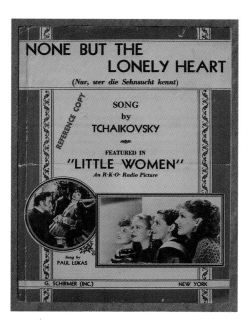

None But the Lonely Heart
Katharine Hepburn was perfectly cast as Jo in *Little Women,* based on the novel by Louisa May Alcott. Cast included, left to right, **Miss Hepburn, Joan Bennett, Frances Dee,** and **Jean Parker. Paul Lukas,** as a musician, sang this Tchaikovsky song in the film. $12 *($44)*

Charlton Heston (born 1924). He studied speech and drama at Northwestern University, and starred in many outstanding television productions for the critically acclaimed series *Studio One* during the late 1940s. In Hollywood movies, he was at his best in historical roles, portraying Moses, Michelangelo, and John the Baptist in stunning Technicolor film spectaculars. He won an Academy Award for Best Actor in the title role of *Ben-Hur* in 1959. Active in Hollywood affairs, he was president of the Screen Actors Guild for six terms, and has served as chairman of the American Film Institute. He is currently the author of a book about the Bible according to Heston.

HESTON MOVIE COVERS: *Dark City*, 1950. *The Far Horizons*, 1955. *Lucy Gallant*, 1955. *The Private War of Major Benson*, 1955. *The Ten Commandments*, 1956. *Three Violent People*, 1956. *The Pigeon That Took Rome*, 1962. *Diamond Head*, 1963. *Fifty-Five Days at Peking*, 1963. *The Agony and the Ecstasy*, 1965. *Major Dundee*, 1965. *The War Lord*, 1965. *Khartoum*, 1966. *Will Penny*, 1968. *Earthquake*, 1974. *Airport 75*, 1975.

Una Momento
Three Violent People co-starred **Charlton Heston, Anne Baxter,** and **Gilbert Roland** in an action-packed Western, with Heston trying to save his ranch from carpetbaggers. $6

William Holden (1918-1981). Starting out as a handsome wide-eyed callow youth, Holden enjoyed a long career in the movies as a popular romantic lead, eventually graduating to a mature action hero and an aging character actor. He won a Best Actor Academy Award for *Stalag 17* in 1953. He traveled extensively all over the world, becoming entranced with Africa where he became a co-owner of the exclusive Mount Kenya Safari Club.

HOLDEN MOVIE COVERS: *I Wanted Wings*, 1941. *Blaze of Noon*, 1947. *Dear Ruth*,

The Peking Theme
Fifty Five Days at Peking was an action film set in 1890s China during the Boxer Rebellion. Its strong cast included (left to right) **David Niven, Charlton Heston,** and **Ava Gardner.** Theme song was by Paul Francis Webster (W) and Dimitri Tiomkin (M). $6 *($13)*

1947. *Dear Wife*, 1949. *Streets of Laredo*, 1949. *Born Yesterday*, 1950. *Sunset Boulevard*, 1950. *You Can Change the World*, 1950. *Escape from Fort Bravo*, 1953. *Forever Female*, 1953. *The Moon Is Blue*, 1953. *The Bridges At Toko-Ri*, 1954. *The Country Girl*, 1954. *Sabrina*, 1954. *Love Is a Many Splendored Thing*, 1955. *Picnic*, 1955. *The Proud and the Profane*, 1956. *The Bridge on the River Kwai*, 1957. *The Key*, 1958. *The World of Suzy Wong*, 1960. *The Counterfeit Traitor*, 1962. *The Lion*, 1962. *Satan Never Sleeps*, 1962. *The Seventh Dawn*, 1964. *Alvarez Kelly*, 1966. *The Devil's Brigade*, 1968. *Wild Rovers*, 1971. *Breezy*, 1973.

I Can't Give You Anything But Love
Born Yesterday was a hilarious comedy brought from Broadway to the screen with **Broderick Crawford** (right) playing a rich junkman who hires **William Holden** to teach "culchur" to dumb blonde **Judy Holliday.** Miss Holliday repeated her stage role, and won an Academy Award as Best Actress for her efforts. $7

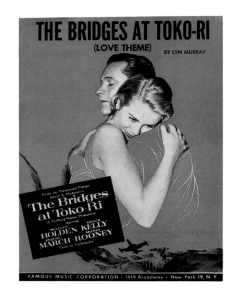

The Bridges at Toko-Ri
William Holden played a brave bomber pilot with a dangerous mission during the Korean war in *The Bridges at Toko-Ri*. The movie was based on James Michener's novel, and had a strong supporting cast including Mickey Rooney, Fredric March, and beautiful **Grace Kelly** as Holden's wife. *Collection of James Nelson Brown.* $10

The Seventh Dawn
William Holden, as a rubber plantation owner in Malaysia, takes on Communist guerrillas in the jungle in *The Seventh Dawn*. The plot develops an interesting triangle between Holden and the two female stars **Susannah York** (left) and **Capucine** (right). $5

Bob Hope (born 1903). One of America's most famous comedians of stage, radio, movies, and television, he was Bing Crosby's sidekick in the famous *"Road"* pictures. He was a frequent emcee of the Oscar presentations and a standing joke was his being overlooked when the awards were given out. In actuality, he won five special awards from the Academy including the prestigious Jean Hersholt Humanitarian Award in recognition for his unselfish services to the motion picture industry and the Academy, for his contribution to the laughter of the world, and his devotion to the American premise. He is also loved and respected for his yearly visits to entertain American troops in far-off lands.

HOPE MOVIE COVERS: *Big Broadcast of 1938. College Swing, 1938. Give Me a Sailor, 1938. Thanks for the Memory, 1938. Some Like It Hot, 1939. Road to Singapore, 1940. Caught in the Draft, 1941. Road to Zanzibar, 1941. Road to Morocco, 1942. Star Spangled Rhythm, 1942. Let's Face It, 1943. They Got Me Covered, 1943. The Princess and the Pirate, 1944. Road to Utopia, 1945. Monsieur Beaucaire, 1946. My Favorite Brunette, 1947. Road to Rio, 1947. Variety Girl, 1947. The Paleface, 1948. The Great Lover, 1949. Honor Caddy, 1949. Sorrowful Jones, 1949. Fancy Pants, 1950. You Can Change the World, 1950. The Lemon Drop Kid, 1951. My Favorite Spy, 1951. Road to Bali, 1952. Son of Paleface, 1952. Off Limits, 1953. Here Come the Girls, 1953. Casanova's Big Night, 1954. The Seven Little Foys, 1955. That Certain Feeling, 1956.*

Silver Bells
Another Damon Runyon story provided the grist for *The Lemon Drop Kid*. **Bob Hope** gets plenty of laughs as a racetrack tipster in trouble with the mob. His leading lady was **Marilyn Maxwell,** a frequent entertainer on his U.S.O. tours. Jay Livingston and Ray Evans wrote the songs, including this hit that has become a Christmas favorite. $5

Two Sleepy People
Bob Hope and **Shirley Ross** were a delightful comedy couple in *Thanks for the Memory*. Their duet of this song in the movie became a smash hit for Frank Loesser (W) and Hoagy Carmichael (M), a hit that has long outlived the movie. $6

Havin' a Wonderful Wish
Bob Hope and **Lucille Ball** co-starred in *Sorrowful Jones*, the Damon Runyon yarn originally filmed as *Little Miss Marker* with Shirley Temple. This time around the little girl was played by Mary Jane Saunders, lower right. Song by Livingston and Evans. $5

Rock Hudson (1925-1985). A leading romantic star of the 1950s and 1960s, Mr. Hudson was equally at ease in dramatic roles like *Magnificent Obsession* and *Giant* (for which he received a Best Actor Academy Award nomination), or zany comedies with Doris Day. His death from complications from AIDS focused public awareness on the disease and fostered fund-raising for research.

HUDSON MOVIE COVERS: *Has Anybody Seen My Gal, 1952. Giant, 1956. A Farewell to Arms, 1957. Written on the Wind, 1957. Pillow Talk, 1959. This Earth Is Mine, 1959. Come September, 1961. The Last Sunset, 1961. Lover Come Back, 1962. Man's Favorite Sport, 1964. Send Me No Flowers, 1964. Ice Station Zebra, 1968. The Undefeated, 1969. Pretty Maids All in a Row, 1971.*

A Farewell to Arms
Rock Hudson played a World War I ambulance driver in a movie remake of *A Farewell to Arms*, based on Ernest Hemingway's moving novel. **Jennifer Jones** was the nurse who became his love interest. Music is by Mario Nascimbene with words added to the theme song by Paul Francis Webster. $7

Pillow Talk
The delightful comedy *Pillow Talk* used the perfect pairing of **Rock Hudson** and **Doris Day** as two singles sharing a party line. Witty dialogue and a clever script brought the writers an Oscar for Best Screenplay, and talented Frank De Vol's music score was also nominated. Title song by Buddy Pepper and Inez James was sung by Hudson and Day in the movie. *Collection of Harold Jacobs.* $15

Man's Favorite Sport?
Rock Hudson is hilarious in *Man's Favorite Sport*, a delightful comedy about a man who has to pretend he's a sportsman to protect his reputation and impress the girl, **Paula Prentiss.** Title song was by Johnny Mercer (W) and Henry Mancini (M). $8

Betty Hutton (born 1921). She sang on street corners for nickels and dimes as a child, eventually becoming a big band singer in her teens. In Hollywood she was known as "The Blonde Bombshell" for her energetic and explosive screen performances. A meteoric rise to fame in the 1940s culminated in her ascension to the Judy Garland title role in *Annie Get Your Gun* when Judy fell ill. Betty Hutton was a major star, earning millions of dollars, when she abandoned her career after a disagreement with the front office. She faded into obscurity until she was found working as a housekeeper in a Catholic rectory in 1974.

HUTTON MOVIE COVERS: *The Fleet's In*, 1942. *Star Spangled Rhythm*, 1942. *Happy Go Lucky*, 1943. *Let's Face It*, 1943. *And the Angels Sing*, 1944. *Here Come the Waves*, 1944. *Incendiary Blonde*, 1945. *The Stork Club*, 1945. *Cross My Heart*, 1946. *The Perils of Pauline*, 1947. *Dream Girl*, 1948. *Red Hot and Blue*, 1949. *Annie Get Your Gun*, 1950. *Let's Dance*, 1950. *The Greatest Show on Earth*, 1952. *Somebody Loves Me*, 1952.

Poppa Don't Preach to Me
Betty Hutton, shown with co-star **John Lund,** was well cast as Pearl White in *The Perils of Pauline*, an entertaining biography about the famous silent film star that used all of Betty's talents. Frank Loesser wrote the great score, including "I Wish I Didn't Love You So," an Oscar nominee that year. $4

Now That I Need You
Betty Hutton co-starred with **Victor Mature** in the musical murder mystery *Red, Hot and Blue*, in which she is the murder suspect. Frank Loesser not only wrote the songs but also appeared in a bit part as one of the gangsters. $4

Doin' What Comes Natur'lly
Betty Hutton did a good job portraying sharpshooter Annie Oakley in a role originally intended for Judy Garland in *Annie Get Your Gun*. The blockbuster movie included the great Irving Berlin songs from the hit Broadway musical. $3

Van Johnson (born 1916). His boyish charm and freckle-faced good looks made him popular with feminine audiences. He started out as a chorus boy on Broadway before coming to Hollywood in the 1940s. His timing was perfect, and he filled the leading man gap left by the actors who were in the service during World War II. Most of his roles were on the lighter side, but he was praised for his effective dramatic acting in *The Last Time I Saw Paris*. Later years have found him playing the lead in a British stage production of *The Music Man*.

JOHNSON MOVIE COVERS: *Thirty Seconds Over Tokyo*, 1944. *Two Girls and a Sailor*, 1944. *Thrill of a Romance*, 1945. *Weekend at the Waldorf*, 1945. *Easy to Wed*, 1946. *No Leave No Love*, 1946. *Till the Clouds Roll By*, 1946. *The Romance of Rosy Ridge*, 1947. *In the Good Old Summertime*, 1949. *Duchess of Idaho*, 1950. *Easy to Love*, 1953. *Remains to Be Seen*, 1953. *Brigadoon*, 1954. *The Caine Mutiny*, 1954. *The Last Time I Saw Paris*, 1954. *The End of the Affair*, 1955. *Miracle in the Rain*, 1956. *Wives and Lovers*, 1963.

Please Don't Say No
Van Johnson played an Air Corps hero, and **Esther Williams** was a swimming instructor in *Thrill of a Romance*, a music-laden movie with opera singer Lauritz Melchior warbling this song by Ralph Freed (W) and Sammy Fain (M). $3

The Last Time I Saw Paris
Van Johnson co-starred with **Elizabeth Taylor** in a romantic version of *The Last Time I Saw Paris*, based on *Babylon Revisited* by F. Scott Fitzgerald. Paris was beautiful, as was Miss Taylor, and Van Johnson excelled in a dramatic role. The haunting title song was originally written by Jerome Kern (M) and Oscar Hammerstein 2nd (W) for the 1941 movie *Lady Be Good*. $7

Jennifer Jones (born 1919). As an aspiring actress, Jennifer Jones and her young husband, actor Robert Walker, came to Hollywood to break into movies. While appearing in nondescript B movies, she was discovered by David O. Selznick, who carefully groomed her for stardom. She won a Best Actress Academy Award for her first major role in *The Song of Bernadette*. Subsequent roles were personally selected by Selznick, who became her second husband in 1949.

JONES MOVIE COVERS: *Since You Went Away*, 1944. *Love Letters*, 1945. *Duel in the Sun*, 1946. *Portrait of Jennie*, 1948. *Ma-*

Portrait of Jennie
Jennifer Jones played the mysterious Jennie, who appeared to an enamored artist, played by **Joseph Cotten** in the wispy, hauntingly beautiful movie *Portrait of Jennie*. The lovely theme song was written by Gordon Burdge (W) and J. Russel Robinson (M). $6

dame Bovary, 1949. *Gone to Earth (a.k.a. The Wild Heart)*, 1950. *Ruby Gentry*, 1952. *Indiscretion of an American Wife*, 1953. *Love Is a Many Splendored Thing*, 1955. *The Barretts of Wimpole Street*, 1957. *A Farewell to Arms*, 1957. *Tender Is the Night*, 1961.

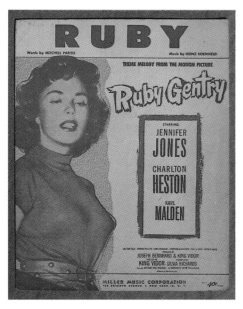

Ruby
Jennifer Jones portrayed a sex-pot who wreaks revenge on Charlton Heston for dumping her in the steamy movie *Ruby Gentry*. The title song was written by Mitch Parish (W) and Heinz Roemheld (M). $4

Tender Is the Night
Jennifer Jones plays a neurotic woman who falls in love with her doctor, **Jason Robards**, in *Tender Is the Night*, a movie based on the F. Scott Fitzgerald story of wealthy but dissolute Americans living in 1920s Europe. Paul Francis Webster (W) and Sammy Fain (M) wrote the title song. $6

Boris Karloff (1887-1969). Though he was a genial handsome fellow off screen, Boris Karloff struck terror into the hearts of movie fans for many years, beginning with his world famous portrayal of the Frankenstein monster in 1931. He was born William Henry Pratt in England and emigrated to Canada in 1909, where he drifted into acting. He appeared in numerous stage productions for the next ten years, then broke into silent movies playing extras and bit parts in 40 films before making his mark in sound movies. In his obituary he was declared by London's *Evening Standard* "the acknowledged king of Hollywood horror films."

Danny Kaye (1913-1987). He was a talented comedian on stage, screen, and television. After gaining early experience on the Catskill Mountain resort circuit, Danny Kaye ended up on Broadway, where he perfected a tongue-twisting routine that became identified with him in subsequent movies. He was enormously popular in 1940s movies that showcased his considerable abilities—pantomime, singing, and impersonation. He was awarded a special Oscar statuette in 1954 for "his unique talents, his service to the Academy, the motion picture industry, and the American people," and the Jean Hersholt Humanitarian Award in 1981 for his work on behalf of UNICEF.

KAYE MOVIE COVERS: *Up in Arms*, 1944. *Wonder Man*, 1945. *The Kid from Brooklyn*, 1946. *The Secret Life of Walter Mitty*, 1947. *A Song Is Born*, 1948. *The Inspector General*, 1949. *On the Riviera*, 1951. *Hans Christian Andersen*, 1952. *Knock on Wood*, 1954. *White Christmas*, 1954. *The Court Jester*, 1956. *Me and the Colonel*, 1958. *Merry Andrew*, 1958. *The Five Pennies*, 1959. *On the Double*, 1961. *The Man from the Diners Club*, 1963.

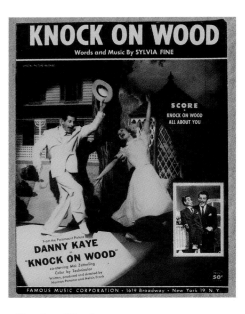

Knock on Wood
Comedian **Danny Kaye** had a knockout with *Knock on Wood*, playing a ventriloquist whose wooden dummy is the repository for secret papers that enemy agents want. **Mai Zetterling** was his co-star. Kaye's wife, Sylvia Fine, wrote the song. $5

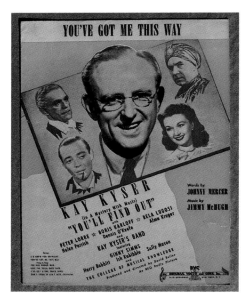

You've Got Me This Way
The great master of "horror" flicks was **Boris Karloff,** seen here on this, his only song cover, with other spook show giants **Peter Lorre** (lower left) and **Bela Lugosi** (upper right). Bandleader **Kay Kyser** and lovely vocalist **Ginny Simms** shared billing in "a mystery with music" *You'll Find Out.* (1940) $8

I Love an Old Fashioned Song
Danny Kaye played a meek milkman, who accidentally becomes a prizefighter in *The Kid from Brooklyn.* Female support came from **Virginia Mayo** (lower left) and **Vera-Ellen.** $6

The Five Pennies
Danny Kaye's performance as jazz great Red Nichols in *The Five Pennies* garnered superlatives all around. It is a special treat for jazz buffs with the real Nichols dubbing for Kaye on the sound track, and support from other legendary jazzmen like **Louis Armstrong**. Sylvia Fine wrote the title song. $6

Howard Keel (born 1917). Gifted with a strong baritone voice and virile good looks, Howard Keel made his movie debut in *Annie Get Your Gun* in 1950. He starred in a string of movie musicals and was a frequent co-star of Esther Williams during the 1950s. Keel also made a few action pictures with straight dramatic parts. He continues to be a popular and well-known singer on stage and television, and on nightclub tours.

KEEL MOVIE COVERS: *Pagan Love Song*, 1950. *Callaway Went Thataway*, 1951. *Show Boat*, 1951. *Texas Carnival*, 1951. *Lovely to Look At*, 1952. *Calamity Jane*, 1953. *Kiss Me Kate*, 1953. *Rose Marie*, 1954. *Seven Brides for Seven Brothers*, 1954. *Jupiter's Darling*, 1954. *Waco*, 1966.

Gene Kelly (1912-1996). He was a gifted song and dance man as well as a talented choreographer on Broadway before making his screen debut in 1942 with Judy Garland in *For Me and My Gal*. He became one of Hollywood's top stars of the 1940s and 1950s, with his brilliant dance routines, homely yet charming singing, and engaging personality. Though Kelly lost out to Ray Milland when nominated for a Best Actor Oscar for *Anchors Aweigh*, the Academy recognized him with a Special Academy Award statuette in 1951 "in appreciation of his versatility as actor, singer, director, and dancer, and especially for his brilliant achievements in the art of choreography on film." He was also honored with the American Film Institute's Lifetime Achievement Award in 1985.

GENE KELLY MOVIE COVERS: *Anchors Aweigh*, 1945. *Living in a Big Way*, 1947. *The Pirate*, 1948. *Words and Music*, 1948. *On the Town*, 1949. *Take Me Out to the Ball Game*, 1949. *Summer Stock*, 1950. *An American in Paris*, 1951. *Singin' in the Rain*, 1952. *Brigadoon*, 1954. *It's Always Fair Weather*, 1955. *The Happy Road*, 1957. *Les Girls*, 1957. *Marjorie Morningstar*, 1958. *What a Way to Go*, 1964. *That's Entertainment*, 1974 and 1976 versions.

You Were Meant for Me
One of **Gene Kelly**'s greatest musicals was *Singin' in the Rain* about Hollywood's transition from silents to sound. He had lots of help from a talented cast that included **Debbie Reynolds** and **Donald O'Connor.** Kelly sang this 1929 standard by Arthur Freed (W) and Nacio Herb Brown (M). $5

Totem Tom-Tom
This version of *Rose Marie* was M-G-M's third mounting of the famous stage operetta. It was filmed in Cinemascope, and benefited from Busby Berkeley's direction of spectacular production numbers like the exotic Totem Tom-tom. Co-stars, left to right, were **Ann Blyth, Howard Keel,** and **Fernando Lamas.** $4

What Makes the Sunset?
The charming M-G-M musical *Anchors Aweigh* followed the adventures of two sailors on leave in Hollywood, and featured the talents of **Frank Sinatra, Kathryn Grayson,** and **Gene Kelly.** Songs by Sammy Cahn (W) and Jule Styne (M) added to the package that also included pianist Jose Iturbi performing in concert at the Hollywood Bowl. Kelly and Sinatra were a pleasing combination and they co-starred again in *On the Town* and *Take Me Out to the Ball Game*, with more hit songs to their credit. $8

I'll Go Home with Bonnie Jean
Lerner and Loewe's Broadway musical *Brigadoon* was brought to the screen complete with its fantasy Scottish village and American visitors portrayed by **Gene Kelly** and **Van Johnson.** $5

Grace Kelly (1929-1982). She, indeed, lived a fairy tale life. She was breathtakingly beautiful, came from a wealthy background, went to all the right schools, and acted on the Broadway stage from whence she embarked on a successful movie career in Hollywood. She won the Best Actress Oscar in 1954 for her unglamorous portrayal of an alcoholic's wife in *The Country Girl*. A year later she met and fell in love with Prince Rainier III of Monaco and retired from films. In a storybook marriage, she reigned as Princess Grace of the small principality until her untimely death in an automobile accident in 1982.

GRACE KELLY MOVIE COVERS: *High Noon*, 1952. *The Bridges At Toko-Ri*, 1954. *The Country Girl*, 1954. *Dial "M" for Murder*, 1954. *Green Fire*, 1954. *Rear Window*, 1954. *To Catch a Thief*, 1955. *High Society*, 1956. *The Swan*, 1956.

My Favorite Memory
Grace Kelly was superb as the wealthy wife of Ray Milland, who cold-bloodedly plans her murder in the Alfred Hitchcock thriller *Dial M for Murder*. Dimitri Tiomkin wrote this theme song with words by Jack Lawrence. *Collection of Harold Jacobs.* $90 ($110)

Dissertation on the State of Bliss
Grace Kelly received the ultimate praise for her performance in *The Country Girl*, as the long-suffering wife of a dipsomaniacal actor played by **Bing Crosby.** She received an Oscar for the year's Best Actress. **William Holden** was effective as the stage director who falls in love with her. Ira Gershwin (W) and Harold Arlen (M) wrote two songs for the film. *Collection of James Nelson Brown.* $40 ($55)

Unexpectedly
To Catch a Thief was another Alfred Hitchcock movie starring **Grace Kelly** and **Cary Grant.** Grant is a reformed cat burglar who falls in love with the lovely Grace as she vacations on the Riviera with her rich Mom. It was filmed on location in southern France, where Grace met the love of her life, Prince Rainier of Monaco. *Collection of Harold Jacobs.* $15

True Love
Grace Kelly shone in *High Society*, opposite the monumental talents of **Bing Crosby** and **Frank Sinatra.** This remake of *Philadelphia Story* was enhanced with songs by Cole Porter. Grace Kelly did her own singing in this duet with Crosby. $4

The Swan
Grace Kelly's swan song was the costume drama *The Swan*, one of her last movies before she became Her Serene Highness Princess Grace of Monaco. Her exquisite beauty is captured on the cover of the theme song by Bronislau Kaper.$15

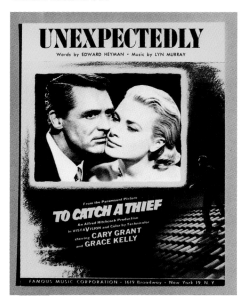

Deborah Kerr (born 1921). A British actress and ballet dancer, Miss Kerr played her first Hollywood part opposite Clark Gable in *The Hucksters*. Usually cast in elegant ladylike roles, she surprised Hollywood by playing a passionate adulteress in *From Here to Eternity*. She subsequently played a broad range of characters, usually portraying the quintessential lady, but with smoldering fire that brought depth to her roles.

KERR MOVIE COVERS: *The Hucksters*, 1947. *If Winter Comes*, 1948. *Quo Vadis*, 1951. *Dream Wife*, 1952. *From Here to Eternity*, 1953. *Thunder in the East*, 1953. *The End of the Affair*, 1955. *The King and I*, 1956. *The Proud and the Profane*, 1956. *An Affair to Remember*, 1957. *Separate Tables*, 1958. *Beloved Infidel*, 1959. *The Sundowners*, 1960. *The Grass Is Greener*, 1961. *The Innocent*, 1961. *Prudence and the Pill*, 1968.

The Ruby and the Pearl
Paramount expected great things from *Thunder in the East*, but despite top names like **Deborah Kerr** playing a blind girl and **Alan Ladd** as an American adventurer in India, the movie bombed. Seen on cover at lower right are other members of the cast, **Charles Boyer** and **Corinne Calvet**. $5

Alan Ladd (1913-1964). He was a handsome bit player struggling for parts in Hollywood, when he married former silent screen actress Sue Carol, who got his career moving in the right direction. His lucky break came when he was cast as a hired killer opposite Veronica Lake in *This Gun for Hire*. Movie fans responded to his "tough guy" roles in 1940s movies, and he remained a star into the 1960s.

LADD MOVIE COVERS: *And Now Tomorrow*, 1944. *Calcutta*, 1947. *Variety Girl*, 1947. *Beyond Glory*, 1948. *Captain Carey U.S.A.*, 1950. *Shane*, 1953. *Thunder in the East*, 1953. *Drum Beat*, 1954. *The Black Knight*, 1954. *The McConnell Story*, 1955. *The Big Land*, 1957. *Boy on a Dolphin*, 1957. *The Proud Rebel*, 1958. *All the Young Men*, 1960.

An Affair to Remember
Deborah Kerr and **Cary Grant** co-starred in *An Affair to Remember*, a romantic remake of *Love Affair*, bringing charm and pathos to the story of lovers who are separated by tragedy. The beautiful theme song was written by Harold Adamson and Leo McCarey with music by Harry Warren. $5

The Call of the Far-Away Hills
The highly acclaimed Western movie *Shane* was one of **Alan Ladd**'s best. He played a mysterious stranger, good with a gun, who came to the aid of homesteaders **Jean Arthur** and **Van Heflin**. Song was written by Mack David (W) and Victor Young (M). $8

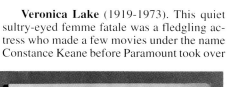

Veronica Lake (1919-1973). This quiet sultry-eyed femme fatale was a fledgling actress who made a few movies under the name Constance Keane before Paramount took over

Born to Love
I Wanted Wings was the first movie in which the young actress Constance Keane was billed as **Veronica Lake**. She played opposite a trio of handsome men, left to right, **Ray Milland**, **William Holden**, and **Brian Donlevy**, who were Air Force trainees, in a movie that won an Oscar for Special Effects. *Collection of Harold Jacobs.* $50

Boy on a Dolphin
The beautifully scenic movie *Boy on a Dolphin* was filmed in the Greek Islands with **Alan Ladd** playing an archaeologist, **Sophia Loren** as a sponge diver who seeks an ancient sunken statue, and **Clifton Webb** as a greedy private collector. Original Greek music was adapted by Hugo Friedhofer with words by Paul Francis Webster. $6

and groomed her for bigger things. She created sparks opposite Alan Ladd in *This Gun for Hire* in 1942, becoming one of Paramount's major stars in the 1940s. She created quite a fashion stir in Hollywood films with her long silky blonde hair worn over one eye in a so-called "peek-a-boo" style. Her Hollywood glory days declined in the late 1940s.

LAKE MOVIE COVERS: *I Wanted Wings*, 1941. *Star Spangled Rhythm*, 1942. *Bring on the Girls*, 1945. *Out of This World*, 1945. *Isn't It Romantic*, 1948.

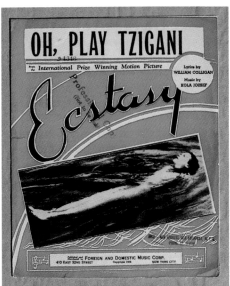

You Moved Right In
Veronica Lake played a gold-digging cigarette girl after millionaire Eddie Bracken's money in *Bring on the Girls*. Left to right on the cover are Veronica, **Marjorie Reynolds, Eddie Bracken,** and **Sonny Tufts,** with **Spike Jones and his City Slickers** in photo at bottom. $5

Oh, Play Tzigani
Hedy Lamarr's husband tried to buy up all existing prints of the film *Ecstasy* to save his wife from embarrassment, but was unsuccessful. The film is still occasionally released, and sheet music with Lamarr *au naturel* on the cover is still floating around. This piece was found in a box of tattered music in a junk store in Salt Lake City. $100

Minnie from Trinidad
The all-star movie *Ziegfeld Girl* chronicled the lives of three beautiful Ziegfeld show girls played by **Hedy Lamarr, Lana Turner,** and **Judy Garland.** It was a lavish production with 100 beautiful girls, fabulous production numbers by Busby Berkeley, and handsome leading men **James Stewart** and **Tony Martin.** Judy Garland did the honors singing this peppy song by Roger Edens. $15

Hedy Lamarr (born 1913). Viennese beauty Hedwig Kiesler was renamed Hedy Lamarr, after the silent screen star Barbara La Marr, when she went to work for Louis B. Mayer. She had already gained fame and notoriety before she came to the United States for appearing completely nude in the 1933 Czech production of the movie *Extase (Ecstasy)*. She was not considered a great actress, but no one really cared, because her exquisite beauty and aura of mystery carried her through a number of good movies.

LAMARR MOVIE COVERS: *Ecstasy*, 1933. *Algiers*, 1938. *Lady of the Tropics*, 1939. *Ziegfeld Girl*, 1941. *White Cargo*, 1942. *Crossroads*, 1942. *The Conspirators*, 1944. *Her Highness and the Bellboy*, 1945. *Samson and Delilah*, 1949. *Copper Canyon*, 1950. *My Favorite Spy*, 1951.

Each Time You Say "Good Bye"
Hedy Lamarr played a half-breed native girl involved with American millionaire **Robert Taylor** in *Lady of the Tropics*. The movie was less than sensational, but Hedy lived up to all of her advance publicity as "the most beautiful girl in the world." *Collection of Harold Jacobs.* $100

Tondelayo
Hedy Lamarr played the exotic temptress Tondelayo in a 1940s version of the tropical scorcher *White Cargo*. This time around it co-starred a jaded Walter Pidgeon and a clean-cut Richard Carlson, who soon falls victim to her charms. *Collection of Harold Jacobs.* $200

Dorothy Lamour (1914-1996). This exotic brunette beauty was only 18 when voted Miss New Orleans. She was an adequate vocalist with a band when she succumbed to the lure of Hollywood. Her first movie, *Jungle Princess*, started her out clad in a sarong, which became her trademark in many movies. She was one of Hollywood's busiest and most popular stars in the 1940s, at her best in the lighthearted *"Road"* series with Bob Hope and Bing Crosby.

LAMOUR MOVIE COVERS: *The Jungle Princess*, 1936. *The Hurricane*, 1937. *Thrill of a Lifetime*, 1937. *The Big Broadcast of 1938*. *Her Jungle Love*, 1938. *Spawn of the North*, 1938. *Tropic Holiday*, 1938. *Man About Town*, 1939. *St. Louis Blues*, 1939. *Johnny Apollo*, 1940. *Moon Over Burma*, 1940. *Typhoon*, 1940. *Road to Singapore*, 1940. *Aloma of the South Seas*, 1941. *Caught in the Draft*, 1941. *Road to Zanzibar*, 1941. *Beyond the Blue Horizon*, 1942. *The Fleet's In*, 1942. *Road to Morocco*, 1942. *Star Spangled Rhythm*, 1942. *Dixie*, 1943. *Riding High*, 1943. *They Got Me Covered*, 1943. *And the Angels Sing*, 1944. *Rainbow Island*, 1944. *Masquerade in Mexico*, 1945. *Road to Utopia*, 1945. *My Favorite Brunette*, 1947. *Road to Rio*, 1947. *Lulu Belle*, 1948. *Slightly French*, 1949. *The Lucky Stiff*, 1949. *The Greatest Show on Earth*, 1952. *Road to Bali*, 1952.

Tangerine
As a glamorous nightclub singer in *The Fleet's In*, **Dorothy Lamour** finally wore something besides a sarong. The popular musical also starred Betty Hutton, William Holden, and Eddie Bracken. This song by Johnny Mercer (W) and Victor Schertzinger (M) was a hit record for Bob Eberly and Helen O'Connell who sang it in the movie with the Jimmy Dorsey Orchestra. British printing. $6

Injun Gal Heap Hep
Dorothy Lamour fans enjoyed her performance as a stripper who is romanced by silver miner **Dick Powell** in *Riding High*. Old-time vaudevillian **Victor Moore** (bottom) also appeared. $10

Burt Lancaster (born 1913). He started out as a circus acrobat, and had his first movie break in *The Killers* in 1946. His athletic abilities stood him in good stead in action westerns and swashbucklers, and his intense portrayals in more serious roles gained the respect of critics. He received a Best Actor Oscar in 1960 for *Elmer Gantry*, and the Venice Film Festival award in 1962 for his sensitive acting in *Birdman of Alcatraz*.

LANCASTER MOVIE COVERS: *I Walk Alone*, 1947. *From Here to Eternity*, 1953. *Apache*, 1954. *His Majesty O'Keefe*, 1954. *Vera Cruz*, 1954. *The Kentuckian*, 1955. *The Rose Tattoo*, 1955. *The Rainmaker*, 1956. *Gunfight at the OK Corral*, 1957. *Sweet Smell of*

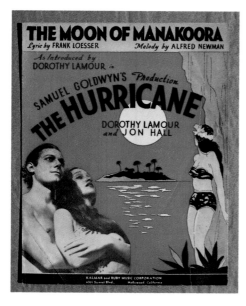

The Moon of Manakoora
Early work by Frank Loesser in Hollywood included the lyrics for this lovely melody by Alfred Newman introduced in Samuel Goldwyn's movie *The Hurricane*. Cover stars are **Jon Hall** and **Dorothy Lamour.** $6

Lovelight in the Starlight
Dorothy Lamour was a jungle maiden on the tropical island where **Ray Milland** crash lands his plane. Nature takes its course, and the two fall in love in *Her Jungle Love*. $5

Vera Cruz
Burt Lancaster and **Gary Cooper** play gunmen in Mexico during the 1866 Revolution, neither trusting the other in *Vera Cruz*, an adventure that ends with a climactic shootout finale. Title song by Sammy Cahn (W) and Hugo Friedhofer (M). $8

Carole Lombard (1908-1942). A delightful blonde comedienne and a fine dramatic actress, Carole Lombard was one of Hollywood's most glamorous stars of the 1930s. She worked her way up the ladder of stardom playing in Westerns and innocuous comedies including a stint with Mack Sennett in the late 1920s. She had extraordinary talent for both screwball comedy and intense drama. Her romance and subsequent marriage to Clark Gable was followed assiduously by legions of fans. Miss Lombard died tragically in a plane crash while flying home from a World War II bond rally.

LOMBARD MOVIE COVERS: *High Voltage*, 1929. *Safety in Numbers*, 1930. *White Woman*, 1933. *Bolero*, 1934. *The Gay Bride*, 1934. *We're Not Dressing*, 1934. *Rumba*, 1935. *The Princess Comes Across*, 1936. *Swing High, Swing Low*, 1937. *True Confession*, 1937. *Fools for Scandal*, 1938. *Made for Each Other*, 1939. *To Be or Not To Be*, 1942.

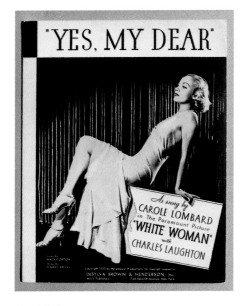

Yes, My Dear
In *White Woman*, **Carole Lombard** played a lady of questionable virtue, who marries Charles Laughton to avoid deportation. The marriage of convenience soon foundered on the rocks of infidelity. Mack Gordon (W) and Harry Revel (M) wrote the song. *Collection of Harold Jacobs.* $95

Panamania
Carole Lombard and **Fred MacMurray** played a married couple in show business who get divorced when conflicting engagements separate them in *Swing High, Swing Low*. All ends well when true love wins out. Sam Coslow and Al Siegel wrote this song. $5

Left:
Made for Each Other
The romantic drama *Made for Each Other* was made to order for **Carole Lombard** and **James Stewart**, as a young married couple adjusting to each other and to their meddlesome in-laws. Title song was written by Harry Tobias (W) and Oscar Levant (M). $60

Bless 'em All
To Be or Not to Be, **Carole Lombard**'s last movie, was released after her death. **Jack Benny** played her husband, the leader of a Shakespearean acting group on tour in Nazi-occupied Poland, who has a great time impersonating a Gestapo officer and a Nazi professor. *Collection of Harold Jacobs.* $40

Woman of the River
Sophia Loren was steamy, sexy, passionate, and beautiful in the foreign film *La Donna del Fiume*, renamed *Woman of the River* in its American release. She attracted favorable attention and her career took off. She is seen on the cover with **Gerard Oury**. $20

Sophia Loren (born 1934) A beautiful, statuesque, voluptuous Italian actress, and a former beauty contest winner in Italy, Sophie Loren was the protégée of Italian producer Carlo Ponti, whom she eventually married. She is an international star, and has made movies in both the United States and Europe. She won a Best Actress Academy Award in 1961 for her moving performance in the Italian film *Two Women*, and a special honorary Oscar from the Academy in 1991.

LOREN MOVIE COVERS: *Woman of the River*, 1955. *Boy on a Dolphin*, 1957. *Legend of the Lost*, 1957. *Scandal in Sorrento*, 1957. *Desire Under the Elms*, 1958. *Houseboat*, 1958. *The Key*, 1958. *The Black Orchid*, 1959. *That Kind of Woman*, 1959. *A Breath of Scandal*, 1960. *It Started in Naples*, 1960. *The Millionairess*, 1960. *Yesterday, Today and Tomorrow*, 1963. *The Fall of the Roman Empire*, 1964. *Lady "L,"* 1965. *Arabesque*, 1966. *Judith*, 1966. *More Than a Miracle*, 1967. *Sunflower*, 1969. *Man of La Mancha*, 1972. *Brass Target*, 1978.

Myrna Loy (1905-1993). Though cast in exotic Oriental roles in her early career, Miss Loy broke out of the rut and found her niche in the 1930s with William Powell in the popular *Thin Man* series. The two were paired as sophisticated detectives Nick and Nora Charles, and also made other movies together. She had a ladylike bearing and poise, and a talent for both comedy and dramatic roles.

LOY MOVIE COVERS: *The Black Watch,* 1929. *The Squall,* 1929. *Cock O' the Walk,* 1930. *Jazz Cinderella,* 1930. *Rogue of the Rio Grande,* 1931. *The Barbarian,* 1933. *The Prizefighter and the Lady,* 1933. *Broadway Bill,* 1934. *After the Thin Man,* 1936. *The Great Ziegfeld,* 1936. *To Mary - With Love,* 1936. *The Rains Came,* 1939. *The Best Years of Our Lives,* 1946. *So Goes My Love,* 1946. *Song of the Thin Man,* 1947. *Mr. Blandings Builds His Dream House,* 1948. *That Dangerous Age,* 1949. *Cheaper by the Dozen,* 1950. *Airport,* 1975.

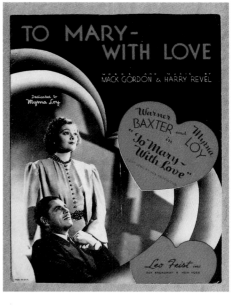

Gypsy Charmer
The Squall starred **Myrna Loy** as a wild Hungarian gypsy who tried to seduce every man in sight until her husband took her in hand. It was an early talking picture made with Vitaphone sound. The song was written by Grant Clarke (W) and Harry Akst (M). $10

To Mary—with Love
Myrna Loy and **Warner Baxter** co-starred in *To Mary With Love,* a marital drama with Myrna remaining steadfast and true to her husband who lets success go to his head. Title song was written by Mack Gordon (W) and Harry Revel (M). $7

The Fall of Love
The incredible lineup of stars in *The Fall of the Roman Empire* was staggering. Besides the luscious **Sophia Loren,** the epic period drama included **Alec Guinness, James Mason, Christopher Plummer, Omar Sharif, Anthony Quayle**, and **Stephen Boyd.** Dimitri Tiomkin, who wrote this song with words by Ned Washington, also composed the score, which was nominated for an Oscar. $5

Arabesque
Sophia Loren and **Gregory Peck** co-starred in the exciting thriller *Arabesque*, with Peck playing an American professor who gets involved in murder and intrigue. Theme music is arranged as a piano solo by composer Henry Mancini. $4

My Dream House
Mr. Blandings Builds His Dream House was a delight from beginning to end. **Myrna Loy** was perfect as the patient wife playing opposite **Cary Grant** as her distraught husband, who decides to build a home in the country with all the attendant woes, including a bungled search for well water and a careful selection of paint. *Collection of Harold Jacobs.* $150

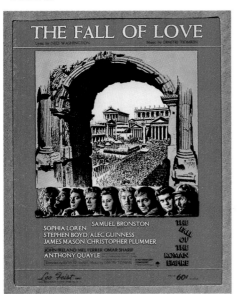

Ida Lupino (1914-1995). This London born actress was the scion of a famous British theatrical family. She started her career in English movies in 1933 but soon went to Hollywood. Though she was a successful dramatic actress at Warner Brothers for many years and was named Best Actress in 1943 by the New York Film Critics for her role in *The Hard Way*, she did not consider herself a great actress. She branched out into the production side of movies and television and enjoyed a second successful career while still acting occasionally in movies and television.

LUPINO MOVIE COVERS: *The Gay Desperado*, 1936. *One Rainy Afternoon*, 1936. *Fight for Your Lady*, 1937. *Moontide*, 1942. *Thank Your Lucky Stars*, 1943. *Pillow to Post*, 1945. *The Man I Love*, 1946. *Deep Valley*, 1947. *Escape Me Never*, 1947. *Road House*, 1948.

The World Is Mine
The Gay Desperado was a musical that featured Metropolitan opera tenor **Nino Martini**, who is kidnapped by a Mexican bandit along with an American heiress, played by **Ida Lupino.** Holt Marvell (W) and George Posford (M) wrote this song performed by Martini in the movie. $8

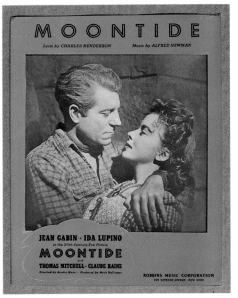

Moontide
In *Moontide,* **Ida Lupino** played a suicidal girl, who is given a reason to live by a rough seaman, **Jean Gabin,** who has problems of his own. The romantic title song was written by Charles Henderson (W) and Alfred Newman (M). $9

Sympathy
This graceful waltz by Rudolf Friml was one of the original songs from the 1912 Broadway operetta *The Firefly*. **Jeanette MacDonald** and **Allan Jones** co-starred in the screen version introducing another generation to the beauty of Friml's music. $4

Smilin' Through
Jeanette MacDonald and her co-star **Gene Raymond** enjoyed making *Smilin' Through,* their only movie together. They were married in real life. This theme song published in England was written by Arthur A. Penn. $9

Jeanette MacDonald (1907-1965). She was a bright star in Broadway musicals before coming to Hollywood in 1929. With grace and charm and a certain glow about her, she became a popular movie star, best remembered as Nelson Eddy's singing partner in several movie operettas, and as the heroine opposite Clark Gable in *San Francisco.*

MACDONALD MOVIE COVERS: *The Love Parade*, 1929. *Let's Go Native*, 1930. *The Lottery Bride*, 1930. *Monte Carlo*, 1930. *The Vagabond King*, 1930. *One Hour with You*, 1932. *The Cat and the Fiddle*, 1934. *The Merry Widow*, 1934. *Naughty Marietta*, 1935. *Rose Marie*, 1936. *San Francisco*, 1936. *The Firefly*, 1937. *Maytime*, 1937. *The Girl of the Golden West*, 1938. *Sweethearts*, 1938. *Broadway Serenade*, 1939. *Bitter Sweet*, 1940. *New Moon*, 1940. *I Married an Angel*, 1942. *Smilin' Through*, 1941. *Cairo*, 1942. *Three Daring Daughters*, 1948. *The Sun Comes Up*, 1949.

You're an Angel
Jeanette MacDonald was *The Lottery Bride* who married a miner in the Yukon, then falls for his younger brother, **John Garrick.** Songs were written by J. Keirn Brennan (W) and Rudolf Friml (M). *Collection of James Nelson Brown.* $40

Dorothy McGuire (born 1918). A lovely leading lady, she starred on the Broadway stage and in radio soap opera before succumbing to Hollywood's entreaties to star in a film version of her stage show *Claudia*. She has been commended for her sensitive in-depth performances in movies for over 30 years, and gracefully moved into more mature roles.

McGUIRE MOVIE COVERS: *The Enchanted Cottage*, 1945. *Till the End of Time*, 1946. *Callaway Went Thataway*, 1951. *Three Coins in the Fountain*, 1954. *Friendly Persuasion*, 1956. *A Summer Place*, 1959. *The Dark At the Top of the Stairs*, 1960. *Flight of the Doves*, 1971.

Till the End of Time
Dorothy McGuire played a war widow opposite current Hollywood heartthrob **Guy Madison** in the romantic wartime movie *Till the End of Time*. Title song was based on a Chopin Polonaise. $4

Shirley MacLaine (born 1934). She started dancing when she was only two years old, and danced her way into a top Broadway show when the lead broke a leg, and Shirley, as understudy, took over. Shortly after, she was summoned to Hollywood to appear in movies. Within a short time she proved herself a capable actress in both comedy and drama, and since has been nominated four times for Best Actress Academy Awards. She finally won in 1983 for her moving performance in *Terms of Endearment*.

MacLAINE MOVIE COVERS: *Ask Any Girl*, 1954. *The Trouble with Harry*, 1955. *Some Came Running*, 1958. *The Apartment*, 1960. *Can-Can*, 1960. *All in a Night's Work*, 1961. *My Geisha*, 1962. *Two for the Seesaw*, 1962. *What a Way to Go*, 1964. *The Yellow Rolls Royce*, 1964. *John Goldfarb Please Come Home*, 1965. *Woman Times Seven*, 1967. *The Bliss of Mrs. Blossom*, 1968. *Sweet Charity*, 1969. *Change of Seasons*, 1980. *Terms of Endearment*, 1983.

Some Came Running Theme
James Jones's novel *Some Came Running* was adapted for the screen with a strong cast, including **Shirley MacLaine** as a good-time party girl who falls for returning GI **Frank Sinatra,** with **Dean Martin** playing a small-time gambler. MacLaine was honored with an Academy Award nomination for Best Actress for her vivid portrayal. Song by Sammy Cahn (W) and James Van Heusen (M). $4

Friendly Persuasion
Dorothy McGuire and **Gary Cooper** co-starred in *Friendly Persuasion*, as a Quaker couple trying to survive the tribulations of the Civil War. The title song was written by Paul Francis Webster (W) and Dimitri Tiomkin (M) who also wrote the score for the movie. $7

If My Friends Could See Me Now!
This song by Dorothy Fields (W) and Cy Coleman (M) was **Shirley MacLaine**'s big number in *Sweet Charity*, a movie about the life of a worldly dance hall hostess and her dreams of domesticity. It was written in 1965 for Bob Fosse's popular Broadway musical. $4

Terms of Endearment Theme
Shirley MacLaine won the Best Actress Academy Award for her role as **Debra Winger**'s mother in *Terms of Endearment*. This sensitive movie also won the Best Picture award, plus additional awards to Jack Nicholson for Best Supporting Actor, and James L. Brooks for Best Director and Best Screenplay. $6

Fred MacMurray (1908-1991). He started his career in show business as a saxophonist and singer with a dance band, and worked as a lowly extra in movies before getting a contract with Paramount in the 1930s. He generally played the lead in light comedies, but could also handle dramatic roles, such as the scheming insurance man in *Double Indemnity* with Barbara Stanwyck. In the 1960s he starred in the popular television series *My Three Sons*, and also appeared in several Disney movies.

MacMURRAY MOVIE COVERS: *The Gilded Lily*, 1935. *The Princess Comes Across*, 1936. *The Texas Rangers*, 1936. *Trail of the Lonesome Pine*, 1936 . *Champagne Waltz*, 1937. *Swing High, Swing Low*, 1937. *Cocoanut Grove*, 1938. *Men With Wings*, 1938. *Sing You Sinners (a.k.a. The Unholy Beebes)*, 1938. *Cafe Society*, 1939. *Little Old New York*, 1940. *Star Spangled Rhythm*, 1942. *The Forest Rangers*, 1942. *And the Angels Sing*, 1944. *Practically Yours*, 1944. *Where Do We Go From Here?* 1945. *A Miracle Can Happen*, 1947. *The Egg and I*, 1947. *Suddenly It's Spring*, 1947. *An Innocent Affair*, 1948. *The Miracle of the Bells*, 1948. *A Millionaire for Christy*, 1951. *Callaway Went Thataway*, 1951. *The Moonlighter*, 1953. *The Caine Mutiny*, 1954. *Woman's World*, 1954. *The Far Horizons*, 1955. *The Absent-Minded Professor*, 1961. *Bon Voyage*, 1962. *Kisses for My President*, 1964. *Follow Me Boys*, 1966.

The Miracle of the Bells
In the sentimental movie *The Miracle of the Bells* **Fred MacMurray** arranges for his deceased love, **Alida Valli**, to be buried in her home town, where a miracle takes place. **Frank Sinatra** portrayed a priest. $7

Steve McQueen (1930-1980). With a troubled childhood including abandonment by his father and a stint in reform school, Steve McQueen rose above it in his early twenties when he discovered his affinity and talent for dramatics. After some noteworthy performances on the New York stage, he started making movies and also made a big splash in TV's *"Wanted" Dead or Alive*. Memorable roles by McQueen include *The Great Escape, The Sand Pebbles*, and *Papillon*. He was a major star when he was cut down in his prime by cancer.

McQUEEN MOVIE COVERS: *The Honeymoon Machine*, 1961. *The War Lover*, 1962. *The Great Escape*, 1963. *Love With the Proper Stranger*, 1964. *The Cincinnati Kid*, 1965. *Nevada Smith*, 1966. *The Thomas Crown Affair*, 1968. *Bullitt*, 1968. *The Honeymoon*, 1968. *Papillon*, 1973. *The Hunter*, 1980.

Nevada Smith
Nevada Smith followed the further exploits of the colorful character in Harold Robbins's novel *The Carpetbaggers*. **Steve McQueen** in the title role tracks down his parents' killers in a taut drama set in California Gold Rush days. The haunting theme song by Hal David (W) and Alfred Newman (M) describes his quest. $4

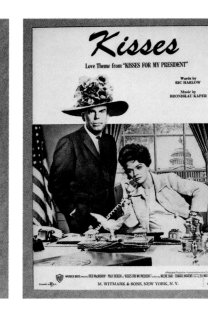

All At Once
Where Do We Go from Here? was a whimsical war movie with **Fred MacMurray** asking a magic genie to get him into the army, but is mistakenly sent to the wrong war at Valley Forge with George Washington. **Joan Leslie** (top) and **June Haver** (MacMurray's future wife) were the two lovely ladies in the piece. Score was written by Kurt Weill with words by Ira Gershwin. $6

Kisses
The amusing premise in *Kisses for My President* is that **Polly Bergen** is the first lady President with husband **Fred MacMurray** in the secondary domestic role. Title song by Ric Harlow (W) and Bronislau Kaper (M). $8

Fredric March (1897-1975). He served as an artillery lieutenant during World War I, after which he studied acting at the University of Wisconsin. Stage work led to a distinguished career in the movies, with two Best Actor Oscars to his credit—for *Dr. Jekyll and Mr. Hyde* in 1932 and *The Best Years of Our Lives* in 1946. He continued a parallel career on the New York stage and won the New York Drama Critics award for *Long Day's Journey Into Night* in 1956.

MARCH MOVIE COVERS: *Good Dame,* 1934. *A Star Is Born,* 1937. *So Ends Our Night,* 1941. *The Best Years of Our Lives,* 1946. *Middle of the Night,* 1959. *Seven Days in May,* 1964.

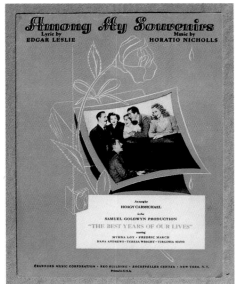

So Ends Our Night
Erich Maria Remarque's book *So Ends Our Night* made a tense dramatic movie co-starring **Fredric March and Frances Dee** (right) as husband and wife and **Margaret Sullavan** as a persecuted Jewish woman fleeing from the Nazi regime. *Collection of Harold Jacobs.* $25 ($200)

Martin and Lewis. This popular comedy team during the 1950s had Dean Martin playing the straight man, and Jerry Lewis the slightly slow-witted misunderstood comic. They made 16 films together before splitting up in 1956, and branching out on independent ventures.

MARTIN AND LEWIS MOVIE COVERS: *My Friend Irma,* 1949. *My Friend Irma Goes West,* 1950. *At War with the Army,* 1951. *Sailor Beware,* 1951. *That's My Boy,* 1951. *Jumping Jacks,* 1952. *The Stooge,* 1952. *The Caddy,* 1953. *Scared Stiff,* 1953. *Money from Home,* 1953. *Living It Up,* 1954. *Three Ring Circus,* 1954. *Artists and Models,* 1955. *You're Never Too Young,* 1955. *Hollywood or Bust,* 1956. *Pardners,* 1956. (Also see listings for **Dean Martin and Jerry Lewis**).

A Star Is Born
Fredric March and **Janet Gaynor** starred in the original version of *A Star Is Born*, about the heartbreak and decline of an actor whose wife's celebrity exceeds his own. The movie received many Oscar nominations, including Best Picture, Actor, Actress, Director, and Assistant Director. With strong competition that year, it only won the writing award for best original story by William Wellman and Robert Carson. *Collection of Harold Jacobs.* $150

You and Your Beautiful Eyes
Hollywood's newest comedy team **Dean Martin** and **Jerry Lewis** co-starred in the comic romp *At War with the Army*, with their usual impossible situations involving the pretty girl, Polly Bergen. Songs were by Mack David (W) and Jerry Livingston (M). $7

Among My Souvenirs
The Best Years of Our Lives was an acclaimed movie winning seven Academy Awards including Best Picture. **Fredric March** won for Best Actor, playing a returning veteran of World War II adjusting to civilian life. Gathered around the piano is the cast—**March, Myrna Loy, Teresa Wright, Dana Andrews, Virginia Mayo, and Hoagy Carmichael** at the keyboard. $5

Never Before
This time around, **Martin** and **Lewis** are in the Navy in the hilarious movie *Sailor Beware*. Their pulchritudinous co-star on the cover is **Corinne Calvet**. Songs by Mack David (W) and Jerry Livingston (M). $6

The Parachute Jump
Jumping Jacks gave Martin and Lewis a great opportunity for their unique clowning. **Jerry Lewis** played a civilian entertainer at a training school for paratroopers who, through a mix-up, ends up jumping from a plane. **Dean Martin** sang the David/Livingston songs to his love interest, pretty **Mona Freeman.** $10

Me 'n' You 'n' the Moon
Martin and Lewis fans loved *Pardners*, a parody of every Western ever made, with Dean Martin playing a ranch foreman fighting the bad guys and Jerry Lewis, an Eastern tenderfoot who tries to help out. Songs for this movie were by Sammy Cahn (W) and James Van Heusen (M). $10

Bells Are Ringing
Dean Martin was a good-looking, capable singer who had no trouble forging a career as a single. The Broadway hit musical, *Bells Are Ringing*, was brought to the screen with Martin rendering the timeless songs of Betty Comden/Adolph Green (W) and Jule Styne (M). **Judy Holliday** was an incandescent talent whose life was snuffed out by cancer after making this, her last movie. $5

Dean Martin (1917-1995). He continued his film career after his partnership with Jerry Lewis folded, maturing into a versatile actor who could handle dramatic parts as well as lighter roles. He was also a top recording star, and a nightclub and television entertainer, popular with his public to the end. (Also see **Martin and Lewis**).

MARTIN MOVIE COVERS: *Ten Thousand Bedrooms*, 1957. *Some Came Running*, 1958. *Career*, 1959. *Rio Bravo*, 1959. *Bells Are Ringing*, 1960. *Oceans Eleven*, 1960. *Who Was That Lady?* 1960. *Ada*, 1961. *All in a Night's Work*, 1961. *Who's Got the Action?* 1962. *Four for Texas*, 1963. *Toys in the Attic*, 1963. *Who's Been Sleeping in My Bed?* 1963. *Kiss Me Stupid*, 1964. *Robin and the Seven Hoods*, 1964. *What a Way to Go*, 1964. *The Sons of Katie Elder*, 1965. *Murderers' Row*, 1966. *The Silencers*, 1966. *Texas Across the River*, 1966. *Rough Night in Jericho*, 1967. *Bandolero*, 1968. *Five Card Stud*, 1968. *Something Big*, 1971.

How Do You Speak to an Angel
Living It Up was a comedy that illustrated the power of publicity. **Jerry Lewis** was built up into a celebrity as a hero suffering from radiation poisoning, though it was really sinus trouble. **Dean Martin** was his doctor. Songs for this movie were by Bob Hilliard (W) and Jule Styne (M). $5 *($16)*

The Devil Rides in Jericho
Normally easygoing, laid-back **Dean Martin** took on an uncharacteristic role as a mean, sadistic bad guy in *Rough Night in Jericho* with **George Peppard** as the U.S. marshal who goes after him, and Jean Simmons as the female lead. $4

Lee Marvin (born 1924). After service in the Marines during World War II, he took up acting. He made his screen debut in 1951, and with his tough demeanor and hard-eyed, no-nonsense face was soon typecast as a heavy in a slew of pictures. He finally reached full-fledged stardom in 1965 with his dual role in *Cat Ballou* for which he was awarded the Best Actor Oscar.

MARVIN MOVIE COVERS: *The Professionals*, 1966. *The Dirty Dozen*, 1967. *Paint Your Wagon*, 1969. *Monte Walsh*, 1970. *Emperor of the North*, 1973.

The Bramble Bush
The Dirty Dozen was a violent wartime action film about 12 soldiers who are convicted of various capital crimes and sentenced to death. They are offered a reprieve, if they liquidate a Nazi generals' hideout, which they proceed to do with great gusto. The 12 convicts appear on the cover with **Lee Marvin,** top left. The theme song has little to do with the movie, but is a pleasing refrain by Mack David and Frank De Vol. $8

The Marx Brothers. Chico (1886-1961), Harpo (1888-1964), Groucho (1890-1977), and Zeppo (1901-1979) came to Hollywood from Broadway's vaudeville stage. They appeared in several nutty comedies in the 1930s, featuring their peculiar brand of slapstick humor that was a big hit with the public. An earlier song cover of some rarity is the large size "Under the Summer Moon" by Leonard (Chico) Marx and Lem Trombley with the four very young brothers, as they appeared in the stage comedy *Home Again*.

MARX BROTHERS MOVIE COVERS: *Animal Crackers*, 1930. *Horse Feathers*, 1932. *A Night at the Opera*, 1935. *A Day at the Races*, 1937. *At the Circus*, 1939. *Go West*, 1940. *The Big Store*, 1941. *A Night in Casablanca*, 1946. *Copacabana (with Groucho only)*, 1947. *Love Happy*, 1950. *Mr. Music (with Groucho only)*, 1950.

Why Am I So Romantic?
The hit Broadway musical *Animal Crackers* was brought to the screen funnier than ever with the crazy antics of the four **Marx Brothers**—Chico, Groucho, Harpo, and Zeppo. This song from the movie was written by Bert Kalmar and Harry Ruby. $50

Ev'ryone Says "I Love You"
The zany **Marx Brothers** pleased their fans with more of their nonsense in *Horse Feathers*. Set on a a college campus, Groucho, as president, tries to build up a football team. $12 *($33)*

Alone
A Night at the Opera is thought by many to be the **Marx Brothers'** funniest film. Chico, Harpo, and Groucho co-starred, providing a laugh a minute. Cover stars **Allan Jones** and **Kitty Carlisle** were the romantic interest who sang this Arthur Freed/Nacio Herb Brown song in the movie. $10

A Message from the Man in the Moon
Crazy goings-on in *A Day at the Races* starred Groucho as a horse doctor, Harpo as a jockey, and Chico as a track tipster. The movie had plenty of good songs with the able singing of **Allan Jones,** seen on cover with **Maureen O'Sullivan.** $20

Who's Sorry Now
Fans of the **Marx Brothers** loved the boys in *A Night in Casablanca*, set in the North African city complete with post-war Nazi intrigue. Groucho managed the Hotel Casablanca, Chico owned the Yellow Camel taxi service, and Harpo worked for an escaped Nazi. This 1923 song used in the film was composed by Bert Kalmar and Harry Ruby (W) and Ted Snyder (M). $20

Virginia Mayo (born 1920). She was a beautiful blonde show girl before entering films in the 1940s. With her vibrant, voluptuous good looks, she was especially suitable for luscious Technicolor movies. She was a frequent co-star of comics Bob Hope and Danny Kaye, and also made a movie with the future President of the United States (Ronald Reagan in *The Girl from Jones Beach*). She was always an asset in her movies and well-liked by audiences.

MAYO MOVIE COVERS: *The Princess and the Pirate*, 1944. *Wonder Man*, 1945. *The Kid from Brooklyn*, 1946. *Out of the Blue*, 1947. *The Secret Life of Walter Mitty*, 1947. *A Song Is Born*, 1948. *Always Leave Them Laughing*, 1949. *The Girl from Jones Beach*, 1949. *She's Working Her Way Through College*, 1952. *She's Back on Broadway*, 1953. *Pearl of the South Pacific*, 1955. *The Proud Ones*, 1956. *The Big Land*, 1957. *Painting the Clouds with Sunshine*, 1959. *Jet Over the Atlantic*, 1960.

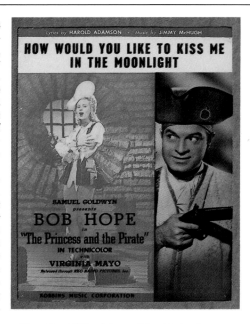

How Would You Like to Kiss Me in the Moonlight
Virginia Mayo as the princess, with comedian **Bob Hope**, tried to elude a throng of evil buccaneers in 1740s Jamaica in *The Princess and the Pirate*. This charming song was written by Harold Adamson (W) and Jimmy McHugh (M). $6

Walter Matthau (born 1920). With his gruff voice, slouchy posture, and craggy rather homely appearance, Mr. Matthau specializes in character and comic roles. In World War II he was a radioman-gunner on Army Air Force bombers, after which he studied acting and began appearing in summer stock, eventually making it to Broadway as star of the big hit show *The Odd Couple*. In Hollywood he won the Best Supporting Actor Academy Award for *The Fortune Cookie* in 1966, and two nominations for Best Actor in *Kotch* (1971) and *The Sunshine Boys* (1975).

MATTHAU MOVIE COVERS: *The Fortune Cookie*, 1966. *A Guide for the Married Man*, 1967. *The Odd Couple*, 1968. *Cactus Flower*, 1969. *Hello Dolly!*, 1969. *Kotch*, 1971. *Plaza Suite*, 1971. *Pete 'n' Tillie*, 1972. *The Front Page*, 1974. *The Survivors*, 1983. *Pirates*, 1986.

Before the Parade Passes By
The hit Broadway show *Hello Dolly!* was brought to the screen with **Barbra Streisand** in the title role of Dolly the Matchmaker and **Walter Matthau** as her swain. Jerry Herman wrote the score that included this big production number that is said to have exceeded $2 million.$6

The Odd Couple
Walter Matthau hit the big time on Broadway in 1965 as one half of *The Odd Couple*, a role created for him by Neil Simon, and one that he repeated with great success on the screen with **Jack Lemmon** as Felix Unger. *The Odd Couple Theme* used throughout the movie was composed by Neal Hefti, with words by Sammy Cahn. $5

Painting the Clouds with Sunshine
Virginia Mayo and **Dennis Morgan** co-starred in *Painting the Clouds with Sunshine*, a remake of 1929's *Gold Diggers of Broadway*, only this time the gold diggers are in Las Vegas. The movie featured lively dance routines by Gene Nelson (bottom center) and songs by Mr. Morgan. $5

Ray Milland (1905-1986). This Welsh-born actor started out in Hollywood in the 1930s playing second leads, but soon graduated to leading man roles. Handsome and debonair, he wasn't taken seriously as an actor until his riveting performance as an alcoholic in *The Lost Weekend* in 1945, a role for which he won the Best Actor Academy Award. His long list of screen credits ranges over 50 years, from 1929 to 1979.

MILLAND MOVIE COVERS: *Gilded Lily*, 1935. *The Big Broadcast of 1937*, 1936. *The Jungle Princess*, 1936. *Three Smart Girls*, 1936. *Easy Living*, 1937. *Her Jungle Love*, 1938. *Men With Wings*, 1938. *Say It in French*, 1938. *Tropic Holiday*, 1938. *French Without Tears*, 1939. *Arise My Love*, 1940. *Irene*, 1940. *I Wanted Wings*, 1941. *The Major and the Minor*, 1942. *Reap the Wild Wind*, 1942. *Star Spangled Rhythm*, 1942. *Kitty*, 1945. *California*, 1946. *Golden Earrings*, 1947. *It Happens Every Spring*, 1949. *Copper Canyon*, 1950. *Circle of Danger*, 1951. *Something to Live For*, 1952. *Let's Do It Again*, 1953. *Lisbon*, 1956. *High Flight*, 1957.

Golden Earrings
Ray Milland played a British intelligence agent on a secret mission who takes refuge in a gypsy caravan with **Marlene Dietrich** playing a seductive gypsy in *Golden Earrings*. Exotic Marlene sang the title song in the film. $4

Robert Mitchum (1917-1997). He portrayed tough characters with an air of casual nonchalance, giving the appearance of not really acting at all. He made approximately 100 films in his lengthy career, and in the 1980s starred as Pug Henry in the multi-chapter television adaptation of Herman Wouk's best-selling novel *The Winds of War* and its sequel *War and Remembrance*.

MITCHUM MOVIE COVERS: *Rachel and the Stranger*, 1948. *Where Danger Lives*, 1950. *His Kind of Woman*, 1951. *One Minute to Zero*, 1952. *Second Chance*, 1953. *Not as a Stranger*, 1955. *Bandido*, 1956. *Foreign Intrigue*, 1956. *Thunder Road*, 1958. *The Wonderful Country*, 1959. *The Grass Is Greener*, 1960. *Home from the Hill*, 1960. *The Sundowners*, 1960. *The Last*

Tonight Will Live
Tropic Holiday was a romantic comedy set in Mexico, starring **Ray Milland** and **Dorothy Lamour**, with a supporting cast that included **Martha Raye** and **Bob Burns.** Song was written by Ned Washington and Agustin Lara. $5

Time I Saw Archie, 1961. *Two for the Seesaw*, 1962. *Man in the Middle*, 1964. *The Way West*, 1967. *Villa Rides*, 1968. *El Dorado*, 1967. *Five Card Stud*, 1968.

Rachel
Robert Mitchum played the stranger in *Rachel and the Stranger*, an American Indian scout who falls in love with co-star Loretta Young over the objections of a jealous William Holden. Waldo Salt (W) and Roy Webb (M) wrote the songs. $18

It Happens Every Spring
Ray Milland plays a scientist who invents a miraculous baseball and becomes famous as a star baseball player in *It Happens Every Spring*. Co-starring in the comedy were **Jean Peters** and **Paul Douglas**. The title song by Mack Gordon (W) and Josef Myrow (M) became a popular hit when recorded by Frank Sinatra. $8

Home from the Hill
Robert Mitchum played a Southern land-owner with two sons, one illegitimate. **Eleanor Parker** was his wife, with **George Peppard** and **George Hamilton** as the sons. Title song was written by Mack David (W) and Bronislau Kaper (M). $6

El Dorado
Robert Mitchum played a sheriff with a drinking problem in the rip-snortin' *El Dorado*. Gunfighter **John Wayne** helps him clean up his act and roust the bad guys out of town. Title song by John Gabriel (W) and Nelson Riddle (M). $8 *($22)*

Marilyn Monroe (1926-1962). In a class by herself, Marilyn Monroe had an extraordinary appeal that enabled her to rise from humble beginnings as an illegitimate child to world renown as Hollywood's newest sex goddess in the 1950s. Beautiful, curvaceous, and sensual, with a touching vulnerability and a riveting screen presence, she became a superstar, only to succumb, as so many had before her, to an overdose of barbiturates and alcohol.

MONROE MOVIE COVERS: *Ladies of the Chorus*, 1949. *Gentlemen Prefer Blondes*, 1953. *How to Marry a Millionaire*, 1953. *Niagara*, 1953. *There's No Business Like Show Business*, 1954. *River of No Return*, 1954. *The Seven Year Itch*, 1955. *Bus Stop*, 1956. *The Prince and the Show Girl*, 1957. *Some Like It Hot*, 1959. *Let's Make Love*, 1960. *The Misfits*, 1961.

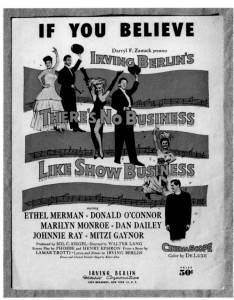

If You Believe
Marilyn Monroe, at her provocative best, was **Donald O'Connor**'s sweetheart in There's *No Business Like Show Business*, the story of a show business family with **Ethel Merman** and **Dan Dailey** as the Mom and Dad, and **Mitzi Gaynor** as the sister. Irving Berlin's songs, both old and new, completed the package. $10

Down in the Meadow
River of No Return co-starred **Marilyn Monroe** and Robert Mitchum in the story of a dance hall girl who finds true love with a farmer in the Canadian wilderness. Songs were written by Ken Darby (W) and Lionel Newman (M). *Collection of Harold Jacobs.* $30

The Bus Stop Song
In *Bus Stop*, **Marilyn Monroe** played the young singer, Cherie, who had pretensions of becoming a movie star in Hollywood. But co-star **Don Murray** has other ideas. He sees her as his angel girl and wants to marry her. Marilyn's big number in *Bus Stop* was "That Old Black Magic," sung in a cheap nightclub to a bunch of rough cowboys. Ken Darby wrote this title song. $35

Let's Make Love
Marilyn Monroe, as a successful Broadway star, is wooed by **Yves Montand** in the lighthearted comedy *Let's Make Love.* Title song was written by Sammy Cahn (W) and James Van Heusen (M). $15

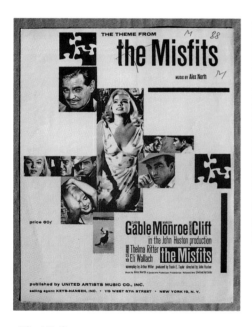

The Misfits
The Misfits, the final movie of two legendary stars, **Clark Gable** and **Marilyn Monroe,** had tragic overtones. Gable and co-star **Montgomery Clift** played a couple of down-and-out cowboys after wild mustangs, to be sold for dog food. Marilyn was the softhearted divorcée, who tried to dissuade them from their cruelty. Gable did his own stunts, which some said contributed to a fatal heart attack a few weeks after the movie was completed. Marilyn died of an apparent drug overdose within the year. $20 *($40)*

Paul Newman (born 1925). A Navy Air Corps radioman in the Pacific during World War II, he later studied economics before changing to acting at the Yale School of Drama. After a successful stage appearance in *Picnic* he was snapped up by Hollywood. He has starred in many critically acclaimed movies, and was nominated several times for an Oscar, finally winning the cherished award in 1986 for *The Color of Money.* His first foray into production was *Rachel, Rachel,* a stellar offering that earned Academy Award nominations for Best Picture, Best Actress, and Best Screenplay, and brought him great honor. He is married to actress Joanne Woodward.

NEWMAN MOVIE COVERS: *Until They Sail,* 1957. *The Long Hot Summer,* 1958. *From the Terrace,* 1960. *The Hustler,* 1961. *Paris Blues,* 1961. *Hud,* 1963. *A New Kind of Love,* 1963. *The Prize,* 1963. *What a Way to Go,* 1964. *The Outrage,* 1964. *Lady "L,"* 1965. *Harper,* 1966. *Torn Curtain,* 1966. *Cool Hand Luke,* 1967. *Hombre,* 1967. *Butch Cassidy and the Sundance Kid,* 1969. *Winning,* 1969. *W.U.S.A.,* 1970. *Sometimes a Great Notion,* 1971. *The Life and Times of Judge Roy Bean,* 1972. *The Sting,* 1973. *Absence of Malice,* 1981.

Torn Curtain Theme
Alfred Hitchcock's 50th film *Torn Curtain* was not considered one of his best. **Paul Newman** gave his usual stellar performance as a scientist on a secret spy mission in East Berlin, with **Julie Andrews** cast as his secretary/lover. John Addison wrote the music to this love song, with words by Jay Livingston and Ray Evans. $7

Jack Nicholson (born 1937). He knocked around Hollywood for several years before getting his first real break in *Easy Rider* (1969), for which he received the first of many Oscar nominations. Other nominations were for the films *Five Easy Pieces, The Last Detail,* and *Chinatown.* He finally won the Best Actor Award for *One Flew Over the Cuckoo's Nest*

Down Here on the Ground
In *Cool Hand Luke,* **Paul Newman** gave a convincing portrayal of a victim of the Southern prison system, and earned a nomination for Best Actor Academy Award. Though he didn't win, George Kennedy, the brutal prison guard, won for Best Supporting Actor. The theme song was by Gale Garnett (W) and Lalo Schifrin (M). $8 *($16)*

Stand By Your Man
Jack Nicholson played a young concert pianist who abandoned his career and his safe niche in a wealthy family to search for his identity in *Five Easy Pieces.* His sensitive portrayal received an Oscar nomination for Best Actor, but he lost out to George C. Scott for *Patton.* The song by Tammy Wynette and Billy Sherrill became a big hit record. $6

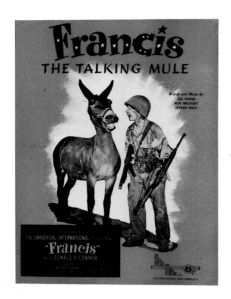

Francis the Talking Mule
Donald O'Connor played a trouble-prone lieutenant who gets involved with a talking mule in *Francis*, the first movie in the popular Francis series. The talking mule, with its voice dubbed by Chill Wills, stole the show and became a drawing card for movie-goers who followed his further adventures in six more *Francis* flicks. *Collection of Harold Jacobs.* $40

Gregory Peck (born 1916). One of Hollywood's most durable stars, Mr. Peck is still a handsome and dependable leading man. He received many Oscar nominations for his fine work, eventually winning the coveted award for his portrayal of a lawyer in *To Kill a Mockingbird* in 1962. He is one of Hollywood's "movers and shakers," a distinguished citizen, active in many causes and an ardent supporter of the film industry. His efforts have been rewarded with the Medal of Freedom Award, the Jean Hersholt Humanitarian Award, and the American Film Institute's Lifetime Achievement Award.

PECK MOVIE COVERS: *Spellbound,* 1945. *Duel in the Sun,* 1946. *Captain Horatio Hornblower,* 1951. *The World in His Arms,* 1952. *Night People,* 1954. *Designing Woman,* 1957. *Beloved Infidel,* 1959. *On the Beach,* 1959. *The Guns of Navarone,* 1961. *How the West Was Won,* 1962. *To Kill a Mockingbird,* 1962. *Arabesque,* 1966. *The Chairman,* 1969. *Mackenna's Gold,* 1969. *I Walk the Line,* 1970. *The Omen,* 1976. *MacArthur,* 1977. *Old Gringo,* 1989.

Gotta Get Me Somebody to Love
Gregory Peck was the bad son and **Joseph Cotten,** the good son, of cattle baron Lionel Barrymore in the epic Western *Duel in the Sun.* **Jennifer Jones** played the half-breed Indian girl who had a love-hate relationship with Peck. Allie Wrubel wrote this song. $8

Maureen O'Hara (born 1920). This beautiful Irish redhead made her first appearance in a Hollywood film as the gypsy Esmeralda in *The Hunchback of Notre Dame.* She was a favorite actress of John Ford, who used her in many of his movies, often opposite John Wayne. With her fiery good looks she was especially effective in the Technicolor medium.

O'HARA MOVIE COVERS: *Dance, Girl, Dance,* 1940. *They Met in Argentina,* 1941. *To the Shores of Tripoli,* 1942. *Ten Gentlemen from West Point,* 1942. *Do You Love Me?* (a.k.a. *Kitten on the Keys*), 1946. *Sitting Pretty,* 1948. *The Quiet Man,* 1952. *The Magnificent Matador,* 1955. *Lisbon,* 1956. *The Wings of Eagles,* 1957. *Our Man in Havana,* 1960. *The Parent Trap,* 1961. *Mr. Hobbs Takes a Vacation,* 1962. *McLintock,* 1963. *The Battle of the Villa Fiorita,* 1965.

I Didn't Mean a Word I Said
The entertaining musical *Do You Love Me?* starred lovely **Maureen O'Hara** as a dowdy dean of a music school who undergoes a transformation into a glamour girl pursued by both bandleader **Harry James** and singer **Dick Haymes.** 20th Century-Fox apparently couldn't decide what title to use for the movie, and sheet music was published under the alternate title *Kitten on the Keys.* $5

Cream Puff
Maureen O'Hara was still a lovely lady playing **James Stewart**'s wife, a mature mother and grandmother, in the pleasant comedy *Mr. Hobbs Takes a Vacation.* **Fabian** sang this song by Johnny Mercer (W) and Henry Mancini (M) in the movie. $8

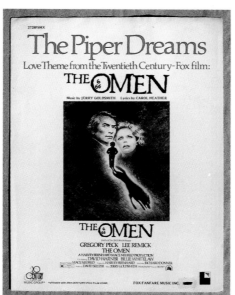

To Kill a Mockingbird
The best-selling novel by Harper Lee, *To Kill a Mockingbird*, was brought forcefully to the screen with **Gregory Peck** playing a sensitive southern lawyer defending a black man on a rape charge, a role that brought him an Oscar for Best Actor. His motherless children were played by 9-year-old **Mary Badham** (nominated for Best Supporting Actress) and 13-year-old **Phillip Alford.** The movie received seven Oscar nominations. $10

The Piper Dreams
Gregory Peck and **Lee Remick** played the parents of a five-year-old child who is the spawn of the devil in *The Omen*, a chilling fantasy/horror movie that almost makes one believe. This love theme was written by Carol Heather (W) and Jerry Goldsmith (M). $6

MacArthur March
Gregory Peck gave a solid performance as General Douglas MacArthur during World War II and the Korean War in the historic movie *MacArthur*. The musical theme was written as a piano solo by Jerry Goldsmith. $4

Walter Pidgeon (1897-1984). He was a solid actor in more than 100 films spanning 50 years. He started out as a professional singer with a good strong baritone voice, but abandoned singing in favor of acting. His glory years were mainly in the 1940s, with such vehicles as *How Green Was My Valley* (1941), *Man Hunt* (1941), and *Command Decision* (1949). He was especially suited as Greer Garson's leading man in at least eight movies including the moving wartime drama *Mrs. Miniver* (1942).

PIDGEON MOVIE COVERS: *A Most Immoral Lady*, 1929. *Her Private Life*, 1929. *Bride of the Regiment*, 1930. *Melody of Love*, 1934. *Society Lawyer*, 1939. *Mrs. Miniver*, 1942. *Weekend At the Waldorf*, 1945. *Holiday in Mexico*, 1946. *The Secret Heart*, 1946. *If Winter Comes*, 1947. *Julia Misbehaves*, 1948. *Voyage to the Bottom of the Sea*, 1961.

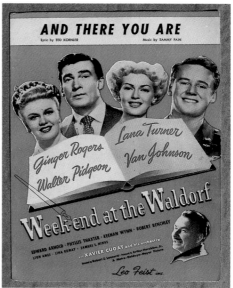

If Winter Comes
Walter Pidgeon starred in the tearjerker *If Winter Comes* with (left to right) **Angela Lansbury** as his wife, **Deborah Kerr** as his true love, and **Janet Leigh** in the supporting cast. Theme song was written by Kim Gannon (W) and Imogen Carpenter (M). $7

And There You Are
Weekend at the Waldorf was an updated remake of M-G-M's 1932 movie *Grand Hotel*, this time set at the Waldorf Hotel in New York City. The all-star cast included (left to right) **Ginger Rogers, Walter Pidgeon, Lana Turner,** and **Van Johnson. Xavier Cugat,** at bottom, provided exotic music. $5

Sidney Poitier (born 1924). He led the vanguard of Hollywood black actors in the 1950s with his output of notable performances. He was nominated in 1958 for the Best Actor Academy Award for his role in *The Defiant Ones*, and subsequently won the prestigious award in 1963 for *Lilies of the Field*.

POITIER MOVIE COVERS: *Porgy and Bess*, 1959. *All the Young Men*, 1960. *Lilies of the Field*, 1963. *A Patch of Blue*, 1965. *The Slender Thread*, 1965. *Duel at Diablo*, 1966. *Guess Who's Coming to Dinner*, 1967. *To Sir with Love*, 1967. *For Love of Ivy*, 1968. *Let's Do It Again*, 1975.

A Patch of Blue
Elizabeth Hartman played a blind white girl who falls in love with **Sidney Poitier,** not knowing he is black, in the sensitive drama *A Patch of Blue*. Shelley Winters won a Best Supporting Actress Oscar as her overbearing mother. Jerry Goldsmith's score was also nominated for an Oscar, but lost to *Doctor Zhivago*. Song is by Goldsmith with words by Bernie Wayne. $5

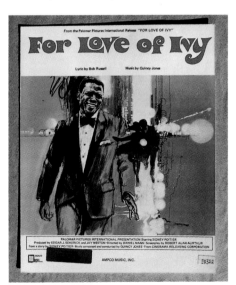

Dick Powell (1904-1963). A successful band vocalist before entering movies, Dick Powell's fine singing voice and clean-cut good looks made him a "natural" for a transition to movie making. He was a big favorite during the 1930s, starring in many entertaining musicals, then graduated in the 1940s to tough-guy detective roles at which he was most convincing.

DICK POWELL MOVIE COVERS: *Blessed Event*, 1932. *College Coach*, 1933. *Footlight Parade*, 1933. *Forty-Second Street*, 1933. *Gold Diggers of 1933*. *The Road Is Open Again*, 1933. *Flirtation Walk*, 1934. *Happiness Ahead*, 1934. *Twenty Million Sweethearts*, 1934. *Wonder Bar*, 1934. *Broadway Gondolier*, 1935. *Shipmates Forever*, 1935. *Thanks a Million*, 1935. *Colleen*, 1936. *Stage Struck*, 1936. *Gold Diggers of 1937*. *Hollywood Hotel*, 1937. *On the Avenue*, 1937. *The Singing Marine*, 1937. *Varsity Show*, 1937. *Cowboy from Brooklyn*, 1938. *Going Places*, 1938. *Hard to Get*, 1938. *Naughty But Nice*, 1939. *Star Spangled Rhythm*, 1942. *Happy Go Lucky*, 1943. *Riding High*, 1943. *True to Life*, 1943. *It Happened Tomorrow*, 1944. *Rogue's Regiment*, 1948. *Station West*, 1948. *Mrs. Mike*, 1949. *Susan Slept Here*, 1954.

Don't Give Up the Ship
Good-looking **Dick Powell** co-starred with his frequent movie sweetheart, pert **Ruby Keeler,** in *Shipmates Forever*, with an authentic setting at Annapolis. The entertaining musical had songs by Al Dubin (W) and Harry Warren (M). $5

For Love of Ivy
Sidney Poitier played the supportive boyfriend of a young domestic servant who wants to better herself by going to secretarial school in *For Love of Ivy*. Theme song, written by Bob Russell (W) and Quincy Jones (M), was sung by the voice of Shirley Horn in the movie. $7

In Your Own Quiet Way
Stage Struck was a backstage musical directed by Busby Berkeley co-starring **Dick Powell** and his real-life wife at the time, **Joan Blondell**. Songs were by E. Y. Harburg (W) and Harold Arlen (M). $7

Eleanor Powell (1912-1982). She was a star tap dancer on Broadway when she was lured to Hollywood in 1935. With her dimpled

I've Got My Eyes on You
What more can you ask for? Lovely **Eleanor Powell,** flashing her dimpled smile and dancing with suave **Fred Astaire,** and a music score by Cole Porter made the movie *Broadway Melody of 1940* a big hit. $8

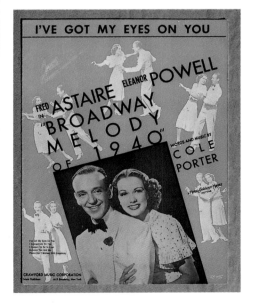

good looks, brilliant smile, shapely figure, and long legs she would have become a star, even if she wasn't also the world's best tap dancer. Her peak of popularity was during the 1930s and 1940s.

ELEANOR POWELL MOVIE COVERS: *Born* to Dance, 1936. *Broadway Melody of 1936.* Rosalie, 1937. *Broadway Melody of 1938.* Honolulu, 1939. *Broadway Melody of 1940. Lady Be Good,* 1941. *Ship Ahoy,* 1942. *I Dood It,* 1943. *Sensations of 1945,* 1944. *Duchess of Idaho,* 1950.

Jane Powell (born 1929). Starting out in movies as a teenager with a beautiful singing voice, Jane Powell moved successfully into delightful Technicolor musicals in the 1940s and 1950s. But she failed to make the transition to more mature roles and retired from the screen in 1958. She has since appeared in nightclubs, starred in a Broadway show, and is an able product spokeswoman on television commercials.

JANE POWELL MOVIE COVERS: *Song of the Open Road,* 1944. *Delightfully Dangerous,* 1945. *Holiday in Mexico,* 1946. *A Date with Judy,* 1948. *Luxury Liner,* 1948. *Three Daring Daughters,* 1948. *Nancy Goes to Rio,* 1950. *Two Weeks with Love,* 1950. *Rich, Young and Pretty,* 1951. *Royal Wedding,* 1951. *Small*

Town Girl, 1953. *Three Sailors and a Girl,* 1953. *Athena,* 1954. *Seven Brides for Seven Brothers,* 1954. *Hit the Deck,* 1955. *The Girl Most Likely,* 1957. *Enchanted Island,* 1958.

My Flaming Heart
Jane Powell falls for rich playboy, **Farley Granger** in the musical *Small Town Girl.* **Ann Miller** was scintillating in a Busby Berkeley production number, "I've Gotta Hear the Beat," and Janie sang the songs of Leo Robin (W) and Nicholas Brodszky (M). $5

Oh! Lady Be Good
Lady Be Good, adapted from the Broadway stage, co-starred **Eleanor Powell, Robert Young,** and **Ann Sothern.** Highlights of the movie were the Gershwin songs, a Busby Berkeley directed dance number of "Fascinating Rhythm" featuring the extraordinary tapping of Miss Powell, and Ann Sothern singing "The Last Time I Saw Paris," Oscar winner for Best Song. $7

It's a Most Unusual Day
A Date With Judy starred the sparkling teenager **Jane Powell** warbling five songs, and competing with beautiful young **Elizabeth Taylor** for the attentions of **Robert Stack.** Cast also included **Wallace Beery,** who learns to dance from **Carmen Miranda, Scotty Beckett** as a callow youth, and the **Xavier Cugat** orchestra. $5

When You're in Love
When **Jane Powell** became **Howard Keel**'s bride in *Seven Brides for Seven Brothers,* she managed to tame his backwoods rowdy relatives. The highly acclaimed musical had songs by Johnny Mercer (W) and Gene De Paul (M). The film score by Adolph Deutsch and Saul Chaplin won an Oscar. $7

Left:
The Last Call for Love
The shipboard World War II musical *Ship Ahoy* had **Eleanor Powell** doing some great tap-dancing, **Red Skelton** and **Bert Lahr** looking for Axis spies, and the **Tommy Dorsey** orchestra with vocalist Frank Sinatra performing this song in the movie. $5

William Powell (1892-1984). This suave and sophisticated actor was active in silent movies typically cast as a villain, a role that he finally was able to shake with the advent of sound. He was paired with cool beauty Myrna Loy in a series of 1930s movies, best known as detective sleuths Nick and Nora Charles in the popular *Thin Man* mystery series. In 1947 he was nominated for the Best Actor Oscar for his warm and funny role in *Life With Father*, but lost out to Ronald Colman in *A Double Life*.

WILLIAM POWELL MOVIE COVERS: *Behind the Make-Up*, 1930. *Paramount on Parade*, 1930. *The Key*, 1934. *Escapade*, 1935. *After the Thin Man*, 1936. *The Great Ziegfeld*, 1936. *Crossroads*, 1942. *The Hoodlum Saint*, 1946. *Life with Father*, 1947. *Song of the Thin Man*, 1947. *Mr. Peabody and the Mermaid*, 1948.

You're Not So Easy to Forget
William Powell and **Myrna Loy** again co-starred as sophisticated sleuths Nick and Nora Charles in *Song of the Thin Man*, the last of their *Thin Man* series. The pretty blonde on the cover is **Gloria Grahame**, who was in the supporting cast. $12

'Til You Return
William Powell played a diplomat in pre-war Paris with **Hedy Lamarr** as his beautiful wife in the suspenseful movie *Crossroads*. **Claire Trevor** and **Basil Rathbone** were devious blackmailers who tried to victimize Powell. $25

Sweet Marie
William Powell was nominated as Best Actor for his performance in *Life With Father*, an engaging period piece that was voted one of the top ten movies of the year by the *New York Times*. The cast was further enhanced by the presence of **Irene Dunne** as his wife, who uses all her wiles to try and get him baptized. Max Steiner's romantic score was nominated for an Oscar. Song by Cy Warman (W) and Raymond Moore (M). $6

Tyrone Power (1913-1958). Both his father and grandfather were distinguished stage actors, and Tyrone Power followed easily in their path. He was extremely handsome with a pleasant unassuming manner, and was very much in demand for leading roles in the 1930s and 1940s. He was a box office favorite at his best as a romantic leading man, but also turned out some strong performances in serious roles. He died at age 45 from a heart attack.

POWER MOVIE COVERS: *Love Is News*, 1937. *Alexander's Ragtime Band*, 1938. *In Old Chicago*, 1938. *Marie Antoinette*, 1938. *The Rains Came*, 1939. *Rose of Washington Square*, 1939. *Second Fiddle*, 1939. *Johnny Apollo*, 1940. *Blood and Sand*, 1941. *A Yank in the R.A.F.*, 1941. *Son of Fury*, 1942. *The Razor's Edge*, 1946. *Captain from Castile*, 1947. *The Black Rose*, 1950. *The Eddie Duchin Story*, 1956. *The Sun Also Rises*, 1957. *Witness for the Prosecution*, 1957.

Amour, Eternel Amour
A sumptuous production of the historical movie *Marie Antoinette* spared no expense. It co-starred Norma Shearer, in the title role, and handsome Tyrone Power, as her lover. Miss Shearer was nominated for the Best Actress Oscar but had some stiff competition, and lost out to Bette Davis in *Jezebel*. $25

THE RAINS CAME

The Rains Came
Tyrone Power played a healer from India who practiced medicine in Ranchipur in *The Rains Came*. **Myrna Loy** and **George Brent** completed the triangle. The movie is most famous for its great flood and earthquake scenes that captured the Oscar for Special Effects, a surprising turn of events in the year that *Gone With the Wind* was also nominated. The theme song was written by Mack Gordon. $50

This Is the Beginning of the End
Clean-cut college graduate **Tyrone Power** opts for a life of crime after his father goes to jail for embezzling in *Johnny Apollo*. He falls in love with **Dorothy Lamour,** who tries to straighten him out. Mack Gordon wrote the theme song. $10 *($30)*

Another Little Dream Won't Do Us Any Harm
Tyrone Power was *A Yank in the R.A.F.*, an immature flyer who joined the British group to be near entertainer **Betty Grable,** a performer at a London club. Combat experience brought him to a new maturity. Song is by Leo Robin (W) and Ralph Rainger (M). $50

Blue Tahitian Moon
Son of Fury was an exciting adventure set in the 1800s, starring **Tyrone Power** as the illegitimate son of an English nobleman who escapes a life of cruelty, finds love with **Gene Tierney** in Polynesia, and becomes rich from pearl diving. The beautiful sheet music cover shows the leading stars in an embrace. Song was written by Mack Gordon (W) and Alfred Newman (M). *Collection of Harold Jacobs.* $100

Elvis Presley (1935-1977). As an idol of teenage girls in the 1950s, he became a famous rock-and-roll star with great charisma, who was equally effective crooning sentimental ballads. He made his screen debut in *Love Me Tender* in 1956, and appeared in many more movies through the 1950s and 1960s. His tragic death at age 42 left many bereft fans. He is recognized throughout the world for his influence on popular music.

PRESLEY MOVIE COVERS: *Love Me Tender,* 1956. *Jail House Rock,* 1957. *Loving You,* 1957. *King Creole,* 1958. *Flaming Star,* 1960. *G.I. Blues,* 1960. *Blue Hawaii,* 1961. *Wild in the Country,* 1961. *Follow That Dream,* 1962. *Girls Girls Girls,* 1962. *Kid Galahad,* 1962. *Fun in Acapulco,* 1963. *It Happened at the World's Fair,* 1963. *Kissin' Cousins,* 1964. *Roustabout,* 1964. *Viva Las Vegas,* 1964. *Girl Happy,* 1965. *Harum Scarum,* 1965. *Tickle Me,* 1965. *Frankie and Johnny,* 1966. *Paradise Hawaiian Style,* 1966. *Spinout,* 1966. *Clambake,* 1967. *Double Trouble,* 1967. *Easy Come Easy Go,* 1967. *Live a Little, Love a Little,* 1968. *Speedway,* 1968. *Stay Away Joe,* 1968. *Change of Habit,* 1969. *Charro,* 1969. *The Trouble with Girls,* 1969. *That's the Way It Is,* 1970.

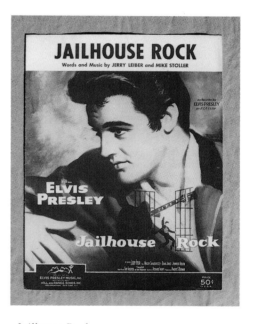

Jailhouse Rock
Thought by many to be his best movie, *Jailhouse Rock* was a perfect vehicle for **Elvis Presley.** He played a convict who learns guitar in prison, becoming a rock star after his release. Songs were by Jerry Leiber and Mike Stoller. Elvis made a No. 1 hit record of the title song. *Collection of James Nelson Brown.* $35

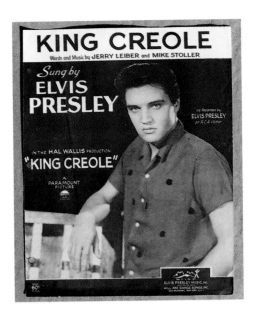

King Creole
Elvis Presley played a nightclub singer in New Orleans who drifts into a life of crime in *King Creole*, a dramatic role that allowed for plenty of good songs from Elvis. The title song was written by Leiber and Stoller. *Collection of James Nelson Brown.* $35

Robert Preston (1918-1987). This handsome and personable actor was type-cast early in his movie career as the second lead, seldom getting the girl. He was always convincing, no matter what the part. He became a superstar on Broadway following his memorable performance in *The Music Man* for which he won a Tony Award, and which was later made into a Hollywood movie. He was nominated for Best Supporting Actor in 1982 for his sensitive role as a gay cabaret performer in *Victor/Victoria*.

PRESTON MOVIE COVERS: *Typhoon*, 1940. *Big City*, 1948. *Tulsa*, 1949. *The Dark at the Top of the Stairs*, 1960. *All the Way Home*, 1963. *Island of Love*, 1963.

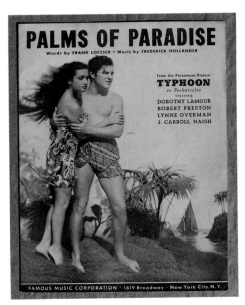

Palms of Paradise
Robert Preston was **Dorothy Lamour**'s co-star in *Typhoon*, a desert island saga complete with marooned sailors, a beautiful native girl, lots of palm trees, and a big storm. Frank Loesser wrote the lyrics to this song, with music by Frederick Hollander. $8

Tulsa
Wildcat drilling in the oil fields is the theme of this action film, co-starring **Robert Preston** and **Susan Hayward** in a passionate quest for "black gold." Theme song was written by Mort Greene (W) and Allie Wrubel (M). $6

The Dark at the Top of the Stairs
Robert Preston and **Dorothy McGuire** co-starred in *The Dark at the Top of the Stairs*, adapted from the William Inge Pulitzer Prize winning play. Set in 1920s Oklahoma, it had Preston torn between his loyal wife, Dorothy McGuire, and Angela Lansbury, the other woman. Max Steiner arranged this piano solo. $5

Anthony Quinn (born 1915). Though he started out in bit parts, he learned his craft well and moved up through the ranks to stardom. He has appeared in more than 100 films during his long career as an actor in Hollywood. He is the winner of two Oscars for Best Supporting Actor in *Viva Zapata* (1952) and *Lust for Life* (1956), and is well remembered for portraying the title role in *Zorba the Greek* in 1964. His prodigious output of movies is reflected in his sheet music covers.

QUINN MOVIE COVERS: *Blowing Wild*, 1953. *The Long Wait*, 1954. *La Strada*, 1954. *The Magnificent Matador*, 1955. *The Ride Back*, 1957. *The River's Edge*, 1957. *Wild Is the Wind*, 1957. *Hot Spell*, 1958. *The Black Orchid*, 1959. *Barabbas*, 1961. *The Guns of Navarone*, 1961. *Requiem for a Heavyweight*, 1962. *Zorba the Greek*, 1964. *High Wind in Jamaica*, 1965. *The Lost Command*, 1966. *The Twenty-Fifth Hour*, 1967. *Guns for San Sebastian*, 1968. *Shoes of the Fisherman*, 1968. *The Secret of Santa Vittoria*, 1969. *A Walk in the Spring Rain*, 1970. *Across 110th Street*, 1972. *Deaf Smith and Johnny Ears*, 1973.

Zorba the Greek Theme
Anthony Quinn was the colorful earthy peasant *Zorba the Greek*, who teaches a young English writer about life and love on the island of Crete. Quinn's memorable interpretation of the lusty Greek earned him an Oscar nomination for Best Actor. Mikis Theodorakis composed the popular theme song. $4

A Walk in the Spring Rain
Anthony Quinn and **Ingrid Bergman,** both middle-aged and married, each to other people, have a romantic liaison in *A Walk in the Spring Rain.* Elmer Bernstein wrote the music and Don Black, the words, for the title song. $5

Luise Rainer (born 1910). She was a native Austrian who acted in a few European films before coming to Hollywood in 1935. She made a meteoric rise to stardom and won two successive Academy Awards, for *The Great Ziegfeld* in 1936, and *The Good Earth* in 1937. Her great talent was lost to the silver screen when she retired from films in the early 1940s.
RAINIER MOVIE COVERS: *Escapade,*1935. *The Great Ziegfeld,* 1936. *The Great Waltz,* 1938.

You're All I Need
Luise Rainer made her American film debut playing opposite **William Powell** in *Escapade,* in a role originally intended for **Myrna Loy.** She acquitted herself nicely, and won rave reviews. $9

You
Luise Rainer copped an Oscar as Ziegfeld's first wife Anna Held in *The Great Ziegfeld.* Co-stars were **Myrna Loy** as Billie Burke, and **William Powell** as the great man himself. The movie also won a Best Picture Oscar, and the opulent "Pretty Girl Is Like a Melody" production number won for Best Dance Direction. Song was by Harold Adamson (W) and Walter Donaldson (M). $6

Tales from the Vienna Woods
Luise Rainer and **Miliza Korjus** were both in love with **Fernand Gravet** as Johann Strauss in *The Great Waltz,* a beautiful movie about the great composer. Korjus (right) was nominated for Best Supporting Actress Oscar, and Joseph Ruttenberg won the award for his outstanding cinematography. British edition. $6

Ronald Reagan (born 1911). He started out as a personable sportscaster on the radio before embarking on a Hollywood movie career. Mr. Reagan appeared in many movies, and received critical praise for his sensitive performance in *Kings Row* in 1942 ("Where's the rest of me?"). During World War II, he served as an officer with the U.S.A.A.F. and starred in the rousing Irving Berlin spectacular *This Is the Army,* a 1943 fundraiser for Army Emergency Relief. He rates a name credit on the sheet music, but no picture. Reagan appeared in more than 50 films before entering politics, making a spectacular rise from president of the Screen Actors Guild to Governor of California to President of the United States.
REAGAN MOVIE COVERS: *Million Dollar Baby,* 1941. *The Girl from Jones Beach,* 1949. *Bedtime for Bonzo,* 1951. *Cattle Queen of Montana,* 1954.

I Found a Million Dollar Baby
Ronald Reagan played a struggling concert pianist in *Million Dollar Baby* opposite **Priscilla Lane.** Reagan, with no keyboard experience, haunted the studio music department, working with a dummy keyboard and a pianist to learn enough basic technique to be convincing in the movie. Also featured was **Jeffrey Lynn.** This song was from the 1931 Broadway revue, *Billy Rose's Crazy Quilt.* $20

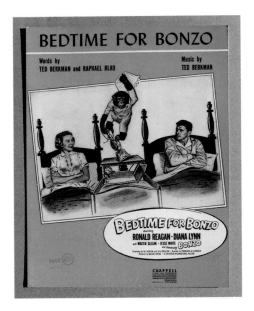

Bedtime for Bonzo
Ronald Reagan portrayed a psychologist in the amusing movie *Bedtime for Bonzo*. As an experiment, he takes a chimpanzee home with him to prove environment is more formative to development than heredity. **Diana Lynn** co-starred, but it was the chimp that stole the show. All of Reagan's sheet music songs are prime collectibles with high value. *Collection of Harold Jacobs.* $200

Robert Redford (born 1937). Despite a baseball scholarship at the University of Colorado, Redford dropped out of college to pursue an artist's career, eventually settling in New York City, where he studied both art and drama. He cut his acting teeth in minor stage parts and on television's *Playhouse 90, Twilight Zone,* and *Alfred Hitchcock Presents.* His first major success on Broadway was in Neil Simon's *Barefoot in the Park,* which he later reprised in the movie of the same name. His acting gained in stature and he became a top box office favorite, popular with both men and women. In 1980 he directed the film *Ordinary People,* winner of three Academy Awards including one to Redford as Best Director.

REDFORD MOVIE COVERS: *Situation Hopeless But Not Serious,* 1965. *The Chase,* 1966. *Inside Daisy Clover,* 1966. *This Property Is Condemned,* 1966. *Barefoot in the Park,* 1967. *Butch Cassidy and the Sundance Kid,* 1969. *Little Fauss and Big Halsy,* 1970. *The Hot Rock,* 1972. *The Way We Were,* 1973. *The Great Gatsby,* 1974. *The Sting,* 1974. *The Great Waldo Pepper,* 1975. *Three Days of the Condor,* 1975. *All the President's Men,* 1976. *The Electric Horseman,* 1979. *The Natural,* 1984. *Out of Africa,* 1986.

The Sting Music Folio
Robert Redford and **Paul Newman** played a couple of con artists in 1920s Chicago who conspire to rip off a racketeer in *The Sting.* The movie won seven Oscars, including Best Picture, Director, Screenplay, and Musical Score. The ragtime music was by Scott Joplin, skillfully arranged by Marvin Hamlisch. $5

The Music of Goodbye
Robert Redford played the English adventurer Denys Finch-Hatton in Oscar-winning *Out of Africa,* an exquisite movie filmed on location in Kenya. **Meryl Streep** played his lover, Karen Blixen, better known as Isak Dinesen, the famous Danish writer. John Barry, winner for Best Original Score, also wrote this love theme with words by Alan and Marilyn Bergman. $6

Burt Reynolds (born 1936). Reynolds acted on television in *M Squad, Gunsmoke, Riverboat,* and also starred in his own series playing the title role *Dan August* in the late 1960s. He attracted favorable critical attention playing a dramatic role in the 1972 movie *Deliverance,* but made an even bigger splash that year when he posed as a nude male centerfold for *Cosmopolitan* magazine. He has since starred in many films, and is popular with the ladies as a sex symbol, and with the men for his macho personality.

BURT REYNOLDS MOVIE COVERS: *Deliverance,* 1972. *Everything You Always Wanted to Know About Sex,* 1972. *The Longest Yard,* 1974. *At Long Last Love,* 1975. *Hustle,* 1975. *Lucky Lady,* 1975. *W. W. and the Dixie Dance Kings,* 1975. *Gator,* 1976. *Smokey and the Bandit I,* 1977. *The End,* 1978. *Starting Over,* 1979. *Smokey and the Bandit II,* 1980. *Paternity,* 1981. *Best Friends,* 1982. *The Best Little Whorehouse in Texas,* 1982. *The Man Who Loved Women,* 1983. *Cannonball Run II,* 1984. *Physical Evidence,* 1989.

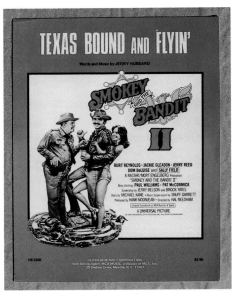

Texas Bound and Flyin'
The comedy *Smokey and the Bandit II* co-starred **Burt Reynolds** and **Sally Field** in the impossible situation of transporting a pregnant elephant to a Republican convention, with **Jackie Gleason** as a disapproving law officer. Song was written by Jerry Hubbard. $4

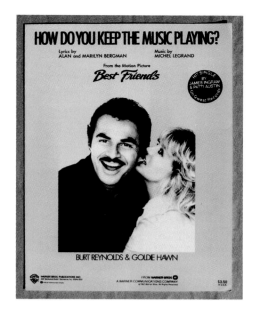

How Do You Keep the Music Playing?
In *Best Friends*, **Burt Reynolds** and **Goldie Hawn,** after living together for five years, decide to marry, with ensuing complications. The song was written by Alan and Marilyn Bergman (W) and Michel Legrand (M). $4

Debbie Reynolds (born 1932). The unsinkable Debbie Reynolds endeared herself to the movie-going public in the 1950 movie *Three Little Words,* in which she portrayed flapper Helen Kane. She followed this with a series of light comedies and musicals that showcased her talent and vivacious personality, especially memorable for *Tammy and the Bachelor* in 1957 and *The Unsinkable Molly Brown* in 1964. She was married to singer Eddie Fisher in what was publicized as an ideal marriage until he left her for Elizabeth Taylor. But she surmounted the attendant pain and embarrassment and continued her successful career with the support of sympathetic fans. In the 1990s she opened a popular nightclub and movie museum in Las Vegas, performing regularly to the applause of her legions of loyal fans.

DEBBIE REYNOLDS MOVIE COVERS: *Two Weeks with Love*, 1950. *Singin' in the Rain*, 1952. *The Affairs of Dobie Gillis,* 1953. *I Love Melvin*, 1953. *Athena*, 1954. *Susan Slept Here*, 1954. *Hit the Deck*, 1955. *The Tender Trap*, 1955. *Bundle of Joy*, 1956. *Tammy and the Bachelor,* 1957. *This Happy Feeling*, 1958. *The Gazebo*, 1959. *It Started with a Kiss*, 1959. *The Mating Game*, 1959. *Say One for Me*, 1959. *The Rat Race*, 1960. *The Pleasure of His Company*, 1961. *The Second Time Around*, 1961. *How the West Was Won*, 1962. *My Six Loves*, 1963. *Goodbye Charlie*, 1964. *The Unsinkable Molly Brown*, 1964. *The Singing Nun*, 1966. *How Sweet It Is*, 1968.

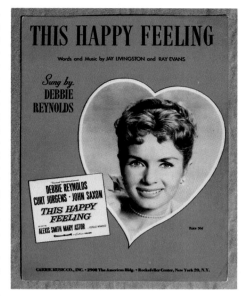

This Happy Feeling
Debbie Reynolds was charming in *This Happy Feeling,* as a young girl in love with an older man. She sang the title song by Jay Livingston and Ray Evans in the film. $6

I Ain't Down Yet
Debbie Reynolds was a knockout in *The Unsinkable Molly Brown* as a backwoods girl who strikes a rich lode of silver and enters society despite her lack of social skills. She was nominated for a Best Actress Oscar for her strong portrayal, losing to Julie Andrews for *Mary Poppins*. The score was composed by Meredith Willson. $5

I Know that You Know
Sailors on leave in San Francisco meet a delectable trio of girls in *Hit the Deck*. The three couples are, left to right, **Jane Powell** and **Vic Damone, Debbie Reynolds** and **Russ Tamblyn,** and **Ann Miller** and **Tony Martin.** Great songs by Vincent Youmans were borrowed from his Broadway shows, including this tune with words by Anne Caldwell from the 1926 musical *Oh, Please!* $5

Edward G. Robinson (1893-1973). Though he played many gangster roles in 1930s movies, his most famous part was Rico Bandello in *Little Caesar*. He was a short, stocky man who dominated the screen with his style and personality. In a movie career that encompassed some 50 years, he was always a forceful and reliable actor, notably effective in psychological dramas like *Double Indemnity*, *The Woman in the Window*, and *Tales of Manhattan*. He was given an Honorary Academy Award statuette in 1972 with the accolade, "Edward G. Robinson, who achieved greatness as a player, a patron of the arts and a dedicated citizen—in sum, a Renaissance man. From his friends in the industry he loves."

ROBINSON MOVIE COVERS: *Barbary Coast*, 1935. *A Hole in the Head*, 1959. *A Boy Ten Feet Tall*, 1964. *Cheyenne Autumn*, 1964.

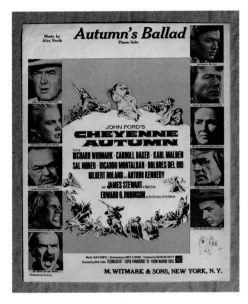

Autumn's Ballad
Cheyenne Autumn was loaded with big name stars, but **Edward G. Robinson**'s cameo role as Secretary of the Interior Carl Schurz was one of the most interesting characterizations. The strong cast also included **James Stewart** and **Richard Widmark**. This piano arrangement of the theme song was composed by Alex North. $5

Ginger Rogers (1911-1995). As an attractive and graceful dancer, she was Fred Astaire's partner in a string of popular musicals. She broadened her horizons in 1940, winning a Best Actress Academy Award for her dramatic portrayal of *Kitty Foyle*. Her versatility in both drama and comedy was evident in many other movies for which sheet music can be found.

GINGER ROGERS MOVIE COVERS: *Queen High*, 1930. *The Sap from Syracuse*, 1930. *Young Man of Manhattan*, 1930. *Broadway Bad*, 1933. *Forty-Second Street*, 1933. *Gold Diggers of 1933*. *Professional Sweetheart*, 1933. *Sitting Pretty*, 1933. *The Gay Divorcée*, 1934. *Twenty Million Sweethearts*, 1934. *In Person*, 1935. *Roberta*, 1935. *Top Hat*, 1935. *Follow the Fleet*, 1936. *Swing Time*, 1936. *Shall We Dance*, 1937. *Carefree*, 1938. *Having Wonderful Time*, 1938. *Vivacious Lady*, 1938. *The Story of Vernon and Irene Castle*, 1939. *The Major and the Minor*, 1942. *Tales of Manhattan*, 1942. *I'll Be Seeing You*, 1944. *Lady in the Dark*, 1944. *Weekend at the Waldorf*, 1945. *Heartbeat*, 1946. *It Had to Be You*, 1947. *The Barkleys of Broadway*, 1949. *Dreamboat*, 1952. *Monkey Business*, 1952. *Forever Female*, 1953. *Tight Spot*, 1955. *The First Traveling Saleslady*, 1956. *Teenage Rebel*, 1956.

Don't Mention Love to Me
Ginger Rogers, portraying a Hollywood star who uses strange disguises to hide from her fans, is miffed when handsome stranger, George Brent, doesn't even know who she is! Songs for *In Person* were by Dorothy Fields (W) and Oscar Levant (M). $7

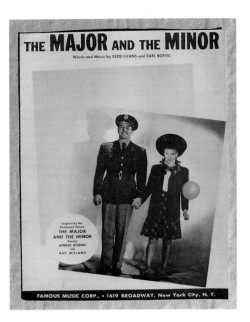

The Major and the Minor
Ginger Rogers ran the gamut of playing a 12-year-old girl, a lovely grown-up woman, and her own mother, complete with spectacles and knitting, in *The Major and the Minor*. **Ray Milland** was the Major, totally taken in by the youngster, much to the disgust of his fiancée, sophisticated Rita Johnson. The title song was by Redd Evans and Earl Bostic. $16

Suddenly It's Spring
The Broadway show, *Lady in the Dark*, was brought to the screen as a spectacular musical with **Ginger Rogers** playing the leading lady, who finds meaning in her exotic dreams. Miss Rogers sang this song by Johnny Burke (W) and Jimmy Van Heusen (M). $5

Roy Rogers (1912-1998). Rogers came to California in 1929 as a migratory fruit picker. He eventually formed a singing group, The Sons of the Pioneers, who performed on Los Angeles radio. He became a popular singing cowboy in the movies, inheriting Gene Autry's title "King of the Cowboys" when Autry entered the military service during World War II. With his horse Trigger, his wife Dale Evans, and his comedic sidekick Gabby Hayes, Roy Rogers made many formula Western movies for Republic Studios in the 1940s and 1950s. Shrewd investments through the years paid off, and the fruit picker retired as a multi-millionaire, living until the ripe old age of 86.

ROY ROGERS MOVIE COVERS: *Shine on Harvest Moon*, 1938. *Under Western Skies*, 1938. *Days of Jesse James*, 1939. *Saga of Death Valley*, 1939. *In Old Cheyenne*, 1941. *Robin Hood of the Pecos*, 1941. *Ridin' Down the Canyon*, 1942. *The Man from Music Mountain*, 1943. *Hands Across the Border*, 1944. *San Fernando Valley*, 1944. *The Yellow Rose of Texas*, 1944. *Along the Navajo Trail*, 1945. *Don't Fence Me In*, 1945. *The Man from Oklahoma*, 1945. *On the Old Spanish Trail*, 1947. *A Gay Ranchero*, 1948. *Night Time in Nevada*, 1948. *The Golden Stallion*, 1949. *Trail of Robin Hood*, 1950. *Trigger Jr.*, 1950. *Son of Paleface*, 1952.

Wing-Ding Tonight
Son of Paleface starred **Bob Hope** as a tenderfoot who goes West to claim an inheritance. **Roy Rogers** is the government agent who tries to help him, and **Jane Russell** runs the Dirty Shame saloon. Songs were written by Jay Livingston and Ray Evans. $8

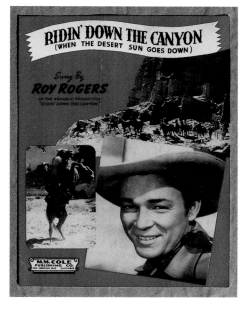

Ridin' Down the Canyon
The popular cowboy star **Roy Rogers** is seen with his horse Trigger on the cover of the title song from the Republic movie *Ridin' Down the Canyon*. The song was written by Nick Manoloff, Gene Autry, and Smiley Burnett. $5

Mickey Rooney (born 1920). As the son of vaudeville performers, he made his stage debut as a 15-month-old infant. He grew up in show business as a singer and dancer and all-round entertainer, and appeared in his first movie when he was barely six. As a teenager, he played the wholesome callow youth, Andy Hardy, in a whole series of Hardy family films. He also starred in fine dramatic roles in productions such as *Captains Courageous, Boys Town, Young Tom Edison*, and *The Human Comedy* for which he received a Best Actor nomination. As a mature performer, he received critical praise and an Oscar nomination for his characterization of a soldier in *The Bold and the Brave* (1956). After announcing his imminent retirement in 1978, he did an about-face and starred in the long-running Broadway hit musical *Sugar Babies*. In 1983 he received a special Academy Award in recognition of his versatility as a performer.

ROONEY MOVIE COVERS: *Thoroughbreds Don't Cry*, 1937. *Boys Town*, 1938. *Love Finds Andy Hardy*, 1938. *You're Only Young Once*, 1938. *Babes in Arms*, 1939. *Andy Hardy Meets Debutante*, 1940. *Strike Up the Band*, 1940. *Andy Hardy's Private Secretary*, 1941. *Babes on Broadway*, 1941. *Girl Crazy*, 1943. *Summer Holiday*, 1948. *Words and Music*, 1948. *The Strip*, 1951. *Sound Off*, 1952. *All Ashore*, 1953. *Off Limits*, 1953. *Twinkle in God's Eye*, 1955. *The Bold and the Brave*, 1956. *Baby Face Nelson*, 1957. *Operation Madball*, 1957. *Andy Hardy Comes Home*, 1958. *Requiem for a Heavyweight*, 1962. *Pete's Dragon*, 1977. *The Magic of Lassie*, 1978.

Have a Heart
Multi-talented Mickey Rooney was still a teenager when he wrote this romantic ballad with Sidney Miller in 1938. He was 18, and one of America's most popular stars at the crest of his career, with memorable performances in *Boys Town* and the *Andy Hardy* pictures. $8

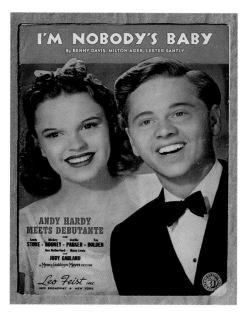

I'm Nobody's Baby
Andy Hardy Meets Debutante starred **Mickey Rooney** in this entry in the popular Andy Hardy series. This situation involved his crush on a Manhattan debutante, while his friend **Judy Garland** gives him moral support. Judy sang this 1921 song by Benny Davis, Milton Ager, and Lester Santly, as only she could sing. $10

153

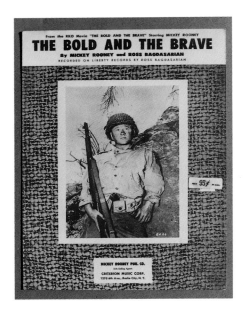

The Bold and the Brave
Mickey Rooney's extraordinary performance as a tough little soldier from New Jersey earned him an Academy Award nomination for Best Supporting Actor in *The Bold and the Brave*. The song was composed by Rooney with Ross Bagdasarian. *Collection of Roy Bishop.*$40

Jane Russell (born 1921). Following a vulgar publicity campaign that capitalized on her ample cleavage, she made her screen debut in Howard Hughes's *The Outlaw* in 1943. An actress with less talent may not have survived, but Miss Russell proved herself a capable actress through the years, typically cast as a worldly, cynical broad. After her retirement from movies in the 1970s she became a television spokeswoman for a bra company.
JANE RUSSELL MOVIE COVERS: *The Outlaw*, 1943. *The Paleface*, 1948. *Double Dynamite*, 1951. *His Kind of Woman*, 1951. *The Las Vegas Story*, 1952. *Montana Belle*, 1952. *Son of Paleface*, 1952. *Gentlemen Prefer Blondes*, 1953. *The French Line*, 1954. *Foxfire*, 1955. *Gentlemen Marry Brunettes*, 1955. *The Tall Men*, 1955. *Underwater*, 1955. *The Revolt of Mamie Stover*, 1956. *Fate Is the Hunter*, 1964. *Waco*, 1966.

Now and Forever
Jane Russell starred in *The Outlaw*, ballyhooed as a "sex Western," playing the role of Billy the Kid's girlfriend Rio. Despite condemnation by the League of Decency for "glamorizing crime and immorality" the movie did well at the box office and Jane became a well-known personality. $10

Tall Men
Clark Gable played a trail driver and **Jane Russell** was on the wagon train in *The Tall Men*. Though strongly attracted to each other, they had a problem about getting him to settle down on a farm. Miss Russell engagingly sang the theme song written by Ken Darby. $10

Cherry Pink and Apple Blossom White
Jane Russell in a skimpy bathing suit was the big attraction in the skin-diving adventure movie *Underwater*. This love theme used in the soundtrack was composed by Louigoy, with English lyrics added by Mack David. $5

Rosalind Russell (1908-1976). A statuesque brunette beauty, Rosalind Russell was the epitome of the stylish wisecracking career woman in many of her movies. She was nominated four times for Best Actress, but failed to win an Academy Award. She was honored with a Special Oscar, the Jean Hersholt Humanitarian Award, for her charity work in 1972.

Jealous
Rosalind Russell played **Don Ameche**'s wife in the sophisticated comedy *The Feminine Touch*. She falls victim to a jealousy attack, suspecting him of having an affair with **Kay Francis** (right). $5

ROSALIND RUSSELL MOVIE COVERS: *The Feminine Touch*, 1941. *The Velvet Touch*, 1948. *The Girl Rush*, 1955. *Rosie*, 1957. *Auntie Mame*, 1958. *A Majority of One*, 1962. *Gypsy*, 1962. *The Trouble with Angels*, 1966. *Oh Dad Poor Dad*, 1967.

The Velvet Touch
In a change of pace, **Rosalind Russell** played a murderess in *The Velvet Touch* whose conscience bothers her when Claire Trevor is accused of the crime. Title song was written by Mort Greene (W) and Leigh Harline (M). $6

Birmin'ham
Rosalind Russell followed her hit Broadway musical *Wonderful Town* with a screen musical, *The Girl Rush*. Songs for the production were written by Hugh Martin and Ralph Blane. $10

George C. Scott (born 1927). Scott served four years in the Marines before venturing into acting. His magnetic stage presence and riveting performances ensured his success in many media including starring roles on both stage and television. But he is best known for his movie work. He was twice nominated for Best Supporting Actor Academy Award for his work in *Anatomy of a Murder* (1959) and *The Hustler* (1961), and finally won the Oscar for Best Actor for his portrayal of *Patton*, an honor he declined. He had little respect for the institution of the Academy Awards and considered the whole election process a "meat parade."

SCOTT MOVIE COVERS: *The Yellow Rolls Royce*, 1964. *Not With My Wife, You Don't*, 1966. *Petulia*, 1968. *Patton*, 1970. *The Last Run*, 1971. *Islands in the Stream*, 1976.

Patton Theme
George C. Scott portrayed Patton in a remarkable performance of the great warrior soldier of World War II that earned him an Oscar for Best Actor. He failed to attend the Awards ceremony claiming he stayed home to watch a hockey game on TV. The distinguished movie won many awards including Best Picture. $8

Riptide
Norma Shearer co-starred with her frequent screen partner Robert Montgomery in *Riptide*, playing a bored rich wife who carries on a dalliance with Montgomery under the eyes of her husband, Herbert Marshall, a stodgy English lord. Title song was written by Gus Kahn (W) and Walter Donaldson (M). $7

The Last Run Theme
As a retired career driver for the mob, **George C. Scott** agreed to one more job in *The Last Run* that cost him his life. The future Mrs. Scott, Trish Van Devere, also starred in the film. This piano arrangement of the theme song was written by Jerry Goldsmith. $4

Norma Shearer (1900-1983). Miss Shearer successfully traversed the road from silent movies to talkies. As the wife of studio executive Irving Thalberg at M-G-M, she became a top star in some of the studio's most prestigious productions. She was a five-time Academy Award nominee and finally won the coveted award for her performance in *The Divorcée* (1930). After her husband's death she made some unwise choices in movie vehicles and, when her career took a downswing, she retired from movies completely.

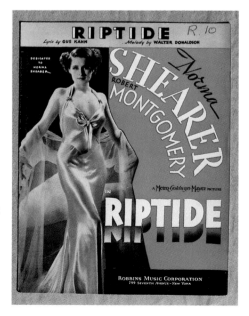

SHEARER MOVIE COVERS: *Pleasure Mad*, 1923. *Pretty Ladies*, 1925. *A Lady of Chance*, 1928. *Hollywood Revue*, 1929. *Their Own Desire*, 1929. *Private Lives*, 1931. *Smilin' Through*, 1932. *The Barretts of Wimpole Street*, 1934. *Riptide*, 1934. *Marie Antoinette*, 1938. *Idiot's Delight*, 1939.

How Strange
Idiot's Delight was a charming adaptation of a Robert Sherwood play that co-starred **Norma Shearer** and **Clark Gable** as former show business partners who meet again in Europe on the eve of World War II. Clark Gable as a hoofer, surprised audiences with a song and dance routine to "Puttin' on the Ritz." $12

Ann Sheridan (1915-1967) was a stunning redhead, who entered movies as a beauty contest winner in 1933, the prize being a part in a Paramount movie. She was given a contract and after gaining acting experience and professional poise was promoted by Warner Brothers studio as the "Oomph Girl." She was a popular star by the late 1930s and proved her acting ability with an in-depth sympathetic performance in *King's Row* (1942). Her movie career slumped in the 1950s, but she was still visible on TV in the soap opera *Another World*.

SHERIDAN MOVIE COVERS: *San Quentin*, 1937. *Naughty But Nice*, 1939. *Winter Carnival*, 1939. *It All Came True*, 1940. *Torrid Zone*, 1940. *Navy Blues*, 1941. *Shine on Harvest Moon*, 1944. *One More Tomorrow*, 1946. *Nora Prentiss*, 1947. *Stella*, 1950. *Come Next Spring*, 1955. *The Opposite Sex*, 1956.

Who Cares What People Say
Ann Sheridan effectively portrayed "the other woman" in *Nora Prentiss*, a melodramatic triangle film with **Kent Smith** (center) as the philandering husband. Also cast were **Robert Alda** (top) and **Bruce Bennett.** $6

Frank Sinatra (1915-1998). Sinatra attracted attention when he won first prize on *Major Bowes Amateur Radio Hour*, which led to singing jobs with the big bands of Harry James and Tommy Dorsey. He became a singing sensation especially popular with young bobby-soxers who followed him avidly, screaming and swooning with delight. After a succession of light musical films in the 1940s, problems developed with his vocal chords and his career faltered. He made a valiant comeback in *From Here to Eternity* in 1953, winning a Best Supporting Actor Academy Award for his dramatic portrayal of Angelo Maggio in the film. His voice recovered better than ever, and his performances of songs "All the Way" in *The Joker Is Wild* (1957) and "High Hopes" in *A Hole in the Head* (1959) won Best Song Academy Awards for songwriters James Van Heusen and Sammy Cahn. Sinatra's superb singing style and colorful personality kept him at the forefront of male pop singers until his demise in 1998.

SINATRA MOVIE COVERS: *Las Vegas Nights*, 1941. *Always a Bridesmaid*, 1943. *Higher and Higher*, 1943. *Step Lively*, 1944. *Anchors Aweigh*, 1945. *The House I Live In*, 1945. *Till the Clouds Roll By*, 1946. *It Happened in Brooklyn*, 1947. *Miracle of the Bells*, 1948. *The Kissing Bandit*, 1948. *Deadly Is the Female*, 1949. *On the Town*, 1949. *Take Me Out to the Ball Game*, 1949. *Double Dynamite*, 1951. *Meet Danny Wilson*, 1952. *From Here to Eternity*, 1953. *Young at Heart*, 1954. *Guys and Dolls*, 1955. *Not As a Stranger*, 1955. *The Tender Trap*, 1955. *High Society*, 1956. *Johnny Concho*, 1956. *The Man with the Golden Arm*, 1956. *The Joker Is Wild*, 1957. *Pal Joey*, 1957. *Kings Go Forth*, 1958. *A Hole in the Head*, 1959. *Some Came Running*, 1959. *Can-Can*, 1960. *Ocean's 11*, 1960. *Come Blow Your Horn*, 1963. *Four for Texas*, 1963. *Robin and the Seven Hoods*, 1964. *Von Ryan's Express*, 1965. *Cast a Giant Shadow*, 1966. *A Man Could Get Killed*, 1966. *The Naked Runner*, 1967. *The Detective*, 1968. *Dirty Dingus Magee*, 1970. *Maurie*, 1973. *That's Entertainment*, 1974 and 1976. *Cannonball Run II*, 1984.

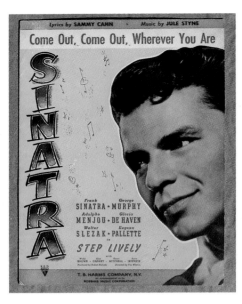

Come Out, Come Out, Wherever You Are
Step Lively was a pleasant remake of the 1938 Marx Brothers comedy *Room Service*. This musical version co-starred **Frank Sinatra** with George Murphy and Gloria De Haven, notable for giving Frank his first screen kiss. Songs were by Sammy Cahn (W) and Jule Styne (M). $4

From Here to Eternity
With his career in limbo, **Frank Sinatra** fought for a chance to portray Angelo Maggio in *From Here to Eternity*. He even offered to work for nothing, just to have the opportunity to prove his dramatic ability. And prove it he did—winning the Best Supporting Actor Oscar. Seen on cover, top to bottom, are **Burt Lancaster, Montgomery Clift, Deborah Kerr, Frank Sinatra,** and **Donna Reed**, winner of the Best Supporting Actress award. The movie won six additional Oscars including Best Director and Best Picture. $11

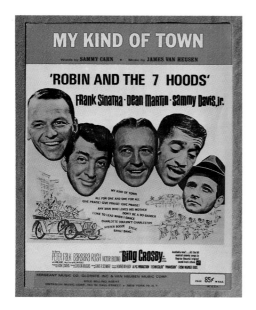

My Kind of Town
Robin and the 7 Hoods was a musical takeoff on the Robin Hood story, with **Frank Sinatra** and his gangster cronies robbing the rich to give to the poor during Prohibition days in Chicago. The all-star cast included (left to right) **Sinatra, Dean Martin, Bing Crosby, Sammy Davis Jr.,** and **Peter Falk.** Songs were by Sammy Cahn and James Van Heusen. $8

Red Skelton (1913-1997). Known as "King of the Clowns," Red Skelton knocked around as an itinerant comic for many years before making his first movie in 1938. He became a popular comedian in 1940s and 1950s movies at M-G-M, and later rose to super stardom on his television show portraying Freddie the Freeloader and Clem Kadiddlehopper.
SKELTON MOVIE COVERS: *Panama Hattie,* 1942. *Ship Ahoy,* 1942. *I Dood It,* 1943. *Bathing Beauty,* 1944. *Neptune's Daughter,* 1949. *Three Little Words,* 1950. *Excuse My Dust ,*1951. *Texas Carnival,* 1951. *Lovely to Look At,* 1952. *Public Pigeon Number One,* 1957.

Barbara Stanwyck (1907-1990). The consummate professional movie actress, Barbara Stanwyck, made more than 80 films from the 1930s to the 1950s, then made the successful transition to television as the star of the series *Big Valley,* for which she won television's Emmy award. Young and beautiful in the 1930s, she moved gracefully into more mature parts in later years. Though nominated for an Oscar four times, she never won, but was honored with a special Academy Award in 1981 "for superlative creativity and unique contribution to the art of screen acting." She was also the recipient of the American Film Institute's Lifetime Achievement Award in 1987.
STANWYCK MOVIE COVERS: *Mexicali Rose,* 1929. *Ten Cents a Dance,* 1931. *The Purchase Price,* 1932. *Red Salute,* 1935. *Banjo on My Knee,* 1936. *A Message to Garcia,* 1936. *This Is My Affair,* 1937. *Lady of Burlesque,* 1943. *Hollywood Canteen,* 1944. *Christmas in Connecticut,* 1945. *California,*

Who's Sorry Now?
Red Skelton portrayed composer Harry Ruby in *Three Little Words,* with **Fred Astaire** as his lyric-writing buddy, Bert Kalmar. The pleasant musical also starred **Vera-Ellen** and **Arlene Dahl** as the songwriters' wives. For Kalmar and Ruby fans, the film featured most of their biggest hits. $5

Star Eyes
Entertaining musical *I Dood It* co-starred **Red Skelton** with **Eleanor Powell**— he as a pants presser and she as a stage star. Vincente Minnelli directed the whole shebang that included knockout dance numbers by Powell, Skelton's unique brand of comedy, and musical interludes by Lena Horne, Hazel Scott, and Jimmy Dorsey with his band. Dorsey singers Bob Eberly and Helen O'Connell performed this Don Raye and Gene De Paul song. $4

1946. *My Reputation,* 1946. *The Strange Love of Martha Ivers,* 1946. *To Please a Lady,* 1950. *Clash by Night,* 1952. *All I Desire,* 1953. *Blowing Wild,* 1953. *The Moonlighter,* 1953. *Cattle Queen of Montana,* 1954. *The Maverick Queen,* 1956. *Forty Guns,* 1957. *Trooper Hook,* 1957. *A Walk on the Wild Side,* 1962.

Take Me Away
A luminous **Barbara Stanwyck** played a worldly torch singer in *The Purchase Price* who runs from her seamy city life to become a farmer's mail-order bride in North Dakota. $20

There's Something in the Air
Barbara Stanwyck and **Joel McCrea** were a young married couple in *Banjo on My Knee,* with him on the run for a murder he didn't commit. Stanwyck sang this song with **Anthony (Tony) Martin**, and also danced with **Buddy Ebsen** in the movie. $4

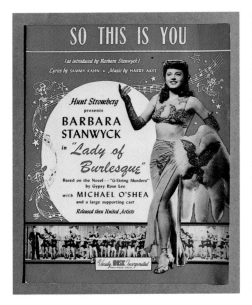

So This Is You
Barbara Stanwyck was delicious as a striptease artist in the murder mystery *Lady of Burlesque* with a maniacal murderer running amok, strangling show girls with their own G-strings. The script was based on the novel *The G-String Murders* written by real-life stripper Gypsy Rose Lee. Songs were by Sammy Cahn (W) and Harry Akst (M). Another song from the movie, "Take It Off the 'E' String," has an alternate cover, but this is the more valuable because of its rarity. *Collection of Harold Jacobs.* $50

California or Bust
The Western melodrama, *California*, starred **Barbara Stanwyck** as a saloon keeper, **Ray Milland** as a wagon master, and **Barry Fitzgerald** as a lovable crusty curmudgeon. The setting was early California before statehood, and the story manages to incorporate some history of the early days. Songs were by E. Y. Harburg (W) and Earl Robinson (M). $8

Seventh Heaven
Nineteen-year-old **James Stewart** and **Simone Simon** co-starred in the remake of the 1927 movie *Seventh Heaven*, the story of a poor struggling couple who find their heaven in a seventh story cold-water flat. Sidney Mitchell (W) and Lew Pollack (M) wrote the title song. $8

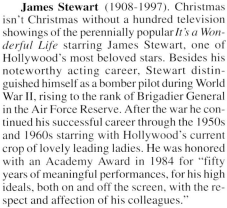

The Wish That I Wish Tonight
The warmhearted comedy *Christmas in Connecticut* starred **Barbara Stanwyck** as a writer who is asked to entertain a returning serviceman, **Dennis Morgan,** with an old-fashioned Christmas at her country home. Unfortunately her magazine column is a fiction, and she can't cook, knows nothing about babies, and has to borrow a country home to keep up the farce. $5

James Stewart (1908-1997). Christmas isn't Christmas without a hundred television showings of the perennially popular *It's a Wonderful Life* starring James Stewart, one of Hollywood's most beloved stars. Besides his noteworthy acting career, Stewart distinguished himself as a bomber pilot during World War II, rising to the rank of Brigadier General in the Air Force Reserve. After the war he continued his successful career through the 1950s and 1960s starring with Hollywood's current crop of lovely leading ladies. He was honored with an Academy Award in 1984 for "fifty years of meaningful performances, for his high ideals, both on and off the screen, with the respect and affection of his colleagues."

STEWART MOVIE COVERS: *Seventh Heaven*, 1937. *Vivacious Lady,* 1938. *Destry Rides Again,* 1939. *Made for Each Other,* 1939. *Pot o' Gold,* 1941. *Ziegfeld Girl,* 1941. *Magic Town,* 1947. *A Miracle Can Happen (a.k.a. On Our Merry Way),* 1948. *The Glenn Miller Story,* 1954. *Rear Window,* 1954. *The Man from Laramie,* 1955. *Strategic Air Command,* 1955. *The Man Who Knew Too Much,* 1956. *Night Passage,* 1957. *Bell, Book, and Candle,* 1958. *Vertigo,* 1958. *The F.B.I. Story,* 1959. *The Man Who Shot Liberty Valance,* 1962. *How the West Was Won,* 1962. *Mr. Hobbs Takes a Vacation,* 1962. *Cheyenne Autumn,* 1964. *The Flight of the Phoenix,* 1965. *Shenandoah,* 1965. *Bandolero,* 1968. *The Magic of Lassie,* 1978.

A String of Pearls
James Stewart totally immersed himself into the character of Glenn Miller in *The Glenn Miller Story*, a charming biographical study of the big bandleader who was lost in a plane wreck during World War II. **June Allyson** played his loving wife. Miller's biggest hits were featured with many of his original musicians backing up. $8 *($18)*

The Man from Laramie
The strong Western drama starred **James Stewart** as *The Man from Laramie*, hell-bent on finding his brother's killers and wreaking revenge. **Cathy O'Donnell** was his love interest. Title song was written by Ned Washington (W) and Lester Lee (M). $6

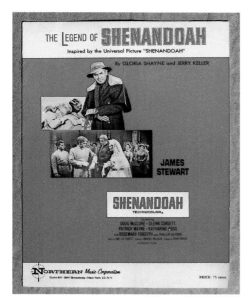

The Shenandoah Theme
In *Shenandoah*, **James Stewart** was effective as the widowed patriarch of a large family who wants to stay isolationist during the Civil War, but is forced by circumstances to take sides. The title song was composed by Gloria Shayne and Jerry Keller. $5

The Phoenix Love Theme
The Flight of the Phoenix was an exciting adventure movie with **James Stewart** as a pilot who crash-lands his plane in the Sahara desert with a motley group of passengers, who show their true colors in the face of daunting hardships. Alec Wilder wrote the title song. $6

Evergreen
Barbra Streisand starred in the third version of *A Star Is Born*, changing the leading characters to pop rock stars instead of movie stars. Streisand's music and Paul Williams's words for this lovely theme took an Oscar for Best Song. $4

Barbra Streisand (born 1942). After her show-stopping performance as Fanny Brice in *Funny Girl* in 1964, Barbra Streisand became one of the biggest names on Broadway. She later repeated her role in Hollywood and won an Academy Award for Best Actress in 1968 in a tie with Katharine Hepburn who also won for Best Actress in *A Lion in Winter*. Streisand's enormous talents and strong personality thrust her into superstardom in the entertainment field.

STREISAND MOVIE COVERS: *Funny Girl*, 1968. *Hello Dolly*, 1969. *On a Clear Day You Can See Forever*, 1970. *The Way We Were*, 1973. *Funny Lady*, 1975. *A Star Is Born*, 1976. *Main Event*, 1979. *Yentl*, 1983. *The Prince of Tides*, 1991.

Places That Belong to You
Barbra Streisand's foray into directing produced *The Prince of Tides*, in which she played a psychiatrist who helps **Nick Nolte** dredge up painful childhood memories. She also recorded this song by Alan and Marilyn Bergman (W) and James Newton Howard (M). $4

Margaret Sullavan (1911-1960). She left her mark on both stage and screen, winning the New York Film Critics' award for best actress in the 1938 movie *Three Comrades*, and the Drama Critics' Award for *The Voice of the Turtle* on Broadway in 1943. She excelled in moving dramatic roles, but was also a gifted comedienne in lighter roles. She was a troubled young woman, married four times, who died tragically by her own hand at age 49.

SULLAVAN MOVIE COVERS: *Only Yesterday*, 1933. *The Moon's Our Home*, 1936. *So Red the Rose*, 1935. *So Ends Our Night*, 1941.

Only Yesterday
Margaret Sullavan made her Hollywood movie debut in the melodrama *Only Yesterday*, as a young woman who, after a night of love with a soldier, bears a child out of wedlock. The soldier, played by **John Boles**, back from the war has no memory of their idyll. Walter Donaldson wrote the title song. $40

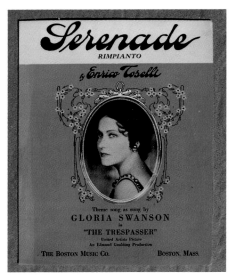

Serenade
Gloria Swanson received a Best Actress nomination for *The Trespasser*, her first talking picture which she also produced. She played a heavy dramatic role as a rejected wife with a baby, and though she lost out to Norma Shearer in *The Divorcée*, the film itself was a big hit with the public. She sang this theme song by Enrico Toselli in the movie. $5

So Red the Rose
Margaret Sullavan played a Dixie belle, patiently awaiting her soldier boyfriend's return from the Civil War battlefield in *So Red the Rose*. Title song was written by Jack Lawrence and Arthur Altman. *Collection of Harold Jacobs.* $25

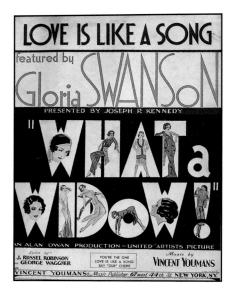

Love Is Like a Song
Gloria Swanson played a lovely spirited widow with a penchant for different men in *What a Widow*, a movie sponsored by her patron Joseph P. Kennedy. The movie was unfortunately a box office dud, despite the good songs and beautiful wardrobe. $10

Elizabeth Taylor (born 1932). Possessor of extraordinary violet eyes and classic brunette beauty, Miss Taylor started out as an enchanting child star in *Lassie Come Home*, graduating into teenager roles, and ultimately into adulthood as a mature actress. In the 1950s she tackled increasingly more complex characterizations, and won Best Actress Oscars for *Butterfield 8* in 1960 and *Who's Afraid of Vir-*

Melody of Spring
Fifteen-year-old **Elizabeth Taylor**'s dazzling photo as a nubile teenager on this song cover from *Cynthia* foreshadows her future as a beauty of world renown. Also appearing in the movie were, top to bottom, **George Murphy, Mary Astor,** and **S. Z. Sakall.** $20

ginia Woolf? in 1966. She had previously been nominated for *Raintree County, Cat on a Hot Tin Roof,* and *Suddenly Last Summer.*

ELIZABETH TAYLOR MOVIE COVERS: *Cynthia,* 1947. *A Date with Judy,* 1948. *A Place in the Sun,* 1951. *Elephant Walk,* 1954. *The Last Time I Saw Paris,* 1954. *Rhapsody,* 1954. *Giant,* 1956. *Raintree County,* 1957. *Butterfield 8,* 1960. *Cleopatra,* 1963. *The VIP's,* 1963. *The Sandpiper,* 1965. *Who's Afraid of Virginia Woolf?* 1966. *The Comedians,* 1967. *Boom,* 1968. *Ash Wednesday,* 1973. *Night Watch,* 1973.

Robert Taylor (1911-1969). This handsome actor was Clark Gable's rival for top romantic leads in the 1930s, and co-starred with some of Hollywood's most beautiful leading ladies. During World War II he served as a flight instructor with the Navy, and was also involved in the production of 17 Navy training films and the documentary *The Fighting Lady.* Back in Hollywood after the war, he continued his career, turning out some solid performances until his death in 1969 from lung cancer.

ROBERT TAYLOR MOVIE COVERS:*Broadway Melody of 1936. Camille,* 1936. *Small Town Girl,* 1936. *This Is My Affair,* 1937. *Broadway Melody of 1938. Lady of the Tropics,* 1939. *Waterloo Bridge,* 1940. *Song of Russia,* 1943. *Undercurrent,* 1946. *The Bribe,* 1949. *Many Rivers to Cross ,*1955. *Saddle the Wind,* 1958. *The Hangman,* 1959. *A House Is Not a Home,* 1964.

I'm Feelin' Like a Million
Robert Taylor was the love interest of **Eleanor Powell** in the star-studded movie *Broadway Melody of 1938.* Young Judy Garland made a splash in her feature debut with other cover stars **Sophie Tucker, George Murphy, Buddy Ebsen,** and **Igor Gorin.** This song by Arthur Freed (W) and Nacio Herb Brown (M) was sung by George Murphy and Eleanor Powell in the movie. $10

Gloria
Elizabeth Taylor was awarded her first Oscar for her role as a sexy model in *Butterfield 8,* co-starred with **Laurence Harvey** (left) as the love of her life, and **Eddie Fisher** (right) as a supportive platonic friend. Theme song was written by Mack David (W) and Bronislau Kaper (M). $12 (*$22*)

Who's Afraid?
Edward Albee's play, *Who's Afraid of Virginia Woolf,* was adapted for the screen with **Elizabeth Taylor** and **Richard Burton** playing the extraordinary couple George and Martha in a tormented relationship. Taylor's towering bitchy performance won her a second Oscar for Best Actress. Alex North wrote the theme song with words by Paul Francis Webster. $10 (*$16*)

Antony and Cleopatra Theme
The expensive production of *Cleopatra* starred **Elizabeth Taylor** in the title role opposite **Rex Harrison** as a mighty Caesar and **Richard Burton** as the ill-fated Antony. Despite its astronomical cost, it failed to win any major Oscars, although it picked up several awards for technical brilliance. Theme song by Alex North was from the Oscar-nominated original music score. $8

And Russia Is Her Name
Robert Taylor portrayed a symphony conductor on tour, who falls in love with beautiful Russian girl **Susan Peters** in *Song of Russia.* The sentiment was pro-Russian in honor of our wartime ally, later regretted by the studio during the Cold War. This was Taylor's last movie before he joined the Navy. Cover song was written by E. Y. Harburg (W) and Jerome Kern (M). $8

161

Undercurrent
After three years in the Navy, **Robert Taylor** returned to star in the suspenseful movie *Undercurrent*. He played **Katharine Hepburn**'s new bridegroom, who shows his evil side after the wedding. The theme song was based on a motif from Brahms's Third Symphony, adapted by Herbert Stothart. $10

Shirley Temple (born 1928). The most famous child star of them all was Shirley Temple, a blonde curly-haired moppet who captivated large audiences with the force of her winning personality. The dimpled darling exuded talent to the extent that some critics accused her of being a midget acting as a little girl. Shirley started out in a series of kiddie short subjects, then was featured in *Stand Up and Cheer* singing "Baby Take a Bow." She became an overnight sensation, and ultimately the most famous child star in the world and a number one box office attraction. She continued to make a few movies during her awkward preteen years and early adulthood, and enjoyed a brief stint on television.

In the 1960s, she entered politics, and had a successful second career in government service. She was appointed representative to the United Nations General Assembly (1969), Ambassador to Ghana (1974), Chief of Protocol of the State Department (1976), and U.S. Ambassador to Czechoslovakia (1989). Shirley Temple sheet music covers are highly prized collectibles valued, from $10 to $25.

TEMPLE MOVIE COVERS: *Baby Take a Bow*, 1934. *Bright Eyes*, 1934. *Little Miss Marker*, 1934. *Now and Forever*, 1934. *Curly Top*, 1935. *The Little Colonel*, 1935. *The Littlest Rebel*, 1935. *Our Little Girl*, 1935. *Captain January*, 1936. *Dimples*, 1936. *Poor Little Rich Girl*, 1936. *Stowaway*, 1936. *Heidi*, 1937. *Just Around the Corner*, 1938. *Little Miss Broadway*, 1938. *Rebecca of Sunnybrook Farm*, 1938. *The Blue Bird*, 1940. *Young People*, 1940. *Kathleen*, 1941. *Since You Went Away*, 1944. *I'll Be Seeing You*, 1945. *Honeymoon*, 1947. *The Bachelor and the Bobby-Soxer*, 1947.

Animal Crackers in My Soup
In *Curly Top*, **Shirley Temple** played an orphan who, with her sister **Rochelle Hudson**, is rescued from the orphanage by **John Boles**. She sang this song during mealtime at the asylum with a chorus of sixty orphans. $15

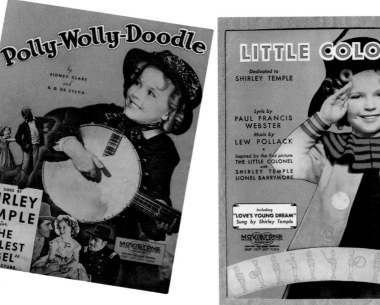

Polly-Wolly-Doodle
As a charming Southern tot, **Shirley Temple** captures the heart of enemy Yankee soldier **Jack Holt** and protects her Confederate officer father, played by **John Boles** in *The Littlest Rebel*. Dance sequences with **Bill Robinson** are especially notable, as well as Shirley's delightful singing. $18

Little Colonel
Shirley Temple co-starred with Lionel Barrymore as her surly old Southern grandfather in *The Little Colonel*. Shirley and the legendary dancer Bill "Bojangles" Robinson got along fine in this movie, dancing their famous staircase dance. $15

Our Little Girl
Shirley Temple, upset at her parents' impending separation, runs away to the circus in *Our Little Girl*. The sentimental movie co-starred Joel McCrea and Rosemary Ames as her parents. Title song was written by Paul Francis Webster (W) and Lew Pollack (M). $25

Left:
At the Codfish Ball
In *Captain January* **Shirley Temple** is rescued from a capsized boat by Guy Kibbee, a salty old sea captain who runs a lighthouse in Maine. Relatives eventually appear to claim her, but not before she has a chance to sing and dance with Buddy Ebsen. $18

An Old Straw Hat
Shirley Temple, as usual, stole the show from co-stars who appear on this alternate cover for *Rebecca of Sunnybrook Farm* (the rarer of the two)—**Phyllis Brooks** and **Jack Haley** (top), **Gloria Stuart** and **Randolph Scott** (center), and **Slim Summerville** (bottom). Mack Gordon and Harry Revel wrote this song. $30

Goodnight My Love
Eight-year-old **Shirley Temple** played a waif with a puppy who is befriended by million-aire **Robert Young** in *Stowaway*. She does indeed stowaway on a cruise ship, singing her tunes and playing cupid with Young and **Alice Faye** before her discovery. Songs are by Gordon and Revel. $15

In Our Little Wooden Shoes
Shirley Temple was perfectly cast in the title role of *Heidi*, the delightful story of an orphan raised by her grandfather in the Tyrolean Alps, who is sold by her aunt as a companion to a wealthy crippled girl. Heidi endures many hardships before reuniting with her beloved grandfather. Shirley sang and danced this number as a little Dutch girl in a dream sequence in the movie. $15 *($25)*

Right:
The Toy Trumpet
Shirley Temple once again danced with Bill Robinson in *Rebecca of Sunnybrook Farm*, doing another staircase routine to this song with music by Raymond Scott and words by Lew Pollack and Sidney D. Mitchell. $15

Around the Corner
In *Kathleen*, **Shirley Temple**, now 13, played an unhappy young lady who lived in a dream world when her busy father ne-glected her. A psychologist is hired to straighten her out, and things end happily as father and psychologist fall in love and Shirley finally has a real home and family. Shirley sang this Roger Edens and Earl Brent song in a dream sequence in the movie. The sheet music is a rarity. $100

The Bachelor and the Bobby-Soxer
Cary Grant played the bewildered bachelor who is attracted to Myrna Loy, but is relentlessly pursued by her sister, 17-year-old bobby-soxer, **Shirley Temple**, who has a crush on him. The movie, *The Bachelor and the Bobby-Soxer* won an Academy Award for writer Sidney Sheldon for the Best Original Screenplay. $22 *($75)*

Gene Tierney (1920-1991). Beautiful and poised, Gene Tierney started her acting career on the Broadway stage, where she was discovered by Darryl F. Zanuck who signed her to a Hollywood movie contract. Her 20 year ca-

I'll Meet You at Sundown
In the wartime movie *Sundown*, **Gene Tierney** plays a gorgeous native girl in Africa opposite **Bruce Cabot**, who thwarts Nazi plans to take over. Jack Betzner and Irving Mills wrote the theme song. *Collection of Harold Jacobs.* $125

reer in movies was highlighted by her portrayal of the hauntingly beautiful heroine in *Laura*, and the psychopathic murderous sister in *Leave Her to Heaven*. Her 1979 autobiography, *Self Portrait*, tells of her dates with John F. Kennedy in his younger Navy days, and candidly discusses her much-publicized mental breakdowns and institutionalism.

TIERNEY MOVIE COVERS: *Sundown*, 1941. *Son of Fury*, 1942. *Laura*, 1944. *The Razor's Edge*, 1946. *The Mating Season*, 1951. *On the Riviera*, 1951.

Laura
Gene Tierney is thought to be dead by hard-boiled detective Dana Andrews in the mystery thriller *Laura*, and he falls in love with her portrait. Johnny Mercer wrote the words to the melodic theme by David Raksin, introduced on the sound track and on radio by **Johnnie Johnston.** $4

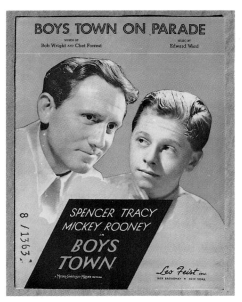

Boys Town on Parade
Spencer Tracy won his second Oscar for his portrayal of Father Flanagan in *Boys Town*, a sentimental story about the founding of the boys' home by a priest who believed there was no such thing as a bad boy. **Mickey Rooney**, a mean and unruly delinquent, tried to prove him wrong, but goodness prevailed. $20

My Lost Melody
Gene Tierney and **John Lund** co-starred as a married couple in *The Mating Season*, but it was Thelma Ritter who stole the show as his mother pretending to be a servant in his household, a richly developed characterization that brought her an Academy Award nomination for Best Supporting Actress. $20

Spencer Tracy (1900-1967). Tracy was a solid and dependable actor in many of M-G-M's finest movie productions. His favorite co-star was Katharine Hepburn, with whom he appeared many times—in *Woman of the Year*, *Keeper of the Flame*, *Without Love*, *The Sea of Grass*, *State of the Union*, *Adam's Rib*, *Pat and Mike*, *Desk Set*, and *Guess Who's Coming to Dinner*. He received Best Actor Academy Awards for his sensitive performances as a fisherman in *Captains Courageous* (1937) and Father Flanagan in *Boys Town* (1938).

TRACY COVERS: *Bottoms Up*, 1934. *Now I'll Tell*, 1934. *Dante's Inferno*, 1935. *They Gave Him a Gun*, 1937. *Boys Town*, 1938. *A Guy Named Joe*, 1943. *Thirty Seconds Over Tokyo*, 1944. *Adam's Rib*, 1949. *The Mountain*, 1956. *The Old Man and the Sea*, 1958. *Judgment at Nuremberg*, 1961. *Guess Who's Coming to Dinner*, 1967.

Farewell, Amanda
Spencer Tracy and **Katharine Hepburn** are husband and wife lawyers on opposite sides of a case in *Adam's Rib*, one of the wittiest of their joint endeavors. **Judy Holliday** (lower left) made her film debut as a blonde airhead who is being tried for shooting her husband. Song was written by the great Cole Porter. $20

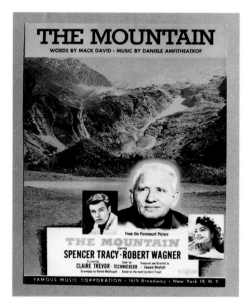

The Mountain
In the suspenseful movie *The Mountain*, **Spencer Tracy**, a simple peasant farmer, is persuaded by his greedy brother, **Robert Wagner**, to make a difficult climb in the Alps to loot a downed airplane. Title song was written by Mack David (W) and Daniele Amfitheatrof (M). *Collection of Harold Jacobs.* $15

Judgment at Nuremberg Theme
Spencer Tracy played the judge in the taut production of *Judgment at Nuremberg*, based on the Nazi war crime trials after World War II. The strong cast included (left to right) **Tracy, Burt Lancaster, Richard Widmark, Marlene Dietrich, Maximilian Schell, Judy Garland,** and **Montgomery Clift.** Theme song was written by Al Stillman (W) and Ernest Gold (M). *Collection of Roy Bishop.* $15

Claire Trevor (born 1909). She studied acting at the American Academy of Dramatic Arts and after successful appearances on the Broadway stage, moved to Hollywood to make movies. Though frequently cast as a gun moll, or hard-boiled babe with a heart of gold, she rose above her material and earned critical respect for her acting ability. She was nominated for a Best Supporting Actress Oscar in 1937 for *Dead End*, and finally received the award in 1948 for her role in *Key Largo*.

TREVOR MOVIE COVERS: *Jimmy and Sally,* 1933. *Baby Take a Bow,* 1934. *Wild Gold,* 1934. *Black Sheep,* 1935. *Dante's Inferno,* 1935. *Song and Dance Man,* 1936. *Star for a Night,* 1936. *Big Town Girl,* 1937. *King of Gamblers,* 1937. *Crossroads,* 1942. *Johnny Angel,* 1945. *The Bachelor's Daughters,* 1946. *The Babe Ruth Story,* 1948. *Stop You're Killing Me,* 1953. *The High and the Mighty,* 1954.

You're My Thrill
Claire Trevor shows off her gorgeous legs on the cover of this song from the Fox film *Jimmy and Sally*, in which she co-starred with **James Dunn**. The torchy cover song was written by Sidney Clare (W) and Jay Gorney (M). $6

Memphis in June
Claire Trevor and **George Raft** teamed up in the movie *Johnny Angel*, a suspenseful melodrama with Raft as a sea captain who solves the mystery of his father's murder. **Hoagy Carmichael** wrote the cover song with words by Paul Francis Webster, and Hoagy also played a part in the film. $5

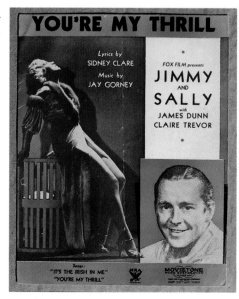

Lana Turner (1920-1995). As a young high-school student she was discovered seated at a Hollywood soda fountain and was signed up for the movies. She managed to surmount many ill-fated marriages and a scandalous affair with a gangster figure to become one of Hollywood's most fabulous and glamorous stars.

In 1958 her disturbed teenage daughter, Cheryl Crane, fatally stabbed her mother's boyfriend, Johnny Stompanato. The girl was acquitted, and the killing was pronounced justifiable homicide at the lurid inquest. Surprisingly the publicity failed to hurt Lana Turner's career, and she continued making movies into her fifties.

TURNER MOVIE COVERS: *Dancing Co-Ed*, 1939. *These Glamour Girls*, 1939. *Two Girls on Broadway*, 1940. *Ziegfeld Girl*, 1941. *Keep Your Powder Dry*, 1945. *Weekend at the Waldorf*, 1945. *The Postman Always Rings Twice*, 1946. *Green Dolphin Street*, 1947. *A Life of Her Own*, 1950. *Mr. Imperium*, 1951. *The Bad and the Beautiful*, 1952. *The Merry Widow*, 1952. *Latin Lovers*, 1953. *Betrayed*, 1954. *Flame and the Flesh*, 1954. *The Prodigal*, 1955. *Another Time, Another Place*, 1958. *Who's Got the Action*, 1958. *Imitation of Life*, 1959. *Bachelor in Paradise*, 1961. *Madame X*, 1966.

By Candlelight
Seductive **Lana Turner** is romanced by nightclub singer **Carlos Thompson** in *Flame and the Flesh*, also starring the fresh young star Pier Angeli. Cover song was written by Jack Lawrence (W) and Nicholas Brodszky (M). $6

Another Time, Another Place
Lana Turner, a newspaper woman in London during World War II is in love with a married man, Sean Connery, who is killed in action. She is comforted by her fiancé, cover star **Barry Sullivan** in *Another Time, Another Place*. Title song was by Jay Livingston and Ray Evans. $7

Jungle Drums
Lana Turner was a glamorous 19-year-old when she made *Dancing Co-ed*, co-starring with the first of her seven husbands, bandleader **Artie Shaw,** and young ingenue **Ann Rutherford.** $8

John Wayne (1907-1979). Beloved by audiences throughout his 40 years as a screen star, John Wayne was a big box office draw. As a young college student, he was on U.S.C.'s football team and worked part-time at Fox studios, where he made friends with director John Ford. He was soon typecast as a cowboy in B-Western movies, which he made for about eight years until his memorable performance in *Stagecoach*, in 1939. Better roles were forthcoming, and his list of outstanding movies is formidable. Wayne's performance as a crusty lawman in *True Grit* earned him a well-deserved Academy Award in 1969.

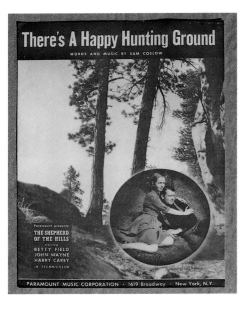

There's a Happy Hunting Ground
Harry Bell Wright's novel *The Shepherd of the Hills* was adapted for a movie starring **John Wayne**, who unknowingly meets and learns to like his father about whom he harbors bitter memories. Film also starred **Betty Field** as the love interest, and Harry Carey as Wayne's long lost father. Song is by Sam Coslow. $7

WAYNE MOVIE COVERS: *The Big Trail*, 1930. *Stagecoach*, 1939. *The Shepherd of the Hills*, 1941. *Reap the Wild Wind*, 1942. *In Old Oklahoma*, 1943. *The Fighting Seabees*, 1944. *They Were Expendable*, 1945. *Fort Apache*, 1948. *She Wore a Yellow Ribbon*, 1949. *Rio Grande*, 1950. *The Quiet Man*, 1952. *Island in the Sky*, 1953. *The High and the Mighty*, 1954. *The Conqueror*, 1956. *The Searchers*, 1956. *Legend of the Lost*, 1957. *The Wings of Eagles*, 1957. *Rio Bravo*, 1959. *The Alamo*, 1960. *North to Alaska*, 1960. *The Comancheros*, 1961. *Hatari*, 1962. *How the West Was Won*, 1962. *The Man Who Shot Liberty Valance*, 1962. *McLintock!* 1963. *The Sons of Katie Elder*, 1965. *Cast a Giant Shadow*, 1966. *El Dorado*, 1967. *The War Wagon*, 1967. *True Grit*, 1969. *The Undefeated*, 1969. *The Shootist*, 1976.

Mush, Mush, Mush, Tural-i-addy
The courtship, Irish-style, of **John Wayne** and **Maureen O'Hara,** along with the antics of lovable **Barry Fitzgerald** brought glory to John Ford in the movie *The Quiet Man*. He took an Oscar for Best Director. *Collection of James Nelson Brown.* $15 *($25)*

Baby Elephant Walk
John Wayne starred in *Hatari!*, an exciting adventure film made in Africa with plenty of action showing the roundup of wild animals to be shipped to zoos around the world. The light-handed directorial touch of Howard Hawks and original background music by Henry Mancini contributed to the enjoyable film. $12 *($22)*

She Wore a Yellow Ribbon
John Wayne played a cavalry officer about to retire who serves one last time to thwart an Indian massacre in *She Wore a Yellow Ribbon*. Actress **Joanne Dru** also starred. Title song was based on an American folk song. $9 *($18)*

The Conqueror
The Conqueror shows **John Wayne** embracing **Susan Hayward** on the cover of the theme song by Edward Heyman (W) and Victor Young (M). This movie has tragic overtones, as it was made near the site of early atomic bomb testing, and many of those connected with the film have since died of cancer, including Wayne himself. $5

True Grit
John Wayne, now 62 years old, won an Oscar for his portrayal of Rooster Cogburn, a crotchety one-eyed codger who helps a young girl avenge her father's murder in *True Grit*. A new young actress, **Kim Darby,** played the gritty tomboy, and **Glen Campbell** backed everybody up. This song by Don Black (W) and Elmer Bernstein (M) was nominated for a Best Song Oscar. $8 *($18)*

Orson Welles (1915-1985). Incredibly gifted in many areas, Mr. Welles was successful on stage, screen, and radio as director, producer, writer, and actor. His movie *Citizen Kane* in 1941 caused an early sensation and is revered yet today for its cinematic innovations. At the time of its release it caused consternation in William Randolph Hearst, who resented the Kane character being based on his life, and tried unsuccessfully to suppress the film. Other notable Welles films were *The Magnificent Ambersons* (1942), *Jane Eyre* (1944), and *The Stranger* (1946). In 1975 he received the American Film Institute's Lifetime Achievement Award. The great man appeared on few movie covers, only *The 3rd Man* (1949) and *The Black Rose* (1950).

Mae West (1892-1980). A legendary figure on the Broadway burlesque stage, Mae West flaunted her sexiness in such plays as *Sex* in 1926, for which she was jailed for ten days on an obscenity charge. In Hollywood films her witty outrageous remarks and sexy mien continued to draw the ire of censors, but she was popular with audiences who enjoyed her tongue-in-cheek humor and double entendre. She was a full figured, buxom lady, who had an inflatable life jacket named after her by pilots and sailors who admired her mammary charms. She cuts a striking figure on her sheet music covers.

WEST MOVIE COVERS: *I'm No Angel*, 1933. *She Done Him Wrong*, 1933. *Belle of the Nineties*, 1934. *Goin' to Town*, 1935. *Go West Young Man*, 1936. *Klondike Annie*, 1936. *Every Day's a Holiday*, 1937. *My Little Chickadee*, 1940. *The Heat's On*, 1943. *Myra Breckenridge*, 1970.

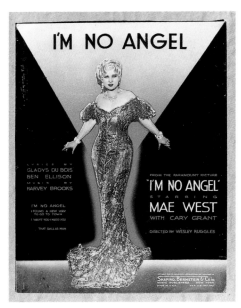

I'm No Angel
Mae West played the carnival girl, Sister Honky Tonk, in *I'm No Angel*, in which she wrote many of her hilarious slightly bawdy one-liners herself, sang five songs, and generally burned up the screen with her torrid personality. $20 *($45)*

Left:
Now I'm a Lady
Mae West, in a rags to riches story, played a poor saloon singer who inherited an oil-rich ranch, and became a social climber. She wrote the script for *Goin' to Town* complete with naughty innuendos, and came up with another box office hit. $50

Occidental Woman
Klondike Annie was an appropriate vehicle for **Mae West.** Running from the law, she switched places with a Salvation Army lass and gave a new interpretation to evangelism. She gave a memorable rendition of this Gene Austin song in the movie. $50

Please Don't Kiss Me
Orson Welles wrote the screenplay for *The Lady from Shanghai*, which he also produced, directed, and starred in with his wife **Rita Hayworth.** It was a steamy *film noir* tour de force with Welles passionately in love with another man's wife, even committing murder for her. Hayworth divorced him shortly after the film was completed. Song by Allan Roberts and Doris Fisher. *Collection of Harold Jacobs.* $60

The 3rd Man Theme
Orson Welles co-starred with **Alida Valli** and **Joseph Cotten** in the moody thriller *The Third Man.* This theme by Anton Karas was played hauntingly throughout the film on a zither. $4

Esther Williams (born 1923). A champion swimmer discovered by M-G-M in the early 1940s, Miss Williams was launched in a series of musical comedies. Brilliantly filmed in Technicolor with lavish song and dance numbers, these movies were a top attraction. No expense was spared in the production of the underwater sequences, and Esther Williams became known as "Hollywood's Mermaid." Her ventures into dramatic roles in the mid-1950s met with a lukewarm reception, and she retired from films in the early 1960s.

WILLIAMS MOVIE COVERS: *Bathing Beauty,* 1944. *Thrill of a Romance,* 1945. *Easy to Wed,* 1946. *The Hoodlum Saint,* 1946. *Fiesta,* 1947. *This Time for Keeps,* 1947. *On an Island with You,* 1948. *Neptune's Daughter,* 1949. *Take Me Out to the Ball Game,* 1949. *Duchess of Idaho,* 1950. *Pagan Love Song,* 1950. *Texas Carnival,* 1951. *Million Dollar Mermaid,* 1952. *Skirts Ahoy,* 1952. *Dangerous When Wet,* 1953. *Easy to Love,* 1953. *Jupiter's Darling,* 1955. *Raw Wind in Eden,* 1958.

Fantasia Mexicana
Esther Williams played a lady matador in *Fiesta,* a Technicolor romp filmed in Mexico, assisted by Cyd Charisse and **Ricardo Montalban.** The theme song was adapted by Johnny Green from Aaron Copland's orchestral suite *El Salon Mexico.* $12

Takin' Miss Mary to the Ball
The romantic musical *On an Island with You,* offered the usual **Esther Williams** package—fabulous production numbers, gorgeous Technicolor, good-looking men like **Peter Lawford** and **Ricardo Montalban,** the comedy of **Jimmy Durante,** dancing by **Cyd Charisse,** and music by **Xavier Cugat** and his orchestra. $6

Jane Withers (born 1926). A child star in the 1930s, Jane Withers possessed a mischievous charm that made her perfect for bratty parts, and a good foil for the sweetness of Shirley Temple. As an adult she became well-known on television commercials as Josephine the Plumber. The sprightly little lady appears on some attractive movie song covers.

WITHERS MOVIE COVERS: *Paddy O'Day,* 1935. *Can This Be Dixie?* 1936. *Little Miss Nobody,* 1936. *The Holy Terror,* 1937. *Rascals,* 1938. *Boy Friend,* 1939. *Shooting High,* 1940. *Golden Hoofs,* 1941.

Then Came the Indians
Little Miss Nobody was a Fox movie starring feisty little **Jane Withers** as a young orphan who gets into trouble and is sent to reform school. But all ends well when the attorney handling her case turns out to be her father. *Collection of Harold Jacobs.* $100

Natalie Wood (1938-1981). Miss Wood was an appealing child star in many 1940s movies including the Christmas perennial classic *Miracle on 34th Street,* in which she played a little girl who discovered there was indeed a Santa Claus. She grew up into a lovely young woman, and an accomplished actress in the

Tumblin Tim
Six-year-old **Natalie Wood** made her film debut in *Tomorrow Is Forever,* playing Orson Welles's pathetic immigrant daughter. Marilyn Lang wrote this cover song with a small photo of the appealing moppet. *Collection of Harold Jacobs.* $25

Let Me Entertain You
The hit stage musical *Gypsy* was brought to the screen with **Natalie Wood** as the legendary Gypsy Rose Lee, **Rosalind Russell** as her ambitious stage mother, and **Karl Malden** as their friend. Songs were by Stephen Sondheim (W) and Jule Styne (M). $5

1950s. As a teenager she packed a wallop in *Rebel Without a Cause*, for which she was nominated for an Academy Award. Her death by accidental drowning in 1981 saddened Hollywood and her fans.

WOOD MOVIE COVERS: *Tomorrow Is Forever*, 1946. *Rebel Without a Cause*, 1955. *A Cry in the Night*, 1956. *Kings Go Forth*, 1958. *Marjorie Morningstar*, 1958. *Splendor in the Grass*, 1961. *Gypsy*, 1962. *Love With the Proper Stranger*, 1964. *Sex and the Single Girl*, 1964. *Inside Daisy Clover*, 1966. *Penelope*, 1966. *This Property Is Condemned*, 1966. *The Last Married Couple in America*, 1979.

Love With the Proper Stranger
Natalie Wood received her third Best Actress nomination for her role in *Love With the Proper Stranger*, opposite **Steve McQueen.** It's the old story of young love, and an unwanted pregnancy handled with sensitivity. Title song, written by Johnny Mercer (W) and Elmer Bernstein (M), was introduced by Jack Jones in the movie. $8

You're Gonna Hear from Me
Natalie Wood does considerable emoting as a young delinquent who turns movie star in *Inside Daisy Clover*. Her co-stars were **Robert Redford** and **Christopher Plummer.** Song was written by Dory Previn (W) and Andre Previn (M). $5

Tom's Theme
Tennessee Williams's play *The Glass Menagerie* was made into an effective movie starring **Joanne Woodward** as Amanda Wingfield. John Malkovich played her son, Tom, and real life husband Paul Newman directed. This theme song was by Henry Mancini. $4

Joanne Woodward (born 1930). After gaining experience acting in high school and college productions, she polished her dramatic skills at the Neighborhood Playhouse in New York. Her first major success in Hollywood was her wide-ranging performance as a schizophrenic with multiple personalities in *The Three Faces of Eve*, for which she won the Best Actress Academy Award in 1957. Her husband, Paul Newman, has been a frequent co-star, and also directed her in *Rachel, Rachel* (1968), which brought her another Oscar nomination.

WOODWARD MOVIE COVERS: *A Kiss Before Dying*, 1956. *The Long Hot Summer*, 1958. *The Sound and the Fury*, 1959. *From the Terrace*, 1960. *A New Kind of Love*, 1963 *The Stripper*, 1963. *A Big Hand for a Little Lady*, 1966. *Winning*, 1969. *W.U.S.A.*, 1970. *The Glass Menagerie*, 1987.

From the Terrace Theme
Joanne Woodward, Paul Newman's real life wife, also played his movie wife in *From the Terrace*, based on the best-selling novel by John O'Hara. Newman portrayed an ambitious businessman who tries to get ahead at any cost, and Woodward was a promiscuous hellion who made his life miserable. The movie theme song was composed by Elmer Bernstein. $10

Teresa Wright (born 1918). As an ingenue on the Broadway stage, Miss Wright was discovered by Samuel Goldwyn who brought her to Hollywood. Her first screen role in *The Little Foxes* received an Academy Award nomination for Best Supporting Actress. The following year she was nominated in two categories—Best Actress for *The Pride of the Yankees* and Best Supporting Actress for *Mrs. Miniver,* which she won. Other praiseworthy parts were in *Shadow of a Doubt* and *The Best Years of Our Lives.* She retired from movies in 1959 with only occasional appearances on the stage and in television.

WRIGHT MOVIE COVERS: *The Pride of the Yankees,* 1942. *Shadow of a Doubt,* 1943. *Casanova Brown,* 1944. *The Best Years of Our Lives,* 1946. *Enchantment,* 1948. *The Men,* 1950. *The Steel Trap,* 1952.

Enchantment
Told in flashback, *Enchantment* recounts a love story relived in the mind of an old man. **Teresa Wright** and **David Niven** were the young lovers of yore, and **Farley Granger** and **Evelyn Keyes** played contemporary lovers. Don Raye and Gene de Paul wrote the theme song. This is an extremely rare piece of great value. *Collection of Roy Bishop.* $150

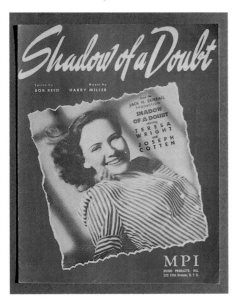

Shadow of a Doubt
Teresa Wright played "young Charlie" in *Shadow of a Doubt,* one of Alfred Hitchcock's best thrillers. She adored her visiting Uncle Charlie (Joseph Cotten) until the dawning of suspicion turned her trust into terror. Title song was written by Bob Reed (W) and Harry Miller (M). *Collection of Harold Jacobs.* $90

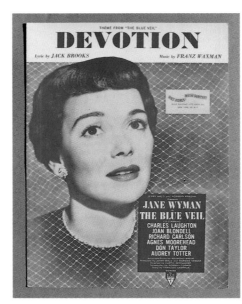

Jane Wyman (born 1914). She started in movies as a cute pug-nosed blonde bit player, and eventually rose above her lightweight material and moved into serious roles. Her talent and ability were recognized with a Best Actress Academy Award for her role as a deaf-mute in *Johnny Belinda* in 1948, and two subsequent nominations for *The Blue Veil* (1951) and *Magnificent Obsession* (1954). She is the former wife of Ronald Reagan.

WYMAN MOVIE COVERS: *Mr. Dodd Takes the Air,* 1937. *Kid Nightingale,* 1939. *Magic Town,* 1947. *A Kiss in the Dark,* 1949. *The Blue Veil,* 1951. *Here Comes the Groom,* 1951. *Just for You,* 1952. *Let's Do It Again,* 1953. *So Big,* 1953. *Lucy Gallant,* 1955. *Miracle in the Rain,* 1956. *Holiday for Lovers,* 1959.

Zing a Little Zong
Jane Wyman starred opposite **Bing Crosby** in *Just for You,* an entertaining musical about a Broadway producer trying to raise two teenagers with the help of his beautiful financée. The movie score was replete with songs by Leo Robin (W) and Harry Warren (M). $6

Devotion
Jane Wyman portrayed a courageous lady in *The Blue Veil,* who, after losing her husband and child, brings new meaning to her life by becoming a children's nanny. She was nominated for a Best Actress Oscar for the dignity and pathos she brought to her role. Cover song was written by Jack Brooks (W) and Franz Waxman (M). *Collection of Harold Jacobs.* $75

Loretta Young (born 1914). She started as a child extra in Hollywood movies, and after schooling in a convent returned to movies as a teenage actress. Before long she was playing leading lady parts, eventually winning the coveted Academy Award as Best Actress in *The Farmer's Daughter* in 1947.

YOUNG MOVIE COVERS: *Fast Life,* 1929. *The Forward Pass,* 1929. *Loose Ankles,* 1930. *Caravan,* 1934. *The Crusades,* 1935. *Ramona,* 1936. *Love Under Fire,* 1937. *Three Blind Mice,* 1938. *Eternally Yours,* 1939. *Love Is News,* 1939. *Wife, Husband, and Friend,* 1939. *And Now Tomorrow,* 1944. *Come to the Stable,* 1949. *Paula,* 1952. *Because of You,* 1952.

Loretta
Loretta Young was the charming hostess of a television drama series, *The Loretta Young Show,* in 1953 that was telecast until 1961. It was a popular show and won several Emmy awards. Loretta swished through the doorway welcoming her viewers each week, exuding glamour and wearing fabulous designer gowns. $25

Isn't It Wonderful, Isn't It Swell
Loretta Young and her two sisters set out to find rich husbands in the entertaining comedy romance *Three Blind Mice.* Loretta meets and falls in love with **Joel McCrea,** and finds that love, not money, is the most important thing. Song is by Sidney D. Mitchell (W) and Lew Pollack (M). $8

BIBLIOGRAPHY

Baxter, John. *Hollywood in the Thirties*. New York: A. S. Barnes and Company, 1980.

Bergan, Ronald. *The United Artists Story*. New York: Crown Publishers, Inc., 1986.

Blum, Daniel. *A New Pictorial History of the Talkies*. New York: G. P. Putnam's Sons, 1973.

Brown, James Nelson. *Star Covers*. Westlake Village, California: 1997.

Cini, Zelda, and Bob Crane. *Hollywood: Land and Legend*. Westport, Connecticut: Arlington House, 1980.

Eames, John Douglas. *The M-G-M Story*. New York: Crescent Books, 1987.

_____.*The Paramount Story*. New York: Crown Publishers, 1987.

Gammond, Peter. *The Oxford Companion to Popular Music*. New York: Oxford University Press, 1993.

Geduld, Harry M. *The Birth of the Talkies*. Indiana University Press, 1975.

Griffith, Richard, and Arthur Mayer. *The Movies*. New York: Simon and Schuster, 1970.

Halliwell, Leslie. *The Filmgoer's Companion*. New York: Hill and Wang, 1977.

Heide, Robert, and John Gilman. *Starstruck, the Wonderful World of Movie Memorabilia*. New York: Doubleday and Company, 1986.

Higham, Charles, and Joel Greenberg. *Hollywood in the Forties*. New York: A. S. Barnes and Company, 1968.

Hirschhorn, Clive. *The Universal Story*. New York: Crown Publishers, 1986.

_____.*The Warner Brothers Story*. New York: Crown Publishers, 1986.

_____.*The Columbia Story*. New York: Crown Publishers, 1989.

Jacobs, Dick and Harriet. *Who Wrote That Song?* Cincinnati, Ohio: Writer's Digest Books, 1994.

Jacobs, Lewis. *The Rise of the American Film*. New York: Harcourt, Brace and Company, 1930.

Jeavons, Clyde. *A Pictorial History of War Films*. Secaucas, New Jersey: The Citadel Press, 1974.

Jones, Ken D., and Arthur F. McClure. *Hollywood at War*. New Jersey: A. S. Barnes and Company, 1973.

Katz, Ephraim. *The Film Encyclopedia*. New York: Perigee Books, 1979.

Knight, Arthur. *The Liveliest Art*. New York: Macmillan Publishing Company, 1978.

Leish, Kenneth W. *Cinema*. New York: Newsweek Books, 1974.

Mast, Gerald. *A Short History of the Movies*. Indianapolis: Bobbs-Merrill Educational Publishing, 1978.

Osborne, Robert. *Sixty Years of the Oscar*. New York: Abbeville Press, 1989.

Shipman, David. *The Great Movie Stars, the Golden Years*. New York: Bonanza Books, 1970.

Spears, Jack. *Hollywood: The Golden Era*. New Jersey: A. S. Barnes, 1971

Stubblebine, Donald J. *Cinema Sheet Music*. North Carolina: McFarland & Company, Inc., 1991.

Taylor, Deems. *A Pictorial History of the Movies*. New York: Simon and Schuster, 1943.

Thomas, Tony, and Aubrey Solomon. *The Films of 20th Century Fox*. New Jersey: Citadel Press, 1985.

Warner, Alan. *Who Sang What on the Screen*. Australia: Angus and Robertson Publishers, 1984.

Wile, Mason, and Dampen Bona. *Inside Oscar*. New York: Ballantine Books, 1988.

SONG INDEX AND VALUE GUIDE

Movie songs are the most popular of collectible sheet music, with prices fluctuating widely depending upon rarity and demand. Most of the popular hit songs from movies are priced relatively low, at around four dollars—not indicative of quality but, of quantity. Well-known songs, including Academy Award winners, had large printings and are quite common in the sheet music marketplace.

The following value guide is based on a combination of dealers' set price lists, published price guides, auction sales, input from knowledgeable collectors, and the author's own experience. Where two prices are given, the prices in *italics* are documented prices known to have been paid at dealers' auctions, which are extremely variable and unpredictable. One can get lucky and pick up a rare piece below market value if the high bidders already have it.

It should be noted that song prices are for the specific song in the illustrated photo. Two songs from the same movie can have a wide disparity in value because of rarity.

The stated price is for illustrated pieces in *excellent* condition, and should be discounted for lower grades as described in the following condition chart.

EXCELLENT—Very clean, paper still crisp, virtually flawless. May have a music store stamp or a price sticker, as old music store stock was routinely price-stickered in the 1960s and 1970s. Full value.

GOOD—Piece in nice shape, desirable for a collection with no immediate need to upgrade. May show some wear—small tears (less than 3/4"), careful taped repair on inside, inconspicuous signature, store stamp, or price sticker on cover. 25% discount.

FAIR—Considerable wear from use, and one or more problems like light soil, creases, tears, frayed edges, separated cover, prominent signatures, stickers, or name stamps. 50% discount.

POOR—Complete, but with one or more mutilation problems, such as ragged edges with large tears or pieces missing, folds and/or creases, heavy soiling, sloppy taped repairs, bold writing or doodling, trimmed down from large size. Generally too worn to be of collectible value, unless rare and in a major collectible category. 90% discount.

175

Song Title	Value	Page	Song Title	Value	Page
Here You Are	$20	111	I'll Sing You a Thousand		
High Hopes	$4	72	Love Songs	$5 *($11)*	91
High Noon	$5	70	I'm an Old Cowhand	$5	39
His Rocking Horse Ran Away	$4	50	I'm Building Up to an		
Hold My Hand (A.Faye)	$6	97	Awful Let-Down	$15	77
Hold My Hand (D.Reynolds)	$5	61	I'm Falling in Love with Someone	$5	31
Hold Your Man	$8	109	I'm Feelin' Like a Million	$10	161
Hollywood Canteen	$7	56	I'm Gettin' Sentimental Over You	$6	53
Home Cookin'	$5	80	I'm in the Market for You	$4	35
Home from the Hill	$6	138	I'm No Angel	$20 *($45)*	168
Honeymoon Hotel	$5	9	I'm Nobody's Baby	$10	153
Hooray for Hollywood	$50 *($120)*	7	I'm Pixilated Over You	$60	38
Horse With the Dreamy Eyes, The	$75	109	I'm Still Crazy for You	$20	107
How About You?	$7	42	I'm the Last of the Red Hot		
How Am I To Know?	$10	103	Mammas	$7	22
How Can You Forget?	$10	37	In Our Little Wooden Shoes	$15 *($25)*	163
How Could You?	$5	40	In the Cool, Cool, Cool of the		
How Do You Keep the Music Playing?	$4	151	Evening	$4	70
How Do You Speak to an Angel	$5 *($16)*	134	In the Park in Paree	$4	85
How Little We Know	$8 *($26)*	79	In the Spirit of the Moment	$7	96
How Long Will It Last	$8	35	In Your Own Quiet Way	$7	144
How Many Times			Indian Love Call	$5	32
Do I Have to Tell You	$5	124	Injun Gal Heap Hep	$10	123
How Strange	$12	156	Innocent Affair, An	$8	36
How Would You Like to Kiss			Is That Good?	$10	54
Me in the Moonlight	$6	136	Isn't It Wonderful, Isn't It Swell	$8	172
Humoresque	$8	104	It Can't Be Wrong	$6	92
Hundred Kisses from Now, A	$75	41	It Had to Be You	$45	40
Hush...Hush, Sweet Charlotte	$8	92	It Happened, It's Over, Let's		
I Ain't Down Yet	$5	151	Forget It	$20	124
I Can't Give You Anything but Love	$7	114	It Happens Every Spring	$8	137
I Could Have Danced All Night	$4	63	It Might as Well Be Spring	$3	69
I Didn't Mean a Word I Said	$5	142	It Only Happens When I		
I Found a Million Dollar Baby	$20	149	Dance With You	$5	105
I Got Rhythm	$8 *($11)*	53	It's a Most Unusual Day	$5	145
I Had the Craziest Dream	$6	107	It's Magic	$5	57
I Hadn't Anyone Till You	$8 *($33)*	48	I've Been Kissed Before	$25	101
I Hum a Waltz	$5	38	I've Got a Date with a Dream	$5	37
I Know, I Know, I Know	$7	53	I've Got My Eyes on You	$8	144
I Know That You Know	$5	151	I've Gotta See for Myself	$45	126
I Love an Old Fashioned Song	$6	118	Ivy	$4	100
I Love to Whistle	$6	26	Jailhouse Rock	$35	147
I Never Knew Heaven Could Speak	$10 *($40)*	36	Janey	$8	60
I Poured My Heart Into a Song	$8 *($16)*	112	Jealous	$5	154
I Surrender Dear	$8	55	Jezebel	$60	91
I Think of You	$6	54	Jingle Jangle Jingle	$4	107
I Want to Be Happy	$6	58	Jitterbug, The	$60	26
I Want You to Want Me	$5	110	Johnny Guitar	$8 *($15)*	58
I Went Merrily Merrily on My Way	$15	141	Judgement at Nuremberg Theme	$15	165
I Wonder Who's Kissing Her Now	$5	110	Jungle Drums	$8	166
If I Had My Way	$7	30	Keep That Twinkle in Your Eye	$25	30
If I Loved You	$4	62	Keepin' Myself for You	$4	21
If I Only Had a Brain	$20	105	Kentuckian Song, The	$5	124
If I'm Dreaming	$5	23	King Creole	$35	148
If My Friends Could See Me Now	$4	131	Kiss to Remember, A	$18	18
If Winter Comes	$7	143	Kisses	$8	132
If You Believe	$10	138	Knock on Wood	$5	118
If You Want the Rainbow	$4	22	La Cucaracha	$7	81
I'll Get By	$4	44	Last Call for Love, The	$5	145
I'll Go Home with Bonnie Jean	$5	119	Last Run Theme, The	$4	155
I'll Meet You at Sundown	$125	164	Last Time I Saw Paris, The		
I'll See You in My Dreams	$8	44	(E.Powell)	$8	68

Song Title	Value	Page	Song Title	Value	Page
Oh, Play Tzigani	$100	122	Seventh Dawn, The	$5	114
Ol' Man River	$4	22	Seventh Heaven	$8	158
Old Acquaintance	$5	92	Shadow of a Doubt	$90	171
Old Glory	$4	56	Shadow Waltz	$4	28
Old Straw Hat, An	$30	163	Shadows on the Moon	$6	32
On Account-a I Love You	$30	29	Shanghai Lil	$6	9
On Golden Pond	$6	99	She Wore a Yellow Ribbon	$9 ($18)	167
On the Atchison, Topeka and			She's Funny That Way	$20	49
the Santa Fe	$6	69	Shenandoah Theme	$5	159
On the Good Ship Lollipop	$10 ($22)	26	Silver Bells	$5	115
On the Waterfront	$40	84	Since You Went Away	$4	44
One Eyed Jacks	$15	84	Sing, Baby, Sing	$6	98
One Kiss	$6	32	Sing Me a Song of the Islands	$4	42
Only Yesterday	$40	160	Singin' in the Bathtub	$4	24
Our Little Girl	$25	162	Singin' in the Rain	$5	21
Our Very Own	$5	82	Sinner Kissed an Angel, A	$7	83
Out of This World	$4	124	Sittin' on a Backyard Fence	$5	9
Over the Rainbow	$15	68	Skippy	$15 ($40)	31
Painting the Clouds with Sunshine	$5	137	Slowly	$4	48
Palms of Paradise	$8	148	Small Fry	$4	141
Panamania	$5	128	Smile When the Raindrops Fall	$60 ($368)	126
Parachute Jump, The	$10	134	Smilin' Through (Shearer)	$5	26
Paradise	$3	19	Smilin' Through (MacDonald)	$9	130
Pass Me By	$4	58	Smoke Dreams	$15	34
Patch of Blue, A	$5	144	Snow White and the Seven		
Patton Theme	$8	155	Dwarfs Folio	$35	31
Peking Theme, The	$6 ($13)	114	So Ends Our Night	$25 ($200)	133
Phoenix Love Theme, The	$6	159	So-o-o-o-o in Love	$6 ($12)	50
Piccolino, The	$10	33	So Red the Rose	$25	160
Pillow Talk	$15	116	So This Is You	$50	158
Pilly Pom Pom Plee	$10	12	Some Came Running Theme	$4	131
Piper Dreams, The	$6	143	Some Enchanted Evening	$4	62
Place in the Sun, A	$20	61	Somebody	$10	127
Places That Belong to You	$4	159	Someday, I'll Meet You Again	$7	45
Please Don't Kiss Me	$60	168	Someone to Care for Me	$10	30
Please Don't Say No	$3	117	Song of the Barefoot Contessa	$10	103
Polly-Wolly-Doodle	$18	162	Song of the Dawn	$4	25
Poppa Don't Preach to Me	$4	116	Song of the Seabees, The	$30	44
Portrait of Jennie	$6	117	Song to Remember, A	$5	141
Put the Blame on Mame	$10	48	Sonny Boy	$4	16
Put Your Arms Around Me Honey	$10 ($18)	42	South of the Border	$6	40
Rachel	$18	137	Speak Low	$4	103
Rains Came, The	$50	147	Spellbound	$5	51
Rat Race, The	$5	90	Spin a Little Web of Dreams	$5	37
Reap the Wild Wind	$40	107	Spring Will Be a Little Late This Year	$8	96
Reckless	$100	109	Stand By Your Man	$6	139
Red River Valley	$5	78	Star!	$4	77
Ride on Vaquero	$6	17	Star Eyes	$4	157
Ridin' Down the Canyon	$5	153	Star Is Born, A	$150	133
Riptide	$7	155	Sting, The	$5	150
'Round and Around	$200 ($350)	87	Strange Lady in Town	$8	106
Ruby	$4	117	Strange Love	$7	49
Ruby and the Pearl, The	$5	121	String of Pearls, A	$8 ($18)	158
Sabrina	$10 ($46)	83	Suddenly It's Spring	$5	152
Sadie Thompson's Song	$6	111	Summer Serenade—Badinage	$5	32
Sayonara	$6 ($15)	58	Sunrise and You	$25	65
Secret Doorway	$50	93	Swan, The	$15	120
Secret Love	$4	70	Swanee	$3	15
Secrets in the Moonlight	$8	90	Sweepin' the Clouds Away	$5	25
Separate Tables	$10	140	Sweet and Lovely	$4	76
September Song	$5	100	Sweet Leilani	$5	67
Serenade	$5	160	Sweet Marie	$6	146

180

STAR AND MOVIE INDEX

183